PENGUIN CANADA

HEALTHY EATING FOR PRETEENS AND TEENS

LESLIE BECK, a registered dietitian, is a leading nutritionist who has helped over 2000 individuals achieve their nutrition and health goals. She is the bestselling author of *Leslie Beck's Nutrition Guide to Menopause*, *Leslie Beck's 10 Steps to Healthy Eating*, *Leslie Beck's Nutrition Guide for Women*, *Leslie Beck's Nutrition Encyclopedia*, and *Leslie Beck's Nutrition Guide to a Healthy Pregnancy* and is a contributing author in *Rose Reisman's Sensationally Light Pasta & Grains*. Leslie writes a weekly nutrition column in *The Globe and Mail*, Canada's national newspaper, is the nutrition expert for CTV's *Canada AM*, and is the host of Discovery Channel's *Foodstuff*, a daily nutrition program aired nationally. She can also be heard two mornings a week on CFRB's *Ted Woloshyn Show*. Leslie runs a private practice at the Medcan Clinic in Toronto.

Leslie has worked with many of Canada's leading businesses and international food companies. She regularly delivers nutrition workshops to corporate groups across Canada and the United States. Having a strong interest in sports nutrition, Leslie has acted as nutrition consultant to the Toronto Raptors and has worked with the Canadian International Marathon (1995–1997). She often holds nutrition workshops for Toronto's marathon and running clinics. Leslie keeps fit herself by running, cycling, and weight training.

Born and raised in Vancouver, B.C., Leslie obtained her bachelor of science (dietetics) from the University of British Columbia and proceeded to complete the dietetic internship program at St. Michael's Hospital in Toronto. She is a member of the Dietitians of Canada, the College of Dietitians of Ontario, and the Consulting Dietitians of Ontario. She lives in Toronto.

Visit Leslie Beck's website at **www.lesliebeck.com**.

Also by Leslie Beck

Leslie Beck's 10 Steps to Healthy Eating

Leslie Beck's Nutrition Encyclopedia

Leslie Beck's Nutrition Guide for Women

Leslie Beck's Nutrition Guide to Menopause

Leslie Beck's Nutrition Guide to a Healthy Pregnancy

Healthy Eating for Preteens and Teens

The Ultimate Guide to Diet, Nutrition, and Food

Leslie Beck RD

PENGUIN
CANADA

PENGUIN CANADA

Published by the Penguin Group

Penguin Group (Canada), 90 Eglinton Avenue East, Suite 700, Toronto, Ontario, Canada M4P 2Y3
  (a division of Pearson Penguin Canada Inc.)

Penguin Group (USA) Inc., 375 Hudson Street, New York, New York 10014, U.S.A.
Penguin Books Ltd, 80 Strand, London WC2R 0RL, England
Penguin Ireland, 25 St Stephen's Green, Dublin 2, Ireland (a division of Penguin Books Ltd)
Penguin Group (Australia), 250 Camberwell Road, Camberwell, Victoria 3124, Australia
  (a division of Pearson Australia Group Pty Ltd)
Penguin Books India Pvt Ltd, 11 Community Centre, Panchsheel Park, New Delhi – 110 017, India
Penguin Group (NZ), cnr Airborne and Rosedale Roads, Albany, Auckland 1310, New Zealand
  (a division of Pearson New Zealand Ltd)
Penguin Books (South Africa) (Pty) Ltd, 24 Sturdee Avenue, Rosebank, Johannesburg 2196, South Africa

Penguin Books Ltd, Registered Offices: 80 Strand, London WC2R 0RL, England

First published 2005

(WEB) 10 9 8 7 6 5 4 3 2 1

LIBRARY AND ARCHIVES CANADA CATALOGUING IN PUBLICATION

Beck, Leslie (Leslie C.)
   Healthy eating for preteens and teens : the ultimate guide to diet, nutrition, and food / Leslie Beck.

Includes bibliographical references and index.
ISBN 0-14-301720-9

1. Teenagers—Nutrition. I. Title.

RA777.B42 2005   613.2'0835   C2005-900220-4

Visit the Penguin Group (Canada) website at **www.penguin.ca**

To Alex and Julien Beck

The "food lady" has done it again.
But this time you've inspired me
to write something especially for you.
The knowledge is yours to use—
to help you eat healthfully over the years to come.

Contents

Acknowledgments

I would like to thank the many people whose encouragement, support, and assistance made this book possible:

- My dedicated and skilled researchers, Anne von Rosenbach and Michelle Gelok, who gathered and organized the scientific and clinical information to support the writing of this book. A special thank you to Michelle, who also organized the recipe section of this book.

- My teenage clients, who over the past few years inspired me to write this book. Their questions about weight control, vegetarianism, sports nutrition, school-cafeteria and summer-camp menus, and eating on campus helped me write a book that is meaningful and relevant for today's preteens and teenagers.

- To everyone who made the What's On Your Plate? High School Nutrition Survey possible: Cathy O'Connor and Donna Bottrell, the dietitians at Chartwells Dining Services, a member of Compass Group Canada; the teachers and principals who opened their classrooms to me; and Vartouhi Jazmaji and Lee Vernich at the Research Services Unit in the Department of Public Health at the University of Toronto, who helped design the survey questions and ran the statistical analyses. And most of all, the 1046 Canadian high school students who took time to complete the survey. The invaluable insights I gained from these teens helped shape this book.

- The team at The Canadian Living Test Kitchen, especially Nancy Baker, who so willingly offered more than 65 nutritious, delicious, and tested till perfect recipes for this book.

- My editors and the production team at Penguin Group (Canada) who continue to support and believe in my work.

- Dawn Bone and Rosemary Chubb, my amazingly proficient and organized assistants who enabled me to manage my busy private practice while writing this book.

- And finally, my family and friends who continue to cheer me on me as I work those extra-long hours while writing my books. As always, I thank you for your support, understanding, and friendship.

Introduction

Adolescence is one of the greatest periods of change during our lifetime. Changes occur in all realms of human development—physical, emotional, intellectual, even spiritual. Body shapes are changing, independent thinking begins, and teenagers take on the social values and roles of adulthood. It's a time of new discoveries and opportunities, but also of anxiety and stress.

On the physical level, adolescence brings on rapid growth and hormonal change. The onset of adolescence is typically associated with the start of puberty and ends when an adult identity and adult behaviours are accepted. The World Health Organization and the Canadian Paediatric Society define adolescence as the period between the ages of 10 and 19 years, and for the purposes of this book, I have adopted this definition. In the chapters that follow I provide nutrient recommendations for preteens and teens aged 9 to 13 years, and older teenagers, those aged 14 to 19 years. Wherever I refer to "teens," I mean to include preteens, unless I specify otherwise.

Most girls begin their growth spurts between the ages of 10 and 13 years, while most boys grow more between the ages of 12 and 15 years. Nearly every organ in the body develops during these times of faster growth, including bones, muscles, and sex organs. That's why the teenage body demands more energy, iron, zinc, and calcium than at any other age.

Fortunately, once the growth spurt begins, teenagers' appetites rev up and they begin to eat more food. And if you have teenage boys, I'm sure you find that keeping the fridge and cupboards full is almost a full-time job. If teenagers make nutritious food choices, they can satisfy both their increased hunger and higher nutrient needs.

Yet, living in the teenage world makes adolescents particularly vulnerable to poor eating habits. As teens assert themselves and become more independent from parents and teachers, their food habits change. Teenagers have more control over their eating habits and more access to foods outside the home, compared to younger children. Lifestyle changes such as having a part-time job, getting a driver's licence, and dating mean that teenagers will spend more time away from home—and from the healthy meals you prepare. Pressure from friends, coaches, and the media can also affect a teenager's food choices.

Many of my clients know that what's good for them is also good for their children. As is the case for adults, teenagers' eating habits can affect their energy level, physical fitness, mental performance, and health. Sure, teenagers are growing and need more calories, but there's no good reason for those calories to come from foods high in fat and sugar.

Over the past 15 years, I have counselled many teenagers about nutrition. I've helped overweight teens slim down and navigate the fat and sugar traps on cafeteria and camp menus. I've educated teenagers about healthy vegetarian diets, and I've advised others about sport-specific nutrition.

There's never been as much demand for nutrition information as there is today. Teenagers and adults are more aware of nutrition than they were even a decade ago. My clients come to me looking for sound, credible, and relevant information about how their food choices affect their well-being.

It's a confusing world out there, sometimes even for a nutritionist like me. Conflicting news stories about nutrition, fad diets, and a growing number of "magic bullet" supplements can make even the most nutrition-savvy person's head spin. Given today's overwhelming amount of health information, it can be a tough task to make sense of the foods you eat.

Growing Up Overfed and Undernourished—and at Risk of Heart Disease

Only recently have researchers, health professionals, and, subsequently, the media taken an interest in the nutritional health of our children. It's unfortunate that it's taken an epidemic of obesity and type 2 diabetes to get our attention. Perhaps we ought to call it the North American Paradox—the fact that we live in an affluent society with access to medical care, nutritious foods, and plenty of open green space, yet so many of our youth are growing up overweight, undernourished, and sedentary.

What's more, today we're witnessing in teenagers the health problems that accompany both over- and under-nutrition. Risk factors for heart disease, including high cholesterol, high blood pressure, and type 2 diabetes, as well as iron deficiency anemia and rickets, a bone disease caused by a lack of vitamin D, are becoming more prevalent among adolescents.

If there is any time in a person's life when he or she is expected to be in the best health, it is during youth. Yet, consider the fact that almost one-third of Canadian adolescents rate their health as no better than "good."[1] Adolescents who are obese, physically inactive, or who eat a poor diet are more likely to convey negative views of their health.

Overweight and obesity is a major concern among Canadian youth. Over the past two decades, rates of obesity have quadrupled among children. In 2001, 5% of kids aged 12 to 19 were considered obese, with the prevalence among boys almost double that of girls. And it seems that many more teens are on their way to obesity: 17% of boys and 10% of girls are now classified as overweight.[2] Statistics for younger children are even more alarming.

These numbers are frightening for a few reasons. For starters, obese adolescents are more likely to become obese adults than are their normal-weight peers. It's estimated that 70% of obese teenagers will remain obese in adulthood. Obese teenagers are also more likely to suffer physical and psychological problems such as high cholesterol, high blood pressure, type 2 diabetes, back and knee problems, low self-esteem, and depression. And finally, adolescent weight problems (along with physical inactivity and poor eating habits) have long-term implications for health in adulthood. It's well documented that obesity increases the risk of heart disease, stroke, diabetes, respiratory illness, and certain cancers.

What's truly worrisome is that so many of these so-called adult diseases are now affecting young people. We are learning that adolescents are not immune to obesity, diabetes, high blood cholesterol, or high blood pressure, conditions that weren't even on the radar screen when it came to adolescent health in the early 1990s because they were considered adult health problems. Indeed, what was only recently called "adult onset diabetes" is now referred to as "type 2 diabetes" because of its diagnosis in children as young as nine years old. It's been said that children growing up in North America today are at risk of becoming the first generation in modern memory that will have a shorter life expectancy than their parents. The reason: an epidemic of obesity and type 2 diabetes.

Physical inactivity, poor eating habits, and parental influences all have a role to play in youth obesity (not to mention nutrient deficiencies in iron, calcium, and vitamin D). Today, only 4 out of 10 teens aged 12 to 19 are physically active, with boys being more active than girls.[3] (Kids considered inactive accumulated less than one hour of walking per day.) Our schools certainly aren't helping our children be physically active. According to a 2002 study, one-half of Canadian schools have a policy of daily physical education, yet only 16% of schools comply. And the number of gym classes offered each week declines with increasing grade.[4]

If kids aren't spending their time being active, what are they doing? Most are sedentary after school, doing homework, reading, surfing the internet, watching television, or playing video games. Research suggests that teens who spend more than two hours each day in front of the television have a significantly lower chance of becoming and remaining active. There's a well-documented link between screen time and body weight. Studies show that watching the tube and playing video or computer games increase the likelihood of being overweight or obese by as much as 61%. On the other hand, participating in sports and other physical activity lowers the odds by 10% to 43%.

When it comes to nutrition, it's hard to get a handle on how Canadian adolescents are eating because so little research has been done. That's why I conducted the What's on Your Plate? High School Nutrition Survey in the spring of 2004. With the help of the dietitians at Chartwells School Dining Services, a member of Compass Group Canada, and the Research Services Unit in the Department of Public Health at the University of Toronto, I asked 1046 Canadian high school students, grades 8 through 12, about their food and exercise habits, as well as about as their nutrition concerns.

It seems that teenagers are quite interested in nutrition. Of the students surveyed, 78% rank nutrition as somewhat or very important when deciding what to eat. A survey conducted in 2002 revealed that 69% of Canadian youth were "slightly" to "far more concerned" with the quality of food they were eating than they were two years earlier.

So many teens are aware of nutrition and food issues. So far, so good. But when I asked high school students about their diets, many came up short in the fruit, vegetable, dairy, and whole-grain departments. Four out of 10 teenagers eat fewer than two vegetable servings per day, and one-half of those surveyed consume no more than two servings of milk. Whole grains aren't that popular, either. One-quarter of the teens say they never opt for 100% whole-wheat or multigrain breads, while 3 out of 10 say they always do.

So why the disconnect? An overwhelming majority of teenagers say nutrition is important, and yet so many have diets that lack nutrient-dense foods. And an increasing number are becoming overweight. It's challenging for teenagers to eat well in our modern world. We live in a toxic food environment, an environment in which we have easy access to a huge variety of highly processed—and inexpensive—foods, all served up in super-sized portions. What's more, these high-fat and sugary foods are marketed directly to teenagers and young children.

Have you ever checked out the menu at your son or daughter's school cafeteria? At summer camp? I encourage you to do so. When I review these menus for my teenage clients, I am usually mortified at what we are feeding our younger generation. Menus geared to teens are often heavy on the white bread, white rice, white potatoes, and sugar, and light on the vegetables, fruit, whole grains, and vegetarian protein options. (Spaghetti and meatless tomato sauce does not cut it—where are the beans and tofu?) Ask your teenager and she'll tell you that healthy food items are hard to find in the cafeteria lineup. And the few choices that do exist—ham sandwiches on brown bread or bruised fruit—are usually hidden among the fries and soft drinks.

Shouldn't we, as adults, know better in this age of skyrocketing obesity rates, trans fats, and high glycemic starches? The good news is that we *are* starting to smarten up. High school cafeterias are changing their menus, prompted by pressure from parents and school boards. Chartwells Dining Services, a member of Compass Group Canada, which holds the market share in contracted high school food service, is committed to bringing healthy foods to the forefront. Students are now seeing more healthy options: whole-grain wrap sandwiches, salads made to order, stir-fries, and grab-and-go veggies. The company is also promoting water and milk in their combo meals rather than sugary pop. And it is piloting healthy eating messages on vending machines.

And there are more signs of change. Provincial governments are cracking down on school boards, mandating the ban of junk foods in vending machines on school premises. The premier of Ontario has even talked about enforcing daily physical education in schools. Fast food joints have added grilled chicken, entree salads, and fresh fruit to their menus. That's a smart move, since adolescents are eating more meals at fast food outlets and restaurants than ever before. Large food manufacturers also seem to be making moves to stem childhood obesity. Kraft Foods announced in January 2004 that it would stop television advertisements for the likes of Kool-Aid, Oreo, and Chips Ahoy! cookies during programming targeted to kids aged 6 to 11 years.

Although it's becoming easier for our teenagers to choose healthy foods when they eat away from home, healthy eating habits begin at home. Parents play an important role in shaping their teenager's health and nutrition habits. We know that overweight among parents is a major factor in excess weight for adolescent boys and girls. Among girls aged 12 to 19 who lived with an obese parent, 18% are overweight and 10% are obese. The situation is similar for boys: 22% of boys with an obese parent are overweight, and 12% are obese.[5]

Aside from weight, other parental habits influence those of their children. These include physical activity, smoking, and eating habits. Canadian teenagers who report a parent who is inactive during leisure time are more likely to be inactive themselves. And if the parent smokes or eats fruits and vegetables infrequently, the teenager is likely to mirror these behaviours.

Clearly, many factors influence the eating habits of teenagers. Another worth mentioning is the lack of knowledge about nutrition. Healthy eating receives little attention in secondary schools. While some teenagers spend a few classes discussing Canada's Food Guide to Healthy Eating, others don't receive any nutrition education at all. It's time we start educating our youth about the importance of good nutrition. Nutrition topics need to be added to the school curriculum. We need to start teaching our kids important life skills such as grocery shopping, label reading, and meal planning. By becoming knowledgeable about nutrition and health, adolescents will be much more likely to take an interest in the foods they eat and make wiser choices when they eat away from home, be it the school cafeteria, the fast food restaurant, or the university dorm. And who knows, maybe as parents you'll be offered more enthusiastic help in the kitchen!

That's where my book comes in—to help educate parents and adolescents about healthy eating in today's fast-paced world. There isn't a book about nutrition out there that is specifically geared to adolescents. Sure, there are weight loss books for teens. But there's a whole lot more to teen nutrition than weight control strategies.

Why This Book Is for *All* Parents of Preteens and Teenagers

To help determine what topics I needed to include in this book, I asked teenagers about their eating habits, their nutrition and food concerns, and their exercise habits. In this book, you'll find information that's relevant for all teenagers. In Part 1, Nutrition Basics, I include essential nutrition information for everyone. You'll learn all about vitamins and minerals (including supplements), carbohydrates, proteins, and fats. You'll also find a chapter on daily water requirements, which includes sections on caffeine and alcohol consumption.

But that's just the start. In Part 2, Making Healthy Food Choices, I give you plenty of practical nutrition advice on helping your teen translate the nutrition basics into healthy food choices—at the grocery store, at the school cafeteria, and the campus dining hall, in ethnic restaurants, and at fast food outlets. You'll even find kitchen tips to help busy teenagers prepare their own healthy meals and snacks.

Part 3, Nutrition for Health and Fitness, offers strategies for kids who need a little more personal nutrition coaching. You'll learn which nutrients need to be paid close attention to if your teenage son or daughter is a lacto-ovo vegetarian or a vegan. I also include a vegetarian food guide to help teens plan a nutritionally adequate diet. There's a chapter dedicated to helping overweight teens make better choices to achieve a healthy weight. And, of course, I've included a chapter on eating disorders, which are far more likely to affect adolescents than adults.

And for those kids who are into sports in a big way, I've included a chapter on sports nutrition. It provides information that will help your child get the fuel he or she needs for the sport of choice, be it basketball, hockey, track and field, swimming, tennis, or dance.

Over 65 Recipes to Keep Busy Teens and Parents Healthy

Every recipe in this book comes from the Canadian Living Test Kitchen. That means they taste great, they're easy to prepare, and of course, they're good for you. Each recipe is accompanied by a nutrient analysis: a breakdown of its calories, fat, protein, fibre, and so on. You'll find recipes for great-tasting breakfasts on the go, bagged lunches, quick dinners on the fly, and plenty of snacks.

There's no question that adopting a healthy lifestyle—even making small changes—can protect a teenager's future health. But healthy eating and becoming physically active (and not smoking) also have immediate benefits for teenagers. A healthy diet and active lifestyle can help teenagers to:

- Increase energy levels

- Improve mental performance

- Boost self-esteem

- Cope with stress and anxiety

- Prevent colds and flu

- Speed recovery from injuries and illness

Eating habits established during adolescence are often carried forward into adulthood. There's no question that a teenager's diet shapes his or her diet later in life. When it comes to getting teenagers, who are striving for independence, to eat healthfully, there's only so much that parents can do. The more we badger our kids about the eating habits they're not implementing, the more our kids will go the other way.

Good nutrition is a shared responsibility between parent and child. As parents, we must try to understand our children's food choices and show respect for their ability to make independent decisions. It's critical that we educate our kids about healthy eating and exercise in a constructive manner. We must encourage and support healthy behaviours in our children by making healthy foods accessible at home and being good role models. Doing so will enable teenagers to make their own food choices with awareness and knowledge. As parents, that's the best we can do for our children.

I truly hope this book helps you and your family adopt and follow a healthy diet. Once you read it, I encourage you to pass this book along to your son or daughter.

Leslie Beck, RD
Toronto, 2005

Part One

———∞∞∞———

Nutrition Basics

1

⸎

How Healthy
Is Your Teen's Diet?

T he teen years are a remarkable period of transformation. During this time, teenagers achieve the final 15% to 20% of their height and gain 50% of their adult body weight. This rapid growth increases the body's demand for energy and nutrients. Indeed, total nutritional needs are higher during adolescence than at any other point in the life cycle.

On average, girls have their growth spurts before boys and, for about two years, are heavier and more muscular than boys of the same age. For females, most physical growth has been completed by about two years after menarche (the first time that a girl menstruates). Most males experience their major growth spurt and increase in muscle mass during middle adolescence.

A healthy diet not only supplies all the nutrients that growing teenagers need but also lays the foundation for future health. Many of us know that a diet that's low in fat and salt, high in fibre, and packed with fruits and vegetables can help prevent obesity, type 2 diabetes, heart disease, and certain cancers. Although these nutrition-related diseases were thought to occur in middle age, many are now on the rise among adolescents.

The importance of healthy eating during the teen years goes beyond disease prevention. Eating the right foods, in the right amounts, at the right times boosts energy levels, keeps the brain alert, and helps the body cope with stress. A steady intake of nutritious foods promotes healthy bone growth and muscle development. And the vitamins and minerals we feed our insides can also affect how we look on the outside. A nutrient-packed diet, along with plenty of water, can help keep our skin and hair looking its best.

It used to be that eating right was simply a matter of common sense. Eat less fat and salt and more fibre and we'd stay healthy and trim. Just follow Canada's Food Guide to Healthy Eating and we'd be sure to get all the vitamins and minerals we needed for good health.

For the most part, these rules still hold true. But we've come a long way in our understanding of nutrition since my early days as a dietitian. As scientists explore the link between the foods we eat and our health, they discover new findings almost daily.

Today we speak of trans fats, omega-3 fats, soluble and insoluble fibres, and phytochemicals, as well as low and high glycemic index carbohydrates. And we're more careful about our food choices than ever before. We read nutrition labels and ingredient lists in search of sodium, sugar, and preservatives. We eat organic foods in an effort to limit our intake of pesticide residues. We take supplements to boost our intake of nutrients that our diets may be lacking.

There is no doubt about it: today we are faced with the task of trying to make sense of an overwhelming amount of health information. Nutrition is an evolving science that unfolds slowly and its advance is seldom steady. For every positive study, there is usually a negative study. In spite of the back and forth, we are making progress. Today, we know far more about how diet affects our health than we did even a decade ago.

Despite the flip-flops in nutrition research and the conflicting news stories about foods, people are more interested in how foods affect their health than they ever have been. According to the Ottawa-based National Institute of Nutrition, almost 9 out of 10 Canadian adults rank nutrition as important when choosing the foods they eat. As adults, we want to eat better, feel better, and stay healthy as we age. We are interested in nutrition not only to help shed unwanted pounds but also to keep up with mounting scientific evidence that certain foods may help cause or prevent disease.

But how do Canadian teenagers feel about nutrition? Are they as interested as their parents? Do they worry about chemicals in their foods? Do they care if they're served french fries instead of salad at the school cafeteria? Do they think twice about reaching for a chocolate bar and Coke after school? Do they think about how the foods they eat will affect their performance on the basketball court or football field?

The What's on Your Plate? High School Nutrition Survey

I asked Canadian high school students in grades 8 through 12 about their food and exercise habits and their nutrition concerns. I encourage you to ask your teenage son or daughter to set aside a few moments to complete the survey, which I've included below. Better yet, have the whole family take the survey. While this survey was specially designed and written for teenagers, it's a great way for every member of your family to assess his or her eating and exercise habits. Questions that were specific to school in the original survey have been modified to accommodate those members of the family in the workforce. Once everyone has completed the survey, share your answers. You just might be surprised what you learn about your children's eating habits, not to mention your own. Use the answers you and your kids provide to stimulate family discussions about healthy eating and exercise.

Nutrition Survey

Part 1: Breakfast, Lunch, and Dinner

1. During a typical school/work week (e.g., Monday to Friday), how often do you—

	Every Day	3–4/ Week	1–2/ Week	Occasionally	Never
a. Eat breakfast?	❑	❑	❑	❑	❑
b. Bring your lunch to school/work?	❑	❑	❑	❑	❑
c. Eat lunch from the school/work cafeteria?	❑	❑	❑	❑	❑
d. Go home for lunch?	❑	❑	❑	❑	❑
e. Skip lunch completely?	❑	❑	❑	❑	❑
f. Eat lunch from a fast food place or restaurant away from school/work?	❑	❑	❑	❑	❑
g. Buy snacks from a vending machine?	❑	❑	❑	❑	❑
h. Eat dinner prepared at home?	❑	❑	❑	❑	❑
i. Eat dinner from a restaurant or fast food place?	❑	❑	❑	❑	❑
j. Skip dinner and snack instead?	❑	❑	❑	❑	❑

Part 2: What's on Your Plate?

2. How many servings of the following do you have on an average day?

Number of Servings per Day

a. Fruits (e.g., 1 medium-sized fruit)

b. 100% fruit juice (1 serving = a 6 oz or 175 ml glass of juice)

c. Vegetables (1 serving = 1/2 cup/125 ml cooked vegetables or 1 cup/250 ml salad)

d. Milk products (1 serving = 1 cup/250 ml milk, 3/4 cup/175 grams yogurt, or 1 1/2 ounces/45 grams cheese)

3. When you eat bread, how often do you choose 100% whole-wheat or multigrain bread instead of white bread?   Never ❑   Sometimes ❑   Always ❑

4. Do you take a calcium supplement?   Yes ❑   No ❑

5. Do you take a multivitamin supplement?   Yes ❑   No ❑

6. In the past 12 months, have you been on a diet to gain weight?   Yes ❑   No ❑

7. In the past 12 months, have you been on a diet to lose weight?   Yes ❑   No ❑

8. In the past 12 months, have you tried a fad diet (e.g., Atkins, South Beach, the Zone)?   Yes ❑   No ❑

9. Are you a vegetarian?   Yes ❑   No ❑

10. If you are a vegetarian, what type of vegetarian are you? (Circle the answer that best suits your situation.)

   a. Vegan (I do not eat any animal products, including red meat, chicken, fish, eggs, or milk.)
   b. Lacto vegetarian (I do drink and eat milk products but not meat, chicken, or eggs.)
   c. Lacto-ovo vegetarian (I do eat and drink milk products and eggs but not meat or chicken.)
   d. Semi-vegetarian (I do eat chicken, fish, eggs, and milk products but not red meat.)
   e. Don't know

Part 3: Eating at the School/Work Cafeteria

11. During a typical week, how often do you eat the following items from your school/work cafeteria?

	Every Day	3–4/ Week	1–2/ Week	Occasionally	Never
a. Hamburgers, hot dogs, pizza	❑	❑	❑	❑	❑
b. Chicken burger or nuggets	❑	❑	❑	❑	❑
c. Sandwiches, subs, wraps	❑	❑	❑	❑	❑
d. Hot meal (e.g., pasta)	❑	❑	❑	❑	❑
e. French fries, potato chips, or nachos and cheese	❑	❑	❑	❑	❑
f. Salad, vegetables, or fruit	❑	❑	❑	❑	❑
g. Cookies, donuts, chocolate bars, candy, or ice cream	❑	❑	❑	❑	❑
h. Pop, sports drinks, or fruit punch	❑	❑	❑	❑	❑

i. Milk, chocolate milk, or yogurt	❑	❑	❑	❑	❑
j. Unsweetened fruit juice	❑	❑	❑	❑	❑
k. Bottled water	❑	❑	❑	❑	❑

Part 4: How Important Is Nutrition to You?

12. When deciding what foods to eat, how important are the following to you?

	Very	Somewhat	Not Very	Not at All
a. Good nutrition	❑	❑	❑	❑
b. Maintaining good health	❑	❑	❑	❑
c. Managing my weight	❑	❑	❑	❑
d. Having energy for my sports/workout	❑	❑	❑	❑
e. Negative news stories about food	❑	❑	❑	❑
f. My diabetes	❑	❑	❑	❑
g. Another health condition	❑	❑	❑	❑

13. When it comes to food and nutrition, how concerned are you with the following?

	Very	Somewhat	Not Very	Not at All
a. Calories	❑	❑	❑	❑
b. Fat	❑	❑	❑	❑
c. Protein	❑	❑	❑	❑
d. Sugar	❑	❑	❑	❑
e. Fibre	❑	❑	❑	❑
f. Vitamins	❑	❑	❑	❑
g. Calcium	❑	❑	❑	❑
h. Iron	❑	❑	❑	❑
i. Salt	❑	❑	❑	❑

14. When it comes to the type of food you eat, how concerned are you with the following?

	Very	Somewhat	Not Very	Not at All
a. Freshness of food	❑	❑	❑	❑
b. Food poisoning	❑	❑	❑	❑
c. Pesticides	❑	❑	❑	❑
d. Use of hormones in foods	❑	❑	❑	❑
e. Use of additives and preservatives in food	❑	❑	❑	❑
f. Genetically modified foods	❑	❑	❑	❑

15. Do you get your nutrition information from any of the following sources?

	Yes	No
a. TV	❑	❑
b. Internet	❑	❑
c. Magazines	❑	❑
d. Friends	❑	❑
e. Parents	❑	❑
f. School	❑	❑
g. Other (e.g., books, doctor, dietitian, newspaper)	❑	❑

Part 5: Exercise Habits

16. During an average school week, how many days do you go to physical education class? (Applicable to preteens and teens only.)

0 ❑   1 ❑   2 ❑   3 ❑   4 ❑   5 ❑

17. Have you been on any school/work sports teams during the past year?   Yes ❑   No ❑

18. Outside of school/work, do you play on any sports teams, take exercise classes, or work out at a gym?   Yes ❑   No ❑

Canadian Teens Are Not Meeting Food Guide Requirements

Now that you've had an opportunity to assess your eating and exercise habits, take a few moments to consider what you've learned. Were you surprised to see that your diet lacks fruit and vegetables? Whole grains? Perhaps you didn't realize just how often you eat fast foods or sugary drinks. Or maybe taking this quiz confirmed for you that you do have a healthy diet. If so, that's great. Keep up the good work!

And what did you learn about the eating habits of the teenagers living in your house? Is nutrition on their radar screen? If your teenagers are like many of the Canadian high school students I surveyed, their diets need improvement. Four out of 10 teenagers surveyed report eating less than two vegetable servings each day, and one-half consume no more than two servings of milk products.

The good news is that teenagers are definitely interested in nutrition and rank it important in terms of staying healthy, controlling weight, and being active. Almost 8 out of

10 students rate nutrition important when deciding what foods to eat. Their top nutrient concerns include fat, calcium, vitamins, and protein.

Not surprisingly, females are more worried about fat and calories than are their male counterparts. When asked if they had been on a diet to lose weight in the past year, 26% of teens said yes, and among the dieters, almost 75% were girls. Interestingly (and thankfully), only 6% said they had tried a fad diet in the past year—be it Atkins, South Beach, or the Zone.

Judging from the survey results, it would appear that weight-conscious teens skip meals in an effort to save calories. Only one-half of teenagers report eating breakfast every day, while 36% say they eat the morning meal no more than twice a week. When it comes to lunch and dinner, almost 2 out of 10 teens skip these meals at least once a week.

Perhaps this explains, in part, why so many of the teenagers surveyed are missing out on their daily share of healthy foods. Canada's Food Guide to Healthy Eating recommends a daily minimum of five servings of fruits and vegetables. That 4 out of 10 teenagers eat less than two fruit and two vegetable servings each day suggests that many are short-changing their bodies of important vitamins, antioxidants, and dietary fibre.

While many teens report a poor intake of fresh fruit, they do seem to be guzzling fruit juice. Seven out of 10 students say they drink at least one serving of juice each day, and about half drink two or more. This suggests that many teens are getting too much sugar and too little roughage.

Also a concern is the reported low intake of dairy products among Canadian teens. Adolescents require 1300 milligrams of calcium each day. In food terms, this translates into roughly four milk servings per day. One serving is 1 cup (250 ml) of milk, 3/4 cup (175 grams) of yogurt, or 1 1/2 ounces (45 grams) of cheese. Only 14% of high school students surveyed report consuming four milk servings each day. The majority—5 out of 10—say they get no more than two daily servings, with girls consuming less than boys.

It would certainly seem that calcium is lacking in the diets of many high school students. When asked if they take a calcium supplement, only 15% said yes. Yet, consuming adequate calcium throughout the teen years is critical to building strong bones, protecting against osteoporosis later in life, and possibly helping ward off obesity.

Whole grains aren't that popular either. One-quarter of teens say they never opt for 100% whole-wheat or multigrain breads, while only 3 out of 10 say they always do.

Other studies have found similar results—many teenagers do not get their daily-recommended servings of fruit, vegetables, and dairy products. Surveys have also found that 60% of female teens are not getting the minimum number of servings of meat and alternatives. These findings clearly imply that many teenagers are at risk of vitamin and mineral deficiencies. And overconsumption of foods high in fat and sugar increases the likelihood of overweight and obesity.

A Food Guide for Teens

How can you ensure your teenager is getting his or her daily share of calories, protein, carbohydrates, vitamins, and minerals? Canada's Food Guide is a great starting point for planning healthy meals and evaluating your family's eating habits. The Food Guide was last revised in 1992, and Health Canada is in the process of updating it to ensure it is based on the latest recommended dietary allowances (RDAs) and current scientific knowledge about nutrition and health. The new guide is expected to be released in spring 2006. In the meantime, our current Food Guide is an excellent tool to help teenagers meet their nutrient needs. The Food Guide is based on these principles:

1. *Eat a variety* of foods to get the energy, protein, vitamins, minerals, and fibre you need for good health.

2. *Emphasize cereals, breads, other grain products, vegetables, and fruit.* These foods are lower in fat and provide carbohydrate for energy, dietary fibre, and many important vitamins.

3. Choose dark green and orange vegetables and orange fruit more often to *support adequate intakes of vitamin A, beta-carotene, and the B vitamin folate.*

4. *Choose lower-fat* dairy products, leaner meats, and food prepared with little or no fat. It's important not to eat too much fat, especially animal fat found in meat, poultry, and dairy products. Too much animal fat can elevate blood cholesterol levels. And too much fat from any source can lead to weight gain.

5. *Achieve and maintain a healthy body weight* by balancing the food you eat with regular physical activity.

6. *Limit salt, alcohol, and caffeine.*

Canada's Food Guide is an outline of what to eat each day. It's not a rigid prescription but, rather, a general guideline. It helps you and your family choose what and how much to eat from each food group to get the nutrients you need and not too many calories, or too much fat, saturated fat, sugar, and sodium.

The Food Guide emphasizes four main food groups: Grain Products, Vegetables and Fruit, Milk Products, and Meat and Alternatives. Each of these food groups provides some but not all of the nutrients you need. For this reason, foods in one group can't replace foods in another. Here is a look at each food group's unique set of nutrients, which you'll read more about in the following chapters.

- Grain Products: carbohydrate, fibre, B vitamins (thiamin, riboflavin, and niacin), iron, magnesium

- Vegetables and Fruit: carbohydrate, fibre, folate (a B vitamin), vitamin A, vitamin C, iron, magnesium

- Milk Products: protein, fat, riboflavin (a B vitamin), vitamin B12, vitamin A, vitamin D, calcium, zinc, magnesium

- Meat and Alternatives: protein, fat, B vitamins, iron, zinc, magnesium

What Counts as a Serving?

You may be wondering what constitutes one Food Guide serving. Here's a selected list to help you determine your daily portions (serving sizes are measured after cooking):

Protein Foods	Amount
Egg whites	2–4
Egg, whole	1–2
Fish, lean meat, poultry, cooked	2–3 oz (50–100 g)
Legumes (beans, chickpeas, lentils)	1/2–1 cup (125–250 ml)
Salmon, canned	1/3–2/3 can (50–100 g)
Soy nuts, roasted	1/4 cup (50 ml)
Tempeh	2/3 cup (150 ml)
Tofu, firm	2/3 cup (150 ml)
Tuna, canned	1/3–2/3 can (50–100 g)
Veggie burger	1
Veggie dog, small	2

Grain Products (choose whole grain)

Bagel	1/4
Bread, whole grain, 1 slice	1 oz (30 g)
Cereal, cold flake or shreddie	3/4 cup (175 ml)
Cereal, hot	1/2 cup (125 ml)
Cereal, 100% bran	1/2 cup (125 ml)
Corn niblets	1/2 cup (125 ml)
Corn on the cob	1/2
Crackers, soda	6
Grains, cooked	1/2 cup (125 ml)
Pasta, cooked	1/2 cup (125 ml)
Pita pocket	1/2
Popcorn, plain	3 cups (750 ml)
Potato	1/2 cup (125 ml)
Rice, cooked	1/2 cup (125 ml)
Roll, large (e.g., Kaiser, 6-inch submarine)	1/2
Tortilla, 6-inch	1

Fruit and Vegetables

Berries	1 cup (250 ml)
Fruit, cut up	1 cup (250 ml)
Fruit, small (plums, apricots)	4
Fruit, whole	1 medium-sized
Juice, unsweetened	1/2–3/4 cup (125–175 ml)
Vegetables, cooked or raw	1/2 cup (125 ml)
Vegetables, salad	1 cup (250 ml)

Milk and Alternatives

Milk, 1% milk fat or skim	1 cup (250 ml)
Cheese, 20% milk fat or less	1 1/2 oz (45 g)
Rice beverage, fortified	1 cup (250 ml)
Soy beverage, fortified	1 cup (250 ml)
Yogurt, 1% milk fat or less	3/4 cup (175 g)

Fats and Oils (Other Foods)

Butter, margarine, mayonnaise	1 tsp (5 ml)
Nuts, seeds	1 tbsp (15 ml)
Peanut and nut butters	1 1/2 tsp (7 ml)
Salad dressing	2 tsp (10 ml)
Vegetable oil	1 tsp (5 ml)

Health
Canada

Santé
Canada

CANADA'S

Food Guide

TO HEALTHY EATING
**FOR PEOPLE FOUR YEARS
AND OVER**

Enjoy a variety
of foods from each
group every day.

Choose lower-
fat foods
more often.

Grain Products
Choose whole grain
and enriched
products more often.

Vegetables and Fruit
Choose dark green and
orange vegetables and
orange fruit more often.

Milk Products
Choose lower-fat milk
products more often.

Meat and Alternatives
Choose leaner meats,
poultry and fish, as well
as dried peas, beans
and lentils more often.

Canada

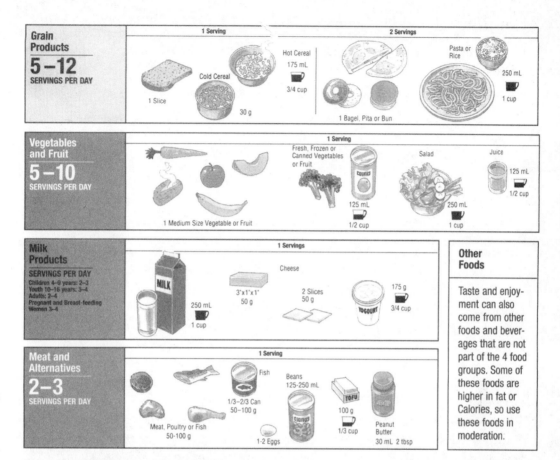

Grain Products **5 – 12** SERVINGS PER DAY	1 Serving		2 Servings	
	1 Slice	Cold Cereal 30 g / Hot Cereal 175 mL 3/4 cup	1 Bagel, Pita or Bun	Pasta or Rice 250 mL 1 cup

Vegetables and Fruit **5 – 10** SERVINGS PER DAY	1 Serving			
	1 Medium Size Vegetable or Fruit	Fresh, Frozen or Canned Vegetables or Fruit 125 mL 1/2 cup	Salad 250 mL 1 cup	Juice 125 mL 1/2 cup

Milk Products SERVINGS PER DAY Children 4–9 years: 2–3 Youth 10–16 years: 3–4 Adults: 2–4 Pregnant and Breast-feeding Women 3–4	1 Servings		
	MILK 250 mL 1 cup	Cheese 3"x1"x1" 50 g / 2 Slices 50 g	175 g 3/4 cup

Meat and Alternatives **2 – 3** SERVINGS PER DAY	1 Serving			
	Meat, Poultry or Fish 50-100 g	Fish 1/3–2/3 Can 50–100 g	1-2 Eggs / Beans 125-250 mL	TOFU 100 g 1/3 cup / Peanut Butter 30 mL 2 tbsp

Other Foods

Taste and enjoyment can also come from other foods and beverages that are not part of the 4 food groups. Some of these foods are higher in fat or Calories, so use these foods in moderation.

Different People Need Different Amounts of Food

The amount of food you need every day from the 4 food groups and other foods depends on your age, body size, activity level, whether you are male or female and if you are pregnant or breast-feeding. That's why the Food Guide gives a lower and higher number of servings for each food group. For example, young children can choose the lower number of servings, while male teenagers can go to the higher number. Most other people can choose servings somewhere in between.

Consult *Canada's Physical Activity Guide to Healthy Active Living* to help you build physical activity into your daily life.

Enjoy eating well, being active and feeling good about yourself. That's VITALIT

© Minister of Public Works and Government Services Canada, 1997
Cat. No. H39-252/1992E   ISBN 0-662-19648-1
No changes permitted. Reprint permission not required.

How Much Food Do Teenagers Need to Eat?

When it comes to food and nutrition needs, no two teenagers are alike. They differ according to:

- Body size—nutrient and calorie needs are greater for those with a larger body size.

- Gender—teenage boys have higher calorie requirements than do girls with similar activity levels, and as result, they need to eat more food. Females, too, have special nutrient needs, particularly for iron.

- Activity level—physically active teenagers will have higher energy and nutrient needs than sedentary kids.

- Individual variation—energy and nutrient needs vary from person to person naturally, even when factors such as age, body size, gender, and activity levels are similar.

That's why Canada's Food Guide gives a range for the number of servings for each food group it recommends, as well as a range for the serving sizes. Teenagers with calorie needs ranging from 1800 to 3200 can choose the number and size of servings appropriate to their nutrient and energy needs. For instance, teens with lower energy needs, such as inactive girls or overweight teens trying to lose weight, can plan their diets around the lower number of servings for each group. But to meet all their vitamin and mineral requirements without consuming too many calories, these teenagers must choose nutrient-rich foods that are lower in fat from each food group.

How much food should your teenager eat? The answer all depends on how many calories, or energy, your son or daughter needs each day. A calorie is a unit of energy that measures how much energy food provides to your body. Some people think calories are a bad thing. But the truth is that everybody needs to get calories from food. Teenagers must consume adequate calories to maintain health, promote optimal growth and maturation, and support physical activity.

The table following lists the recommended calorie intakes for teenagers of varying activity levels (these numbers are based on a standard height for each age). First, you need to figure out what activity level matches your teenager's daily activity pattern. Ask your son or daughter which of the following best describes his or her *daily* activity. Consider active time in gym class, team practice and games, and workouts in the gym. Keep in mind that most people overestimate how active they are.

ACTIVITY TABLE

Sedentary	No regular activity*
Low active	Up to 30 minutes of physical activity per day
Active	30 to 60 minutes of physical activity per day
Very active	More than 60 minutes of physical activity per day

*Brisk walking, swimming, cycling, jogging, in-line skating, dancing, team sports, etc.

CALORIE NEEDS OF PRETEENS AND TEENAGERS: FEMALES

	Activity Level			
Age (years)	Sedentary	Low Active	Active	Very Active
11	1540	1810	2070	2500
12	1615	1910	2180	2640
13	1685	1990	2280	2760
14	1720	2035	2335	2830
15	1730	2055	2360	2870
16	1730	2060	2370	2885
17	1710	2040	2350	2870
18	1690	2025	2335	2860

You'll notice that females have high energy needs up until the age of 15, at which time most growth and development has occurred. That's why the calorie requirements for ages 16 through 18 don't increase. (You might have noticed that they actually decrease; this is because the extra calories for growth are no longer needed.) Teenagers aged 19 have calorie requirements similar to adults. Gender, body weight, and daily physical activity level will determine how many calories 19-year-olds should consume.

CALORIE NEEDS OF PRETEENS AND TEENAGERS: MALES

	Activity Level			
Age (years)	Sedentary	Low Active	Active	Very Active
11	1690	1985	2280	2640
12	1800	2110	2425	2815
13	1935	2275	2620	3040
14	2090	2460	2830	3285
15	2225	2620	3015	3500
16	2320	2735	3152	3665
17	2365	2795	3225	3755
18	2385	2825	3265	3805

How Many Servings Are Right for Teenagers?

Now that you know how many calories your son or daughter needs each day, you can figure out how many servings from each food group he or she should be getting every day. Here are some sample diets for teenagers with varying calorie needs:

NUMBER OF FOOD GUIDE SERVINGS FOR DIFFERENT CALORIE LEVELS

	Lower: 1600–1700	Moderate: About 2200	Higher: About 3200
Grain products	5	9	12
Vegetables	3	4	6
Fruit	2	4	6
Milk products	3	4	4
Meat and alternatives	2 (or 6 oz/170 g)	2 (or 6 oz/170 g)	3 (or 9 oz/255 g)
Fats and oils (teaspoons)	4	6	7

In addition to milk, yogurt, and cheese, the Milk Products food group includes calcium-enriched soy beverages. All teenagers require 1300 milligrams of calcium each day. In food terms, that's four servings of milk products each day. You'll notice that I've listed only three servings for the lower-calorie-level diet. The remaining calcium can come from calcium-fortified fruit juice or a calcium supplement. Eating leafy green vegetables and almonds are other ways to bump up calcium intake.

You're probably thinking that 5 to 12 servings from the Grain Products group sounds like a lot, but it's really not. Just consider what one serving looks like—one slice of bread, 1/2 cup (125 ml) cooked rice or pasta, or 3/4 cup (175 ml) hot cereal. (For more information on serving sizes of grain products, see Chapter 2.)

You'll notice that I have added a new food group, Fats and Oils, which is not included in Canada's Food Guide. Added fats such as vegetable oils, non-hydrogenated margarine, butter, and salad dressings provide calories, too. You'll learn more on how to choose the healthiest fats in Chapter 4. In Canada's Food Guide, added fats and oils are found in the Other Foods category, a group of foods and beverages that are not part of any food group.

And don't forget that teenagers will get additional calories from added sugars in sweets, candy, soft drinks, and fruit drinks. These are incorporated into the Other Foods category along with fatty junk foods such as potato chips and french fries. Teenagers should keep their intake of these foods to a minimum.

Does Your Teen Need Extra Vitamins?

The teenage body needs more than 45 nutrients to grow and stay healthy. A diet that's low in fat and rich in vegetables, fruit, and whole grains will provide teenagers with plenty of vitamins and minerals. But most parents agree that busy teens don't always eat healthy. Between classes, homework, a part-time job, extracurricular sports, and family obligations, it can be tough to fit in a serving of yogurt or vegetables. For many teens, grabbing a fat-laden muffin mid-morning at school is more convenient than sitting down to a bowl of whole-grain cereal with milk before leaving for classes. Indeed, dietary surveys suggest that many teenagers, especially females, don't consume enough calcium, iron, and zinc—key nutrients for proper growth and development. To help your family eat a diet that's brimming with vitamins and minerals, use the following guide to choose nutrient-packed foods.

KEY VITAMINS	NEEDED FOR	BEST FOOD SOURCES
Vitamin A	Vision, growth, and development; healthy skin, hair, nails, bones, teeth	Beef liver, eggs, oily fish, cheese, milk Beta-carotene*: apricots, mangos, peaches, broccoli, carrots, kale, spinach, sweet potato, winter squash
Vitamin B1 (thiamin)	Converting food into energy; healthy nerve, muscle, and heart function	Beef liver, pork, fish, enriched breakfast cereals, legumes, nuts, wheat germ, whole grains and breads
Vitamin B2 (riboflavin)	Converting food into energy; vision; healthy skin and red blood cells	Red meat, eggs, cheese, fortified soy or rice milk, milk, yogurt, legumes, nuts, whole grains
Vitamin B3 (niacin)	Converting food into energy; healthy skin; digestion; nerve function	Beef liver, red meat, poultry, fish, eggs, dairy products, peanuts, almonds, enriched breakfast cereals, wheat bran
Vitamin B6	Breaking down protein and fat; red blood cell formation	Beef liver, red meat, poultry, eggs, fish, legumes, nuts, seeds, whole grains, avocados, bananas, green leafy vegetables, potatoes
Vitamin B12	Building and repairing DNA (genetic material of cells); making red blood cells; nerve function	Red meat, poultry, eggs, fish, dairy products, fortified soy or rice milk
Folate	Breaking down protein; red blood cell formation	Legumes, seeds, orange juice, artichokes, asparagus, spinach

Vitamin C	Forming connective tissue, bones, teeth, gums; absorbing iron; immune function; wound healing	Cantaloupe, citrus fruit and juices, kiwi, strawberries, bell peppers, broccoli, cabbage, cauliflower, tomato juice
Vitamin D	Strong bones and teeth	Milk, egg yolks, oily fish, fortified soy or rice milk
Vitamin E	Cell membranes, immune function, and red blood cell production	Nuts, seeds, soybeans, vegetable oils, wheat germ, whole grains, avocados, leafy green vegetables
Vitamin K	Blood clotting and bone formation	Beef liver, broccoli, cabbage, green peas, leafy green vegetables

* Beta-carotene is a natural chemical found in orange- and green-coloured fruits and vegetables. The liver converts some of the beta-carotene we consume from foods into vitamin A. There is no official daily requirement for beta-carotene. However, studies suggest that foods rich in beta-carotene may help prevent heart disease, cataracts, macular degeneration (an eye disease), and possibly lung cancer.

KEY MINERALS	NEEDED FOR	BEST FOOD SOURCES
Calcium	Building bones and teeth; muscle and nerve function; blood clotting; maintaining a healthy blood pressure	Canned salmon (with bones), sardines, dairy products, fortified soy or rice milk, almonds, legumes, tofu, fortified fruit juice, broccoli, leafy green vegetables
Iron	Formation of hemoglobin, which transports oxygen to body tissues; making brain chemicals that aid in concentration	Red meat, poultry, eggs, salmon, tuna, baked beans, lentils, enriched breakfast cereals, whole grains, raisins, blackstrap molasses
Magnesium	Heart, muscle, and nerve function; protein building; bone growth	Legumes, tofu, almonds, Brazil nuts, sunflower seeds, whole grains, dates, figs, prunes, leafy green vegetables
Potassium	Maintaining fluid balance in body; muscle and nerve function; maintaining healthy blood pressure	Avocados, bananas, cantaloupes, oranges, orange juice, peaches, broccoli, Brussels sprouts, green peas, lima beans, spinach, tomato juice
Zinc	Growth; sexual development; immune function; wound healing	Beef, lamb, pork, milk, yogurt, legumes, cashews, pumpkin seeds, wheat bran, wheat germ, whole grains, enriched breakfast cereals

Many of my clients ask me if their teenager should take a multivitamin and mineral supplement. My answer is always yes. Many health professionals contend that if you eat a well-balanced diet, there's no need for vitamin pills. I agree that a healthy diet is better for you than a handful of supplements, but there are a few reasons why a daily multivitamin and mineral supplement is a smart idea for growing teenagers.

For starters, as I mentioned above, dietary surveys show that many Canadian teenagers don't get enough fruits, vegetables, and dairy products. A national study also revealed that a surprisingly large proportion of teenage boys and girls don't meet the Food Guide recommendations for Meats and Alternatives. Taken together, these findings suggest that many teenagers are not meeting their daily requirements for vitamins A, C, and D; folate; calcium; and iron—all important nutrients for growth and development.

And no matter how good you are at planning your family's meals, there will be hectic days when eating right is a challenge. What's more, as a parent, you can't control how well your teenage son or daughter eats when away from home. Teens eat many meals outside the family home—when they're at sports tournaments, working at part-time jobs, or hanging out with friends.

A multivitamin supplement helps teenage girls meet their daily iron and folate requirements. Teens who skip meals or diet to lose weight also need insurance that they're meeting their daily requirements for most vitamins and minerals (though a multivitamin won't supply teens with every nutrient they need, in particular calcium). And vegetarian teens will get extra iron and vitamin B12 from a multivitamin, two nutrients that meat-free diets may be lacking.

Choosing a Multivitamin

It can be frustrating shopping for a multivitamin when there are so many product choices. You might wonder how anyone without a nutrition degree is expected to know which one to choose. Unfortunately, specially tailored multivitamins that meet teen nutrient needs do not yet exist. Teenagers should take an adult multivitamin formula, rather than a children's product. That's because children's multivitamins contain amounts of vitamins and minerals that are too low for growing teens. As well, many children's multivitamins don't contain iron or zinc.

Most multivitamin and mineral supplements will provide 100% to 300% of the recommended dietary allowance, or RDA, for most vitamins and minerals (with the exception of calcium, magnesium, and iron). However, mega, super, and high-potency formulas usually provide higher doses of B vitamins and antioxidants (vitamins C and E, beta-carotene, selenium).

Women's formulas should offer extra folic acid, which is the synthetic form of folate (0.6 to 1.0 milligrams), calcium (200 to 300 milligrams), and iron (15 to 18 milligrams), but they do not always include the full range of minerals. That's because adding more calcium to a formula takes up space, often at the expense of other nutrients. There are complete women's multivitamin and mineral products that contain all vitamins and minerals, but be warned—it's probably going to be a fairly large pill. Women's formulas with extra iron are suitable for teenage girls who are menstruating and losing iron each month. Formulas will vary by manufacturer, so be sure to check the ingredient list to see what you're paying for.

You can also choose between tablets, capsules, and chewable multivitamins. This choice comes down to personal preference. I like capsules because I find them easier to swallow than big tablets. If your teen prefers chewable multivitamins, he will probably have to chew two of these tablets to meet his recommended daily nutrient intake. Check the instructions for use on the label.

Here are some tips for choosing a multivitamin for teenagers:

- Choose a product containing vitamins A, C, D, E, B1, B2, niacin, B6, folic acid, and B12. Choose a formula that provides the RDA for vitamins B6 (1.0 to 1.2 milligrams), B12 (2.4 micrograms), and folic acid (0.4 milligrams).

- Avoid products that supply more than 5000 IU (international units) of vitamin A from retinol (often called vitamin A palmitate or acetate). Excess vitamin A from supplements may harm bone health. There's no evidence that beta-carotene is harmful to bones.

- Choose a product containing the minerals chromium, copper, iron, magnesium, selenium, and zinc. If your teen's diet lacks calcium, he or she should take a separate supplement, since most multivitamins contain less than 200 milligrams.

- Don't waste money on extras such as ginseng or ginkgo. Even if these herbs do boost energy and memory, the amounts added to a multivitamin are too small to help. The same goes for lutein (for eye health) and lycopene (for prostate health). When it comes to these natural plant chemicals, research suggests that it's foods containing these nutrients that are protective, not supplements.

- Make sure the expiry date is valid over the period you intend to use the product.

Choosing a Calcium Supplement

Here are some tips for choosing for a calcium supplement:

- Calcium citrate supplements generally supply 300 milligrams of calcium and can be taken any time of day, even on an empty stomach.

- Calcium carbonate supplements generally supply 500 milligrams of calcium and should be taken with meals for better absorption.

- If more than one calcium supplement is needed, spread calcium intake over the course of the day. Absorption from supplements is best in doses of 500 milligrams or less because the percentage of calcium your body absorbs decreases as the amount in the supplement increases.

- If your son or daughter is adverse to swallowing pills, try a chewable, liquid, or effervescent calcium supplement. These supplements dissolve well since they're broken down before entering the stomach.

- To prevent gas, bloating, and constipation, ensure your teen's diet provides adequate fluids and fibre. If this doesn't help, try another brand or form of calcium.

- If calcium intake needs to be increased, it should be done gradually. Start with 500 milligrams for one week, then add more calcium slowly if needed.

- Teens (and adults) should not consume more than 2500 milligrams of calcium per day from food and supplements combined. Taking too much calcium can cause stomach upset, high blood calcium levels, impaired kidney function, and decreased absorption of other minerals.

Remember, a multivitamin is meant to support your teen's diet, not replace it. So encourage your teen to eat right first, then supplement with a multivitamin.

How Healthy Is Your Teen's Body Weight?

One of the most common questions that teenagers ask me is, "What's the right weight for my height?" The truth is, there's no single number that's right for a specific height. Teenagers have different body types—some are more muscular and some are more developed than others. As adolescents go through puberty, the amount of muscle, fat, and bone in their bodies can change dramatically. Children's body fatness changes as they grow, and boys and girls differ in the amount of fat they carry as they mature. And let's not forget that teenagers can grow as much as 10 inches (25 centimetres) during puberty before reaching full adult height.

For adults, we use a measure called the body mass index (BMI) to assess weight. But unlike adults, a child's BMI value varies with age and gender. That's why a calculation called BMI-for-age is used to assess underweight, overweight, and the risk of becoming overweight in children and teenagers, aged 2 to 20 years. BMI-for-age is gender and age specific; it takes into account that teenagers' bodies are growing, developing, and changing (see charts on pages 23 and 24). The tool was developed by the Centers for Disease Control and Prevention in the United States and it is recommended for use for children by the Canadian Paediatric Society.

To determine your teenager's BMI-for-age, you must first calculate his or her BMI, as follows (you'll need a calculator):

1.	Determine body weight in kilograms	Weight in kilograms
	(Divide weight in pounds by 2.2)	
2.	Determine height in centimetres	Height in centimetres
	(Multiply height in inches by 2.54)	
3.	Determine height in metres	Height in metres
	(Divide height in centimetres by 100)	
4.	Square height in metres	Height in metres^2
	(Multiply height in metres by height in metres)	
5.	Now, calculate the BMI	BMI
	(Divide weight in kilograms by height in metres^2)	

The next step involves plotting the BMI on a gender-specific BMI chart. BMI charts contain a series of lines, which indicate percentiles.

A teenager's BMI percentile indicates how his or her measurements compare with other teens in the same age group. For example, let's say your 14-year-old daughter has a BMI of 24. Once you plot this value on the BMI-for-age chart for girls, you'll see that her BMI places her between the 85th and 90th percentile. This means that approximately 87% of other girls her age have a lower BMI than 24. Here's what BMI percentiles indicate:

BMI-FOR-AGE PERCENTILE	MEANS
Less than 5th percentile	Underweight
Between 85th to 95th percentile	At risk for overweight
Greater than 95th percentile	Overweight

Recent studies have shown that risk factors for heart disease are linked with BMI-for-age. Many children with a BMI-for-age greater than the 95th percentile have at least one obesity-related condition, such as high blood pressure, high cholesterol, or high insulin levels (a risk factor for type 2 diabetes).

Your teen's BMI-for-age should be calculated at every doctor's checkup. If your family doctor has not begun keeping track of your child's BMI, ask your doctor to do so. It will allow your teen to monitor his or her weight over time. Measuring BMI also presents an opportunity for the doctor to talk to your teenager about eating and exercise habits.

CDC Growth Charts: United States

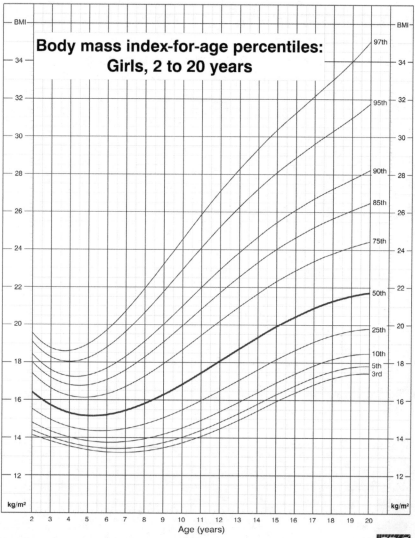

Body mass index-for-age percentiles: Girls, 2 to 20 years

Published May 30, 2000.
SOURCE: Developed by the National Center for Health Statistics in collaboration with the National Center for Chronic Disease Prevention and Health Promotion (2000).

CDC
SAFER·HEALTHIER·PEOPLE™

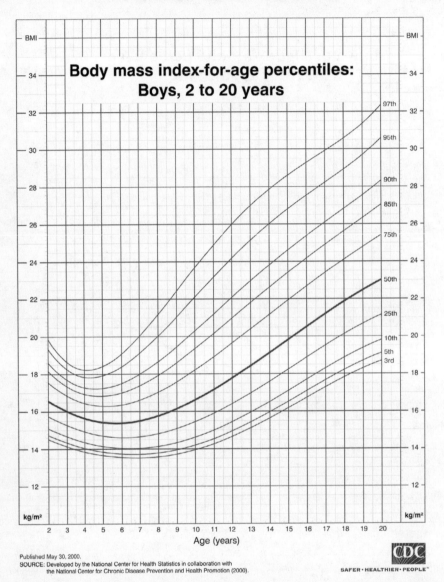

CDC Growth Charts: United States

Body mass index-for-age percentiles: Boys, 2 to 20 years

Published May 30, 2000.
SOURCE: Developed by the National Center for Health Statistics in collaboration with the National Center for Chronic Disease Prevention and Health Promotion (2000).

SAFER · HEALTHIER · PEOPLE™

Helping Your Teen Eat a Healthier Diet

There are no easy solutions to improving your teenager's diet. It's difficult to convince children of the benefits of healthy eating when there are so many competing forces at play.

Young people are exposed to powerful messages from food advertisements as well as to peer pressure. And let's face it—many teenagers like to go out with their friends and eat fast foods. Often teenagers see other activities or being with their friends as more important than having a family meal that you've taken the trouble to prepare.

Adolescence is also a time when teens may experiment more with food and begin new ways of eating, such as vegetarianism. And finally, it's a time of breaking away from family routines, doing things differently, and not wanting to be told what to do.

Leslie's Tips for Getting Teens to Eat Healthy

1. Set a good example. The way you take care of yourself sends a powerful message to your kids. When it comes to healthy eating, lead by example.

2. Encourage regular physical activity, including walking or bike riding instead of getting a ride or taking the bus. Encourage your kids to feel good about themselves—their size, their shape, and their other personal qualities.

3. Respect your teenager's opinion if he wants to eat differently than the rest of the family. If your child has expressed an interest in going vegetarian, ask why and encourage him to learn more about the diet.

4. Provide healthy foods and snacks in the home. Your teenager can then decide the amount she needs and what she wants to eat.

5. Get your teenager active in the kitchen. Get him involved in grocery shopping, menu planning, and meal preparation.

6. Teach food safety in the kitchen. Hand washing, and proper food storage and cooking practices are essential to good health.

Now it's time to help your teen adopt the healthiest diet possible. You've already completed step one—you've assessed your family's food and exercise habits, as well as each member's nutrition concerns. And I've given you a general template outlining what and how much food teenagers need to eat each day.

But that's only a start. Next, you'll learn how to make the healthiest food choices in each food group. From carbohydrates to protein-rich foods to fats and oils, I'll tell you the top picks of each. The remaining chapters will give you the tools and information you need to assist your teen in learning about healthy eating so he is able to make informed food choices when away from home.

2

––––⬥⬥⬥––––

All About Carbohydrates

Carbohydrate-rich foods are often called the staff of life, and for good reason. Carbohydrates, or "carbs" as they're often referred to, provide about half of all the energy that muscles, nerves, and other body tissues use. Carbohydrate is also the brain's preferred fuel source—it relies on a steady supply of glucose (the form of carbohydrate in the bloodstream) to function properly. It's for these reasons that eating an adequate amount of carbohydrate is necessary for growing teens. If it weren't for carbohydrate, teenagers would not have the energy to concentrate on their homework or play on the school sports team.

When teens think of carbohydrate-rich foods, they tend to think of starchy foods such as bagels, breakfast cereals, cereal bars, and french fries. That's only natural, since these foods make up a large part of many teenagers' diets. But teens can't live on starch alone. They also need carbohydrates from fruit, vegetables, whole grains, legumes, nuts, and dairy products.

What Are Carbohydrates?

Plants make the carbohydrates we eat from carbon dioxide, water, and the sun's energy. Carbohydrate is composed of carbon, hydrogen, and oxygen. The carbohydrate family includes simple sugars, starches, and dietary fibre.

Simple sugars are classified as monosaccharides ("mono" meaning one and "saccharide" meaning sugar) or disaccharides (two sugars). Monosaccharides are the simplest form of carbohydrate because they consist of only a single sugar molecule. The three monosaccharides important to nutrition are glucose (also called dextrose and blood sugar), fructose (found in fruit, honey, and corn syrup), and galactose. Galactose rarely occurs by itself in foods; instead, it's attached to another sugar unit to form the disaccharide called lactose. The disaccharides are pairs of monosaccharides linked together. Maltose (malt sugar), sucrose (table sugar), and lactose (milk sugar) are disaccharides that we consume in foods every day.

Starches are more complex arrangements of carbohydrate. Starches in foods are long chains of hundreds or thousands of glucose units linked together. These giant molecules are stacked side by side in a grain of rice, a slice of bread, or a flake of breakfast cereal. Other starchy foods include potatoes, wheat, rye, oats, corn, and legumes (chickpeas, kidney beans, black beans, soybeans, lentils, and so on). Starchy foods give your body energy but, as you'll learn later in this chapter, not all starchy foods are created equal when it comes to good nutrition and health.

Dietary fibres are the structural parts of vegetables, fruit, grains, and legumes. Pectins, lignans, cellulose, gums, and mucilages are the scientific names given to different types of fibres found in plants. Our digestive enzymes cannot break down the chemical bonds that link the building blocks of fibre. When undigested fibre arrives in your large intestine (colon), resident bacteria ferment these fibres and break them down. Now you know why flatulence can be a problem when you begin eating high-fibre foods.

How Much Carbohydrate Do Teens Need?

Adolescents need carbohydrate to provide energy to all cells in the body, especially brain cells. Carbohydrate-rich foods fuel an active brain as well as developing muscles and body tissues. And teenagers who are physically active have higher carbohydrate needs for sustaining their increased calorie requirements.

Children aged 12 to 19 years require at least 130 grams of carbohydrate each day (the same amount adults need). This daily requirement is based on the average minimum amount of carbohydrate, in the form of glucose, that's used by the brain. But most parents don't need to worry that their teenager isn't getting enough—teens typically exceed their minimum carbohydrate requirements. And unless overweight or obesity is an issue, this is not a concern. Here's how much food a day it takes to get 130 grams of carbohydrate:

Breakfast	Carbohydrate (grams)
1 1/2 cups (375 ml) ready-to-eat breakfast cereal	30
1 cup (250 ml) milk	16
1 cup (250 ml) unsweetened orange juice	24
Lunch	
Sandwich with 2 slices of whole-grain bread	40
3/4 cup (175 g) fruit-bottom yogurt	33
1 medium banana	27
Snack	
1 large muffin or bagel	60
Dinner	
4 oz (115 g) chicken	0
1 cup (250 ml) rice, pasta, or potato	30–45
1/2 cup (125 ml) vegetables or 1 cup (250 ml) tossed salad	2
1 cup (250 ml) milk	16
1 medium apple	20
Total daily carbohydrate intake:	*298–313*

Many teens snack more often than once a day, boosting their carbohydrate intake even higher than this chart shows. Teenagers at risk for not getting enough include those who skip meals, those who cut carbs in an effort to lose weight, and athletes who have very high calorie needs.

What Are the Best Carbohydrates to Eat?

Contrary to what advocates of low-carb diets say, not all carbohydrates make you fat, nor do they all increase your risk for health problems such as diabetes and heart disease. When it comes to weight control and health, what is most important is the *quality* of carbohydrate-rich foods you eat. In fact, populations around the world that enjoy the lowest rates of disease actually eat a high-carbohydrate, low-fat diet. Mediterranean, Asian, and vegetarian diets—often called vegetarian-style, high-carb diets—all provide at least 55% of calories from carbohydrate-rich foods such as grains, beans, fruits, and vegetables. However, these high-carbohydrate diets are very different from our North American version.

The high-carb diet we consume is often referred to as a low-fat convenience food diet. That's because the hallmark foods of the North American diet include refined and processed foods: low-fat cookies and muffins, cereal bars, pretzels, crackers, baked tortilla chips, bagels with fat-free cream cheese, low-fibre breakfast cereals, and so on. (Just think of all those snack foods your teenagers munch on.) Refined grains (e.g., white flour, white rice) are derived from whole grains (e.g., whole-wheat flour, brown rice) that have been milled. Modern milling of whole cereal grains removes the germ and bran layers, which contain 90% of the nutritional content of the kernel. That leaves only the starchy inner layer, called the endosperm. This starch is then ground and the result is "refined" flour. These overly processed foods lack fibre, nutrients, and antioxidants. They're certainly a far cry from the whole grains, legumes, fruit, and vegetables that define a healthy high-carb diet.

Research shows that a vegetarian-style high-carb, low-fat diet does not raise cholesterol or other blood fats (known as triglycerides). In fact, it actually tends to lower blood fats and promote weight loss. Nor do these diets depress your level of HDL cholesterol, considered good cholesterol because it does not accumulate on artery walls. (I discuss blood cholesterol in more detail in Chapter 4). That's because this type of high-carb diet is loaded with fibre, vitamins, minerals, antioxidants, and protective plant chemicals, all of which help keep you healthy and trim. On the other hand, a steady intake of refined carbohydrates can trigger your appetite, promote weight gain, and raise blood triglycerides. What's more, a steady intake of refined carbs is linked with a higher risk of heart disease, type 2 diabetes, and colon cancer.

Go for Whole Grains

A common thread to these healthy high-carb diets is that they all contain plenty of whole-grain foods. Eating foods made from whole grains means you're getting all parts of the grain: the outer bran layer where nearly all the fibre is; the germ layer, rich in nutrients such as vitamin E; and the endosperm, which contains the starch. When whole grains are milled, scraped, refined, and heat processed into flakes, puffs, or white flour, all that's left is the starchy endosperm. That means you end up with significantly less vitamins, minerals, antioxidants, protective plant chemicals, and fibre.

The more that grains are altered and stripped of their natural parts, the more quickly our bodies are able to digest them, leaving us soon hungry again. Intact whole grains are digested less rapidly and enter our bloodstream more slowly than refined grains.

When we eat refined grains and other foods that are rapidly digested and converted into blood glucose, the pancreas releases excessive amounts of the hormone insulin into the bloodstream. Insulin's job is to move glucose from the blood to your cells, where it's needed for energy. A number of studies have found that people who eat a steady diet of whole grains have a lower risk of developing type 2 diabetes, a disease that's increasing among teenagers. A 2003 study from the University of Minnesota found that compared with adolescents who consumed less than one whole-grain serving per day, those teens who ate at least one daily serving had a lower body mass index (an assessment of weight) and greater sensitivity to insulin, the body's sugar-clearing hormone.[1] The association was the strongest among the heaviest teenagers. High body mass index and insulin insensitivity are two risk factors for type 2 diabetes.

Favouring whole grains instead of refined carbohydrate foods is also linked with protection from heart disease, stroke, and certain cancers.

Until recently, the health benefits of whole grains were attributed to their fibre content. But scientists have identified other protective ingredients in whole grains. Antioxidant compounds such as vitamin E, tocotrienols, and flavonoids may discourage the formation of blood clots and may also prevent LDL (bad) cholesterol from sticking to artery walls. The antioxidants in whole grains, along with naturally occurring plant estrogens, may also protect from cancer. Whole grains are also important sources of zinc, selenium, copper, and iron—minerals that keep our immune systems healthy.

How to Add Whole Grains to Your Teen's Diet

According to the research, you need to eat only two or three servings of whole grains each day to reap their health benefits. Encourage your teens to eat at least three servings of whole grains each day. What's a serving? One serving of whole grain is equivalent to:

1 slice whole-grain bread	3/4 cup (175 ml) ready-to-eat whole-grain breakfast cereal
1/4 whole-grain bagel	
1/2 whole-wheat pita pocket	1/2 cup (125 ml) cooked whole grain (e.g., barley, bulgur)
1/2 cup (125 ml) 100% bran cereal	1/2 cup (125 ml) cooked whole-wheat pasta
1/2 cup (125 ml) cooked oatmeal	1/2 cup (125 ml) cooked brown rice

If whole grains are so healthy, why do so many of us eat so few of them? And why are teenagers even worse than adults when it comes to eating whole grains? Surveys show that most teens choose refined breads and cereals over whole grains. One reason may be that many people don't know what whole grains are. You probably understand that a refined grain has all of its fibre removed. But you might be hard-pressed to figure out if Kellogg's Special K cereal is refined (yes), a bread labelled "multigrain" is whole grain (not always), or if unbleached wheat flour is white flour in disguise (always).

When it comes to whole grains, it's hard to know what's what. Is that pumpernickel bagel from the bagel shop whole grain? And what about that bran muffin from the bakery—does it contain any whole-wheat flour? Shopping for whole grains can be a challenge when an overwhelming number of rapidly digested refined-grain products— cereals, crackers, breads, pastas—dominate grocery store shelves. And knowing what's whole grain and what's not can be a challenge because you won't always find this information on nutrition labels of food packages. To help, here's a list of selected grains and grain products.

Whole Grains	Refined Grains
Brown rice	Cornmeal
Bulgur	Pasta, white
Corn	Pearl barley
Emmer	Rice flour
Farro	Rye flour
Flaxseed	Unbleached wheat flour
Kamut	Wheat flour
Kasha (buckwheat groats)	White rice
Millet	
Oat Bran	
Oatmeal, Whole oats	
Popcorn	
Pot barley	
Quinoa	
Spelt	
Wheat berries	
Whole or cracked wheat	
Whole rye	
Wild rice	

How do you sleuth out whole grains among a sea of refined foods? Start by reading labels carefully. Look for claims such as "100% whole wheat." Foods whose packaging states "whole grains" may contain only tiny amounts. Next, check the ingredient list. If the whole grain is listed first, the product is predominately whole grain. If a whole grain is listed second, you might be getting only a little or nearly half whole grain.

When buying bread, look for whole-wheat flour or whole-rye flour on the list of ingredients. Wheat flour or unbleached wheat flour as an ingredient means it's a refined food. Don't be fooled by healthy sounding names such as 7 Grain, Multigrain, Prairie Bran, Oat and Honey, or Pumpernickel. Once you read the ingredient list, you'll find that many consist mostly of refined flour.

When choosing breakfast cereals, look for cereals that are whole grain and contain at least 4 grams of fibre per serving. Cereal fibres help prevent constipation, and they're linked with protection from heart disease and type 2 diabetes. You might be surprised to learn that your bowl of 100% bran cereal is not whole grain. Look at the ingredient list, and you won't find one whole grain listed. However, you can consider these cereals as whole grain since they are a concentrated source of bran that's missing from refined grains.

Whole grains add variety and flavour to meals. Take a break from the usual side of white rice or potatoes; be adventurous and introduce the following into your family's diet:

Buckwheat Kasha, also called roasted buckwheat groats, has a nutty taste that boosts the flavour of any meal. It is quick cooking and very versatile. Simmer 1 part kasha with 2 parts water brought to a boil, for 15 minutes. Try it in soups, stews, stuffing, pilaffs, and stir-fries.

Bulgur If you've eaten Middle Eastern cuisine, chances are you've met bulgur in tabouli salad. It's another quick cooking grain. Simmer 2 parts bulgur per 5 parts liquid brought to a boil over low heat for about 25 minutes. Remove from the heat and let stand covered for about 10 minutes. Bulgur is high in iron, calcium, and fibre, and great in pilafs, soups, and stuffings.

Cracked wheat This grain takes a little longer to cook, but it's worth the effort. Simmer 1 part cracked wheat in 2 parts water brought to a boil for about 40 minutes. Enjoy as a side dish or add it (uncooked) to quick-bread recipes.

Kamut Kamut is related to the wheat family, but it has less potential for causing an allergic reaction. The grain is about two or three times the size of a wheat berry and has more fibre and protein than most grains. Its chewy texture and buttery flavour make it great for salads. It's also ground into flour, used for baked goods, cereals, and pasta.

Quinoa Sacred to the Incas, this fluffy grain is sold as a pasta or whole grain. Quinoa is lower in carbohydrate and higher in protein than most grains. Try it in pilafs, salads, casseroles, and stir-fries. Rinse, then cook 1 part quinoa per 2 parts water or stock. Bring to a boil, then cook over medium-low heat for 12 to 15 minutes.

Spelt Touted as a grain well tolerated by people with a wheat sensitivity, you'll find this age-old staple sold as whole grain, flour, bread, breakfast cereal, and pasta. Try using spelt flour in baking and cooking. It adds a delicious nutty taste to pizza crusts and multigrain breads.

Teens, Carbohydrates, and the Glycemic Index

I mentioned earlier that whole grains are digested more slowly than refined grains. As a result, the carbohydrate (glucose) from these foods enters your bloodstream more gradually. We are learning that the health benefits of whole grains may also be due to the rate at which they are digested and absorbed into the bloodstream.

The glycemic index (GI) is a relatively new—and complicated—concept in the world of carbohydrates. It is a scale that ranks carbohydrate-rich foods by how fast they raise blood sugar levels compared with a standard food. The number tells you whether a food raises your blood glucose rapidly, moderately, or slowly. The standard food usually used is pure glucose, which is ranked 100 (fast acting).

Foods with a high GI value are digested quickly and cause a rapid rise in blood sugar, and therefore, an outpouring of insulin. This surge of insulin can trigger hunger and overeating. What's more, a steady intake of fast-acting carbohydrates can lead to chronic high insulin levels and eventually insulin resistance, a precursor for type 2 diabetes.

Foods that rank high on the GI scale (70 or higher) include white bread, whole-wheat bread, baked russet potatoes, refined breakfast cereals, instant oatmeal, cereal bars, Pop-Tarts, raisins, dates, ripe bananas, carrots, honey, and sugar.

Foods with a low GI (less than 55) release their sugar more slowly into the bloodstream and don't produce a rush of insulin. Such foods include grainy breads with seeds, steel-cut oats, 100% bran cereals, brown rice, sweet potatoes, pasta, apples, citrus fruit, grapes, pears, legumes, nuts, milk, yogurt, and soy milk (refer to page 35 for a longer list of foods and their GI values).

A diet based on low GI foods—foods that are digested slowly—might help overweight teenagers eat smaller portions and lose weight. Short-term studies indicate that eating fast-acting, high GI foods actually increases hunger and triggers overeating in teens. Researchers from the Children's Hospital in Boston fed overweight teenage boys a low, medium, or high GI lunch. The boys were then given access to snack foods for the next five hours. Compared with the boys who ate the low GI lunch, those who were given the high GI meal ate a whopping 81% more calories over the course of the afternoon.[2]

A one-year study published in 2003 found that a low glycemic diet helped obese teenagers lose more weight and body fat than did a standard low-fat, high-carb diet. The teens following the low glycemic diet also experienced less insulin resistance (a risk factor for type 2 diabetes) than the adolescents on the low-fat meal plan.[3] In still another study, researchers prescribed either a low GI or standard low-fat diet to 107 obese children for four months. At the end of the study, the children on the low GI regime dropped more weight and had a lower body mass index than those on the standard high-carb, low-fat diet.[4]

It seems that slowly digested carbohydrates keep you feeling full longer. The prolonged presence of food in your stomach can stimulate receptors that tell your brain you're full. You stop eating sooner and feel satisfied longer. Think about it: doesn't a bowl of oatmeal (low GI) keep your hunger at bay much longer than two slices of white toast (high GI)?

How to Adopt a Low Glycemic Diet

Eating more low GI foods needn't require a calculator or memorizing a lengthy list of glycemic index values. Here are a few tips to help you incorporate low GI foods into your family's meals:

- Keep in mind that unprocessed fresh foods such as whole grains, legumes, nuts, fruits, and vegetables will have a low GI value. High glycemic foods are usually highly processed and may have a concentrated amount of sugar.

- Include at least one low GI food per meal, or base two of your family's meals on low GI choices (see the table below).

- Pay attention to breads and breakfast cereals, since these foods contribute the most to the high glycemic value of our North American diet; this is especially true for teenagers.

- Encourage your teen to avoid snacking on high GI foods such as pretzels, corn chips, and rice cakes, as these can trigger hunger and overeating. Instead have fresh fruit, low-fat dairy products, nuts, or unbuttered popcorn within easy reach.

- Use salad dressings made with vinegar or lemon juice, as acidic foods have a lower GI.

- Keep in mind that combining a high GI food with a low GI food will result in a meal with a medium GI value.

- Remember that not all high GI foods are unhealthy, nor should they be avoided. Take whole-wheat bread, for example. It's definitely a more nutritious choice than fluffy white bread, but because both are finely milled, they both have a high GI. Carrots have a high GI but are loaded with the antioxidant beta-carotene. The same goes for bananas (high in potassium) and dates (high in magnesium), two nutrient-packed foods linked with healthy blood pressure.

- By the same token, keep in mind that not all low GI foods are good for you. Sure, ice cream comes in at 38 and white chocolate scores a 44, but health foods they aren't.

- Don't forget about portion size. When it comes to weight control, excess calories add up regardless of their glycemic index.

Below is a list of foods ranked by their GI value, from lowest to highest. Here's what the GI numbers mean:

Less than 55	Low GI
55–70	Medium GI
Greater than 70	High GI

GLYCEMIC INDEX VALUES OF SELECTED FOODS

Bread and Crackers

Bagel, white	72
Baguette, French	95
Breton Wheat Crackers	67
Cracked-wheat bread	53
Enriched white bread, Wonder	73
Kaiser roll	73
Light rye bread, Silverstein's Bakery	68
Flaxseed/Linseed rye, Rudolph's	55
Melba toast	70
Pita bread, white	57
Pumpernickel bread, whole-grain	46
Rice cakes	78
Rye bread	65
Rye bread, whole-meal	58
Rye crispbreads	64
Soda crackers	74
Sourdough rye bread	53
Stoned Wheat Thins	67
Water crackers	71
White bread	70
Whole-wheat bread	71

Breakfast Cereals

All-Bran Original, Kellogg's	42
All-Bran Bran Buds, Kellogg's	47
Bran flakes	74
Cheerios	74
Corn Bran Squares, Quaker	75
Corn flakes	81
Cream of wheat	66
Cream of wheat, instant	74
Crispix, Kellogg's	87
Grape-Nuts, Post	71
Oat bran	50
Oatmeal, instant	66
Porridge made from rolled oats	49
Raisin bran	61
Red River	49

Shredded Wheat, Weetabix	75
Special K, Kellogg's	54

Cookies, Cakes, and Muffins

Angel food cake	67
Arrowroot cookies	65
Banana bread	47
Blueberry muffin	59
Digestive biscuits	59
Graham wafers	74
Oat bran muffin	60
Oatmeal cookies	54
Oatmeal muffins, made from mix	69
Sponge cake	46

Pasta, Grains, and Potatoes

Barley	25
Bulgur	46
Corn, sweet	53
Couscous	65
Fettuccine, egg	32
Millet	71
Potato, french-fried	75
Potato, instant, mashed	86
Potato, new, unpeeled, boiled	78
Potato, red-skinned, boiled	88
Potato, red-skinned, mashed	91
Potato, white-skinned, baked	60
Rice, basmati	58
Rice, brown	55
Rice, instant	69
Rice, long-grain, white	56
Rice, risotto	69
Rice, white, converted, Uncle Ben's	45
Spaghetti, white	41
Spaghetti, whole-wheat	37
Sweet potato, boiled	59

Legumes, Nuts, and Seeds

Baked beans	48
Black beans	30

Black bean soup	64
Chickpeas, canned	42
Kidney beans	28
Lentils, green	30
Lentil soup, canned	44
Peanuts	14
Soybeans	18
Split pea soup	66

Fruit and Unsweetened Juices

Apple	34
Apple juice	40
Apricot, dried	31
Banana	55
Cherries	22
Dates, dried	103
Grapefruit	25
Grapes	43
Kiwi	53
Mango	51
Orange	42
Orange juice	46
Peach	28
Pear	38
Pineapple	59
Raisins	64
Tomato juice	38
Watermelon	72

Milk Products and Milk Alternatives

Milk, chocolate	34
Milk, skim	32
Milk, whole	27
Ice cream, premium	38
Ice cream, regular	61
Soy beverage, full-fat	40
Soy beverage, low-fat	44
Tofu-based frozen dessert	115
Yogurt, low-fat, aspartame	14
Yogurt, low-fat, sugar	33

Snack Foods and Sugary Drinks

Cola	58
Corn chips	63
Gatorade	78
Popcorn	72
Potato chips	54
Pretzels	83
Sports Bar, PowerBar, chocolate	56

Sugars

Fructose (fruit sugar)	19
Glucose	99
Honey	55
Lactose (milk sugar)	46
Sucrose (table sugar)	68

Foster-Powell, K, et al. International tables of glycemic index and glycemic load values: 2002. *Am J Clin Nutr* 2002, 76(1): 5–56. Adapted with permission by the *American Journal of Clinical Nutrition.* © AM J Clin Nutr American Society for Clinical Nutrition.

Why It's Important for Teens to Boost Their Fibre Intake

Carbohydrate foods can contain a little or a lot of fibre. Certainly, whole grains have more fibre than their refined counterparts. But fruit, vegetables, and legumes can also supply a fair amount of fibre to your diet. A high-fibre diet is important for a number of reasons. For starters, boosting your fibre intake can keep you regular. By absorbing water and adding bulk, fibre helps move food through your digestive tract faster. Not only does this bulking action prevent constipation, it can also reduce the exposure of cells in your colon to cancer-causing substances. Dietary fibre may also inactivate these harmful compounds before they can harm your colon. And certain types of fibre can act to help keep your cholesterol levels in check, too.

Fibre is classified according to the physical properties it exerts on the body. Foods are made up of two types of fibre, soluble and insoluble. Both are always present in varying proportions in plant foods, but some foods are rich in one or the other. For instance, dried peas, beans, lentils, oats, barley, psyllium husks, apples, and citrus fruits are good sources of soluble fibre. Soluble fibre forms a gel in your stomach and slows the rate of digestion and absorption. As soluble fibre passes through the digestive tract, its gel-like property can trap substances related to high cholesterol. There's plenty of evidence to show that oats, beans, and psyllium lower elevated blood cholesterol levels.

Diets rich in soluble fibre also may help prevent type 2 diabetes. Because soluble fibre delays the rate at which food empties from your stomach into the intestine, your blood sugar level will rise more slowly after eating a meal that contains carbohydrate. (Remember, carbohydrate in foods gets broken down into small sugar units—glucose— before it enters the bloodstream.) If, after a meal, your blood sugar rises gradually, rather than quickly, less wear and tear is put on your pancreas, the organ that secretes the sugar-clearing hormone insulin.

If your teenager suffers from constipation, he or she needs to eat foods rich in wheat bran, as well as whole grains and plenty of vegetables. These foods contain mainly insoluble fibre, the type of fibre that retains water and acts to increase stool bulk and promote regularity. By preventing constipation, a high-fibre diet can also prevent diverticulitis, a condition in which bulging pouches in the colon become inflamed or infected, causing abdominal pain, fever, nausea, and a change in bowel habits. (Diverticulitis occurs mainly in older adults. But since teenage eating habits are often carried into adulthood, encouraging teens to choose higher-fibre foods now can help prevent the condition later in life.)

A high-fibre diet might also help overweight teenagers lose weight. That's because high-fibre diets are lower in calories and larger in volume than low-fibre diets. A fibre-rich meal takes longer to eat, and its presence in the stomach may bring on a feeling of fullness sooner. This means filling up on fewer calories. Studies show that obese men and women eat less fibre than their healthy weight peers.

How Much Fibre Do Teenagers Need?

Data suggest that North American kids and teens, like adults, eat too little fibre. It's important that teenagers add fibre-rich foods to their diets to promote normal laxation, to help keep cholesterol levels in check, and to reduce the risk of obesity and type 2 diabetes. Daily fibre requirements are based on how many calories you consume. For instance, compared with teenage girls of the same age, adolescent boys consume more calories each day and therefore should be getting more fibre in their diets. Here are the daily fibre requirements for teenagers.

Age	Daily Fibre (grams)
9–13 years, boys	31
9–13 years, girls	26
14–19 years, boys	38
14–19 years, girls	26

If your teen's diet is low in fibre, make sure he increases fibre intake gradually, to prevent bloating and gas. And remember that fibre needs fluid to work, so be sure to encourage him to drink at least one glass of water with each high-fibre meal and snack. Use the list of fibre-rich foods to plan your family's meals. You'll notice that high-fibre food choices also tend to have a low glycemic index.

FIBRE CONTENT OF SELECTED FOODS (GRAMS)

Legumes

Beans and tomato sauce, canned, 1 cup (250 ml)	20.7
Black beans, cooked, 1 cup (250 ml)	13.0
Chickpeas, cooked, 1 cup (250 ml)	6.1
Kidney beans, cooked, 1 cup (250 ml)	6.7
Lentils, cooked, 1 cup (250 ml)	9.0

Nuts

Almonds, 1/2 cup (125 ml)	8.2
Peanuts, dry roasted, 1/2 cup (125 ml)	6.9

Cereals

100% bran cereal, 1/2 cup (125 ml)	10.0
Bran flakes, 3/4 cup (175 ml)	6.3
Grape-Nuts, Post, 1/2 cup (125 ml)	6.0
All-Bran Bran Buds, Kellogg's, 1/3 cup (75 ml)	13.0
Corn Bran Squares, Quaker, 1 cup (250 ml)	6.3
Oat bran, cooked, 1 cup (250 ml)	4.5
Oatmeal, cooked, 1 cup (250 ml)	3.6
Red River, cooked, 1 cup (250 ml)	4.8
Shreddies, 3/4 cup (175 ml)	4.4

Bread and Other Grain Foods

Bread, 100% whole-wheat, 2 slices	4.0
Flaxseed, ground, 2 tbsp (25 ml)	4.0
Pita pocket, whole-wheat, 1	4.8
Rice, brown, cooked, 1 cup (250 ml)	3.1
Spaghetti, whole-wheat, cooked, 1 cup (250 ml)	4.8
Wheat bran, 2 tbsp (25 ml)	3.0

Fruits

Apple, 1 medium with skin	2.6
Apricots, dried, 1/4 cup (50 ml)	2.6
Banana, 1 medium	1.9
Blueberries, 1/2 cup (125 ml)	2.0
Figs, dried, 5	8.5
Orange, 1 medium	2.4
Pear, 1 medium with skin	5.1
Prunes, 3	3.0
Raisins, seedless, 1/2 cup (125 ml)	2.8
Strawberries, 1 cup (250 ml)	3.8

Vegetables

Broccoli, 1/2 cup (125 ml)	2.0
Brussels sprouts, 1/2 cup (125 ml)	2.6
Carrots, 1/2 cup (125 ml)	2.2

Corn niblets, 1/2 cup (125 ml)	2.3		Potato, 1 medium, baked, with skin	5.0
Green peas, 1/2 cup (125 ml)	3.7		Sweet potato, mashed, 1/2 cup (125 ml)	3.9
Lima beans, 1/2 cup (125 ml)	3.8			

Source: *Nutrient Values of Some Common Foods,* table titled "Fibre Content of Selected Foods," Health Canada (© 1999, reprint 2002). Reproduced with the permission of the Minister of Public Works and Government Services Canada, 2005.

Share these tips with your teenager to help her add more fibre to meals and snacks:

- Strive to eat five or more servings of fruits and vegetables each day.

- Leave the peel on fruits and vegetables whenever possible (but wash thoroughly).

- Eat at least three servings of whole-grain foods each day.

- Buy high-fibre breakfast cereals. Aim for at least 4 grams of fibre per serving (check the nutrition information panel on the cereal packaging). If your teenager's favourite cereal is low in fibre, suggest she mix it with one that's higher in fibre. You'll find a list of ready-to-eat breakfast cereals and their fibre contents on the following pages.

- For a real fibre boost at breakfast, choose a 100% bran cereal, which packs 10 to 13 grams of fibre per 1/2 cup (125 ml) serving.

- Top breakfast cereals with fresh berries, dried cranberries or blueberries, or raisins.

- Add 1 to 2 tablespoons (15 to 25 ml) of natural wheat bran, oat bran, or ground flaxseed to cereals, yogurt, applesauce, casseroles, and soup.

- Eat legumes more often. Add white kidney beans to pasta sauce, black beans to tacos, chickpeas to salads, lentils to soup.

- Add a handful of seeds, nuts, or raisins to salads.

- Add cashews or peanuts to a vegetable stir-fry.

- Reach for high-fibre snacks such as plain popcorn, dried apricots, or dates. Dried apricots and almonds make a great after-school snack; these can be prepackaged in resealable snack bags so they're ready to throw into a backpack.

Best Bets for High-Fibre Breakfast Cereals

Let's face it: most teenagers love cereal. They'll eat it for breakfast and then happily devour a couple of bowls as an after-school snack. Cereal is a great way for growing teenagers to get energy, iron, and calcium (from the milk). And fibre, too. But once you start reading nutrition labels, you'll see that all cereals are not created equal. The ideal ready-to-eat breakfast cereal is low in fat and sugar, high in fibre, and made with whole grains (oats, whole wheat, whole rye, barley, flaxseed, brown rice, kamut, and so on). Per serving, my top picks have:

- Usually no more than 8 grams of sugar

- At least 4 grams of fibre

- No more than 4 grams of fat

In addition, they are made from whole grains.

The numbers given for sugar on the cereal package's nutrition labels include both added sugars and sugars occurring naturally in fruit. That means there are some exceptions to the 8 grams of sugar cut-off. You'll notice that some of my top picks listed below have more than 8 grams of sugar per serving. Cereals with dried fruit, for example raisins and cranberries, will have higher sugar contents, but they'll also have more fibre, which is a good thing.

Other exceptions to my sugar limit include very-high-fibre cereals, such as All-Bran. High-fibre cereals usually pack in more sugar. It's added by the manufacturer to make your bowl of bran more palatable. In my opinion, it's more important to choose a cereal that's high in fibre, even if it has a few extra grams of sugar, than not get enough fibre because you are trying to avoid the sugar. Eating a bowl of bran cereal each morning can put a big dent in your daily fibre requirement.

The cereals (and the serving sizes) listed below all contain no more than 4 grams of fat per serving.

Cereal	Calories	Sugars (grams)	Fibre (grams)	Whole Grains
Breadshop's Granola Crunchy Oat Bran with Almonds and Raisins, 1/2 cup (125 ml)	222	8.8	5	Yes
Grain Shop High Fibre Crisp, 1/2 cup (125 ml)	116	5	4	Yes
Health Valley Organic Golden Flax, 2/3 cup (150 ml)	205	9	5.5	Yes
Kashi Golean, 1 cup (250 ml)	140	6	10	Yes
Kashi Golean Crunch!, 1 cup (250 ml)	190	6	10	Yes
Kashi Good Friends, 1 cup (250 ml)	170	9	12	Yes
Kellogg's All-Bran Bran Buds, 1/3 cup (75 ml)	70	8	12	No
Kellogg's All-Bran Flakes, 1 cup (250 ml)	110	4	5	Yes
Kellogg's All-Bran Original, 1/2 cup (125 ml)	90	7	12	No
Kellogg's Raisin Bran, 1 cup (250 ml)	180	16	6	Yes
Nature's Path 8 Grain Synergy Multigrain, 2/3 cup (150 ml)	100	5	6	Yes
Nature's Path Flax Plus, 3/4 cup (175 ml)	100	6	7	Yes
Nature's Path Heritage Multigrain, 3/4 cup (175 ml)	100	4	6	Yes
Nature's Path Optimum Power, 1 cup (250 ml)	190	16	10	Yes

Nature's Path Optimum Slim, 1 cup (250 ml)	180	10	11	Yes
Nature's Path Optimum Zen, 3/4 cup (175 ml)	200	14	10	Yes
Our Compliments Nutri-Crisp, 3/4 cup (175 ml)	115	6.6	5.5	Yes
PC Extra Raisin Raisin Bran, 1 1/4 cup (300 ml)	149	14	4	Yes
PC Blue Menu Fibre First Multi-Bran Cereal, 1/2 cup (125 ml)	94	5.4	13	No
Post Bran Flakes, 3/4 cup (175 ml)	107	5	4.5	Yes
Post Grape-Nuts, 1/3 cup (75 ml)	110	0	4	Yes
Post 100% Bran, 1/2 cup (125 ml)	107	7.8	10	No
Post Selects Great Grains Raisin, Dates, Pecan, 1/2 cup (125 ml)	160	10	4	Yes
Post Spoon Size Shredded Wheat, 2/3 cup (150 ml)	110	0	4	Yes
Post Shredded Wheat 'N Bran, 2/3 cup (150 ml)	110	0	5	Yes
Post Original Shredded Wheat, 1 biscuit	90	0	4	Yes
Quaker Corn Bran Squares, 1 cup (250 ml)	116	6.1	4.8	No
Weetabix Shredded Wheat, 2 biscuits	133	1.7	4.6	Yes

Does Your Teen Eat Too Much Added Sugar?

Added sugars are sugars and syrups added to foods during the manufacturer's processing and preparation. They're not to be confused with naturally occurring sugars, such as lactose in milk and fructose in fruit. Many of us are afraid that added sugars will cause us to put on weight, develop diabetes, and develop heart disease.

The truth is, when eaten in small amounts, sugar has not been found to cause any of these health problems. It's when you eat too much sugar along with too much fat and have too little fibre in your diet that health problems occur.

And that's exactly what we are doing. We're swallowing more sugar today than ever before. The Canadian Sugar Institute estimates that the average Canadian consumes 16 teaspoons (80 ml) of added sugars per day—about 13% of our daily calories. It's certainly less than our American neighbours, who consume as many as 20 teaspoons (100 ml) each day.

But once you factor in the part of the population that eats far less sugar, it becomes clear that many Canadians are getting far more than 16 teaspoons (80 ml) of sugar each day. And thanks to the popularity of soft drinks, many teenagers are at the high end of the sugar scale.

A joint Canada–U.S. report released in September 2002 suggests that we should get no more than 25% of daily calories from added sugars. This is more lenient than recommendations put forward by the World Health Organization in April 2003. The WHO report suggests we limit our added sugars to less than 10% of our daily calories.

Sugar is everywhere today. It's found in soft drinks, fruit drinks, cakes, cookies, muffins, breakfast cereals, decadent coffee drinks, dairy desserts … the list goes on. On a food package, you'll find added sugars listed as brown sugar, granulated sugar, cane sugar, honey, rice syrup, maple syrup, malt syrup, corn syrup, corn sweeteners, high fructose corn syrup, dextrose, and molasses.

It's frightening how accessible sugar has become. You can grab a cold soda pop or fruit drink at the grocery store, the video store, the gas station, and, of course, the high school vending machine. And we're not talking about a small serving size, either. Soft drink servings have grown over the past 50 years. In the 1950s, the average serving of pop at a fast food restaurant was about 7 ounces (210 ml). And there was no such thing as medium or large—there was one size only. Today, that original size is now smaller than, or equal to, the smallest size sold.

A kids'-size pop at Wendy's provides 10 ounces (295 ml) of sugary beverage. That's 30% more than the fast food soft drink served in the 1950s. Wendy's Biggie soft drink is 16 fluid ounces (475 ml) and almost 14 teaspoons (70 ml) of sugar. And here's a shocker: 7-Eleven's Super Big Gulp delivers 44 ounces (1.3 litres) of soda and 50 teaspoons (250 ml) of sugar. I won't even mention the Double Big Gulp! That's a whole lot of sugar. And a steady diet of sugary foods and drinks can certainly affect a teenager's health status.

Sugar and Weight Control

Recent reports say our increased use of sugar over the past 20 years coincides with our nation's rapid rise in obesity. While these studies can't prove that sugary drinks cause more weight gain than other foods, they do give you reason to think twice before you reach for that can of pop.

Each gram of carbohydrate, whether it's refined sugar, fruit sugar, or starch, supplies four calories. One teaspoon (5 ml) of table sugar has 4 grams of carbohydrate, and therefore 16 calories. It may not sound like a lot, but refined sugar is usually consumed in a concentrated form, so those calories can add up quickly.

Think about this: if you drink a 12 ounce (355 ml) can of Coke each day, you'll gulp 150 calories and almost 10 teaspoons (50 ml) of sugar. Over the course of one year, that adds up to almost 55,000 calories and 3,650 teaspoons (18 litres) of sugar. And guess how many pounds? Well, considering it takes an excess of 3600 calories to one's daily requirement to make one pound of body fat, we're talking about 15 pounds. That means if a teenager adds one can of Coke to his diet every day for one year, and doesn't burn off those extra calories, he could gain 15 pounds (6.8 kilograms) by the end of the year.

There's also the mistaken thinking that regardless of their sugar content, fat-free foods don't have an impact on the bathroom scale. A classic example is candy, often chosen over a high-fat chocolate bar. Eat a 75 gram package of Twizzlers and you'll get 280 calories (not to mention 18 teaspoons/75 ml of sugar)—roughly the same number of calories found in most chocolate bars.

Many teenagers get their calorie hits from sugar-fat combinations, or sweetened fats, as I like to call them. These are the popular items sold at the school cafeteria or after-school hangouts. Many teenage girls I talked to said they always skip the greasy burgers and fries at lunch, but they do line up for a cookie or a muffin. Here's how these calories add up.

CALORIES IN POPULAR SUGAR-FAT FOODS

Saint Cinnamon cinnamon bun	700
Ben & Jerry's Cherry Garcia ice cream, 1 cup (250 ml)	520
Starbucks Chocolate Brownie Frappuccino, grande	488
Bagel (generic) and cream cheese, 1 1/2 oz (42.5 g)	450
Starbucks blueberry scone	440
Tim Hortons chocolate chip muffin	440
Starbucks oatmeal raisin cookie	390
Tim Hortons cherry cheese Danish	380
Snickers bar	270
Krispy Kreme glazed cruller	239
Tim Hortons chocolate chip cookie	155

A few hundred extra calories might not be a problem if your teenager is a growing male or an athlete who burns off a few thousand calories each day. But many teenagers aren't that active, and teenage girls don't need as many calories as boys.

Sugar and Nutrition

A steady diet of candy, soda pop, and other sugary foods can impact the nutritional quality of a teenager's diet. It probably comes as no surprise that if your teenager gets a big chunk of her calories from sugar-fat foods, she's likely missing out on fruit, vegetables, whole grains, and dairy products, as sugary foods force more nutritious foods out of the diet. And that means it's harder for her to meet daily requirements for important vitamins and minerals. Over the long term, this can increase the risk of nutrient deficiencies, for example, iron and calcium deficiencies, as well as increase the risk of heart disease and cancer.

Sugar and Bone Health

There's more at risk than weight control when it comes to a steady intake of soft drinks. According to surveys, American teenagers drink twice as much pop as milk. The average American teenage girl gets 40% less calcium than she needs. We don't have hard data for Canadian teens, but studies do consistently reveal that teenage diets, especially those of females, are lacking in the calcium department. And considering that most bone mass is built by the age of 18, teenagers who don't get the calcium they need run the risk of developing osteoporosis later in life.

Sugar and Diabetes

Eating candy every now and again or drinking the occasional soda pop won't cause your teenager to develop diabetes. However, if your teen's usual diet is high in sugar *and* low in fibre, he may be at greater risk of developing type 2 diabetes. A recent eight-year study published in the *Journal of the American Medical Association* found that compared with young and middle-aged women who consumed less than one sugar-sweetened beverage per month, those who drank one or more per day were much more likely to develop type 2 diabetes.[5] These women were also much more likely to report weight gain.

Sugar, Cavities, and Gum Disease

Yes, too much sugar *can* cause cavities. Once you eat carbohydrates, they begin breaking down into sugars in the mouth. Bacteria in the mouth ferment these sugars and, in the process, produce an acid that erodes tooth enamel. The damage caused by sugar depends on how much sugar is consumed and how long it stays in the mouth.

The worst foods for their cavity-promoting potential include sticky candies, rolled-up fruit snacks, fruit leather, and raisins. Regular snacking on carbohydrate foods throughout the day keeps the bacteria working, too. Eating non-sugary foods can help remove sugar from the surface of the teeth. (This is why cheese is said to help prevent cavities. The protective properties of cheese are attributed to several factors. The texture of cheese increases the secretion of saliva, while the nutrient content—protein, calcium, and phosphorus—neutralizes cavity forming acids.) The best defence your teenager has against cavities? Rinsing her mouth and brushing teeth after eating.

Since the introduction of fluoridated water, cavities have become more a question of geography than age. Most urban centres fluoridate their water, so city-raised kids of any age tend to have few cavities. Kids in rural areas who drink well water and kids from immigrant families who were not exposed to fluoridation in their countries of origin are the most likely to have cavities.

When it comes to brushing and flossing, the bigger issue is gum disease. If kids don't brush and floss and see the dentist regularly, plaque builds up on their teeth and irritates the gums, causing puffiness, bleeding, infection, and ultimately bone erosion and tooth loss.

Kids start to care about brushing when they begin to care about their appearance and about being attractive to others. (That's why ads for Crest Whitestrips feature good-looking teenagers.)

If your teenager doesn't have a regular brushing and flossing routine, tell him that brushing will remove plaque (resulting from all foods, not just sugary foods), which causes bad breath, puffy gums, and gum infections. Who wants to kiss someone with a dirty mouth and bad breath? Plaque will also cause teeth to look yellow. In fact, a surprising number of kids are already whitening their teeth with bleaching kits; according to dentists, this is not a good thing to start at a young age. Dentists recommend teens wait until the age of 16, when tooth enamel has fully calcified. If teeth have matured early, it might be okay for teens as young as 14 to use bleaching kits, but the only way to know for sure if bleaching is safe for your teen's teeth is to ask his or her dentist.

Okay, back to the sugar issue. A healthy teenage diet should minimize the consumption of table sugar, soft drinks, fruit drinks, fruit leather, candy, and other sweets. Parents should help their kids understand that these foods are considered treats and so should not be eaten on a regular basis. Here are a few strategies to help curb your teen's sugar intake:

- Limit soft drinks. Don't bring them into the house. Instead make water, low-fat milk, vegetable juice, and unsweetened fruit juice available.

- When grocery shopping, stay clear of fruit drinks, fruit cocktails, and fruit beverages, which are little more than sugar and water.

- Encourage your teen to snack on fresh fruit rather than on candy, cakes, cookies, and pastries. Even fat-free desserts can have as much sugar and as many calories as their full-fat counterparts.

- When your teen does splurge on sweets, have him pay attention to portion size. King-sized desserts such as store-bought muffins, coffeeshop cookies, and movie-theatre candy bars are loaded with added sugar.

- Choose breakfast cereals that have no more than 8 grams of sugar per serving (the exception being very high-fibre cereals or those with dried fruit).

Leslie's Tips for Incorporating Healthy Carbohydrate Foods into Your Teen's Diet

1. Include carbohydrate-rich foods at each meal and in snacks so your teen gets adequate energy for growth, sports, and brain power. Overweight teens can omit starchy foods from dinner as long as they eat plenty of vegetables along with their meat, chicken, fish, or vegetarian protein food (for more meat alternatives for vegetarian teens, see Chapter 8, page 153).

2. Encourage your teen to eat at least three servings of whole grains each day. Choose a breakfast cereal made with whole grains, and try brown rice or whole-wheat pasta at dinner.

3. Buy bread and crackers that list whole wheat or whole rye as the first ingredient.

4. Gradually add low glycemic index carbohydrate foods to your family's diet so that eventually you're including one low GI food in two meals each day. Use the list on page 35 to help you choose low GI foods.

5. To boost fibre, add natural wheat bran, oat bran, or ground flaxseed to hot cereal, yogurt, applesauce, and home baking. Choose breakfast cereals that have at least 4 grams of fibre per serving.

6. Read ingredient lists. The nutrition label doesn't tell you how much *added* sugar a food contains. Rather, it declares the grams of total sugars (added sugars plus naturally occurring sugars). Added sugars can be found on the ingredient list under these names: corn syrup, dextrose, fructose, fruit juice concentrate, glucose, glucose-fructose, high fructose corn syrup, honey, invert sugar, malt, maltose, molasses, sucrose, and syrup.

7. As a rule, keep sugary foods such as candy, chocolate bars, store-bought cookies, breakfast pastries, and rich desserts out of the house. Limit these to weekly treats for the whole family.

8. Replace soda pop with water, tea, low-fat milk, calcium-enriched soy or rice milk, or vegetable juice.

9. When your kids do eat sweets—and of course they will—discourage them from indulging in super-sized portions. Avoid bulk-sized packages when buying treats for the family. Instead, buy single-sized servings to help prevent overeating.

3

⚏⚏⚏

A Primer on Protein

Since its discovery in the late 19th century, protein has had a strong hold on our culture and cuisine. Parents worry that their children may not be getting enough, as do many teenage boys who are interested in "beefing up." Getting enough protein is also a concern that many vegetarian teenagers have—not to mention the parents of these growing teens.

Protein is definitely an important nutrient that every teenage body needs for good health. Teens need an adequate protein intake to ensure healthy growth and development of muscles and bones—even skin and hair relies on a steady intake of protein-rich foods. Getting enough dietary protein is especially important for younger teens, whose body tissues are growing quickly.

Most of us know that protein is found in foods, and we're pretty good at naming best food sources. Meat, poultry, eggs, milk, yogurt, cheese, beans, tofu, and other soy products are the richest sources of protein in the diet. Grains and vegetables, though not nearly as good a source, also provide some protein. The only foods that are truly protein deficient are fruit, fats, and sugars.

But did you also know that protein is found throughout the body? Thanks to the proteins you get from foods, proteins in your body are able to perform hundreds and hundreds of vital tasks.

Why Do Teens Need Protein?

During the process of digestion, your body breaks down food proteins into their individual building blocks, amino acids (discussed in more detail below). These amino acids are then absorbed by your intestine and eventually make their way to your body's cells. Here, amino acids are repackaged into between 10,000 and 50,000 different kinds of body proteins, each one playing a unique and important role in your health.

Proteins form structural components in the body—muscle tissue, connective tissue, and the support tissue inside bones and teeth are all derived from the protein we eat. Scars, tendons, and ligaments are made of collagen, one of the body's key structural proteins. The cells of your skin, hair, and fingernails consist mainly of protein. Many of these body proteins are in a continual state of breakdown, repair, and maintenance. During adolescence, all body tissues are growing and rely on a steady intake of protein. If your diet is chronically low in protein, protein rebuilding and repair slows down.

Amino acids in food are also used to make hormones, important proteins that regulate hundreds of body processes. Thyroid hormones control metabolism, the speed at which the body burns calories. The hormones insulin and glucagon closely regulate the level of sugar in your bloodstream. When your blood sugar rises after eating, insulin ensures that this sugar enters your cells, where it's needed for energy. On the flip side, if you haven't eaten for hours and your blood sugar becomes too low, glucagon helps release sugar that's stored in your liver into your bloodstream.

Enzymes are another group of body proteins that control billions of chemical reactions taking place in your body every day. Enzymes not only break down large molecules into smaller ones, they also build compounds and transform one substance into another. The digestive enzyme lactase breaks down lactose, the natural sugar in milk, into smaller sugar units so they can be absorbed by your small intestine. Teenagers who participate in endurance sports such as running and cycling need protein to make glycogen synthetase—the enzyme that rebuilds muscle glycogen (carbohydrate) stores. During a workout or team practice, muscles break down glycogen to get fuel. If it weren't for glycogen synthetase (and recovery foods such as energy bars and sports drinks, foods to eat after exercise to replenish used muscle glycogen), your teen's muscles wouldn't be prepared to exercise the next day.

Protein also helps teens' immune system defend their bodies against viruses and bacteria. Amino acids derived from foods are used to make antibodies, giant protein molecules that attack foreign invaders and ward off infection. In healthy teenagers, antibodies work so quickly that most infections never have a chance to get started. But if your teen's diet lacks protein, his body cannot maintain its resistance to illness. Other types of body proteins help maintain fluid balance, transport nutrients in the bloodstream, and aid in blood clotting.

The body uses protein for energy, too. In Chapter 2, you learned that carbohydrate-rich foods, for example, grains and fruit, play an important role in providing energy (glucose) to all body tissues. But if your teen's diet doesn't supply enough carbohydrate (perhaps because he's following a low-calorie diet to lose weight), his liver is forced take the protein he eats and convert it to glucose for fuel. Turning protein into glucose for energy is a normal process that happens inside the body every day. It happens when we skip a meal, or go for a long period without eating.

But if your son's diet is chronically low in calories and carbohydrate, his body will break down muscle and other important proteins to make needed glucose. The end result can include muscle wasting, a sluggish metabolism, delayed healing from an injury, and a weakened immune system. If your son lifts weights at the gym and he doesn't eat enough carbohydrate-rich foods, he won't get the muscle-building results he's looking for. That's because some of the protein he eats must to be used to make energy for his body, rather than building muscle.

The Building Blocks of Protein: Amino Acids

Protein-rich foods supply your body with 20 amino acids, all of which are needed for good health. Eleven of these can be manufactured by your body and are called non-essential amino acids. The remaining nine, however, must be supplied by your diet because your body cannot synthesize them on its own. They are called, as you may have guessed, essential amino acids.

If the diet does not supply enough of these essential amino acids, the body's rate of protein building and repair will slow down. Eventually the body will have to break down its own proteins (such as muscle tissues, hormones, and enzymes) to get these much-needed amino acids.

Animal and plant proteins have very different amino acid profiles. Animal protein foods contain all the essential amino acids in sufficient quantities to support growth, repair, and maintenance of body tissues. For this reason, animal proteins are considered complete proteins, or high-quality proteins. All plant-based foods are low in at least one of the nine essential amino acids our bodies need to get from food. In some plant foods, an essential amino acid will be totally absent. Plant proteins are considered incomplete proteins, or low-quality proteins.

If you're the parent of a vegetarian teenager, I can hear your next question, and it's one I often get from parents: "If my vegetarian son/daughter eats only tofu, soy products, and beans for protein, how can he/she get all the amino acids needed for proper growth?"

It's a good question. We used to think that vegetarians needed to combine different plant protein foods at the same meal (e.g., brown rice with beans, or peanut butter on whole-grain bread) to get an adequate supply of essential amino acids. Sounds like a lot of work, right? But we now know that as long as a variety of protein foods are eaten over the course of a day or two, there's no need to worry about combining plant protein foods at every meal. You can read all about vegetarian nutrition in Chapter 8.

How Much Protein Do Teens Need?

We all need to consume enough protein each day to make up for the amount our body loses. The amount of protein in your diet needs to be matched with the amount you lose in urine, skin, hair, and nails, and in your muscles during exercise. The recommended dietary allowances (RDAs) for protein are rather low compared with what we get from our diet, and they change very little according to a person's age. The exception: the RDA for protein is higher for boys and girls just before the teen years, when their tissues are growing at a fast rate. As you'll see below, protein requirements for teens are based on body weight.

RECOMMENDED DAILY PROTEIN INTAKES FOR PRETEENS AND TEENAGERS

9 to 13 years	0.43 grams per pound (0.95 grams per kilogram) body weight
14 to 18 years	0.38 grams per pound (0.85 grams per kilogram) body weight
19+ years, sedentary	0.36 grams per pound (0.80 grams per kilogram) body weight

National Academy of Sciences, Institute of Medicine, Food and Nutrition Board. Dietary Reference Intakes. Energy, Carbohydrate, Fiber, Fat, Fatty Acids, Cholesterol, Protein, and Amino Acids. National Academy Press, Washington, DC, 2002.

So, how much protein does your son or daughter need each day? Here are a few examples:

- A 120-pound 13-year-old boy needs 52 grams of protein (120 × 0.43 grams protein)

- A 130-pound 15-year old girl needs 49 grams of protein (150 × 0.38 grams protein)

- A 140-pound 17-year old girl needs 53 grams of protein (140 × 0.38 grams)

- A 195-pound 18-year old boy needs 74 grams of protein (195 × 0.38 grams protein)

If more than the daily requirement of protein is eaten, the excess gets excreted or stored as body fat (not muscle).

What about sports? Do teenagers need more protein if they're on the track or swim team, if they play football, or if they work out at the gym? That's a tough question to answer because so little research has been conducted with adolescent athletes. At this time it is unclear whether teenage athletes need more protein than their sedentary peers for normal growth and development and optimal performance.

Some studies have shown that adults who engage consistently in endurance and strength training may benefit from more protein. Despite this, the most recent recommendations for protein, released by the National Academies of Science in 2002, state that no additional dietary protein is needed for healthy, physically active adults. And there just isn't compelling enough evidence to the contrary.

But when it comes to children and teenagers, the research is scant. French researchers found that a daily protein intake of 0.71 grams per pound (1.57 grams per kilogram) of body weight maintained a positive protein status in 15-year-old male soccer players. This one study does suggest that there's a need for higher protein requirements among adolescent athletes, or among soccer players anyway. But that's not a lot of evidence to go on.

The most important thing to ensure is that teenagers—active or inactive—are meeting their daily protein targets. Studies of young athletes indicate that those who must make a weight class to qualify for their sport (e.g., wrestling) by cutting calories may be short-changing their diets of protein. If your teen participates in a weight-conscious sport such as wrestling, figure skating, gymnastics, or swimming, pay attention to his or her protein intake. (For more information on sports nutrition, see Chapter 10.)

What Are the Best Foods for Protein?

Okay, so know you know how many grams of protein your son or daughter should be getting from his or her diet every day. But in food terms, what does that look like? It's time to translate the RDA for protein into servings of protein-rich foods.

PROTEIN CONTENT OF SELECTED FOODS (GRAMS)

Poultry, Meat, and Fish

Chicken, 3 oz (90 g)*	21
Meat, 3 oz (90 g)	21–25
Salmon fillet, 3 oz (90 g)	25
Sole, 3 oz (90 g)	17
Tuna, canned and drained, 1/2 cup (125 ml)	30

Eggs

Egg white, 1 large	3
Egg, whole, 1 large	6

Dairy Products

Cheddar cheese, 1 oz (30 g)	10
Milk, 1 cup (250 ml)	8
Yogurt, 3/4 cup (175 g)	8

Legumes and Soy Foods

Baked beans, 1 cup (250 ml)	13
Black beans, cooked, 1 cup (250 ml)	16
Kidney beans, cooked, 1 cup (250 ml)	16
Lentils, cooked, 1 cup (250 ml)	19
Soybeans, cooked, 1 cup (250 ml)	30
Soy ground round, cooked, 1/3 cup (55 g)	11
Tofu, firm, 6 cm × 4 cm × 4 cm piece (80 g)	13
Veggie burger, 1 (85 g)	17
Veggie dog, 1 small (46 g)	11

Nuts and Seeds

Almonds, 1/2 cup (125 ml)	12
Mixed nuts, 1/2 cup (125 ml)	13
Peanut butter, 2 tbsp (25 ml)	9

Peanuts, 1/2 cup (125 ml)	18
Sunflower seeds, 1/3 cup (75 ml)	8
Tahini (sesame butter), 2 tbsp (25 ml)	2

Other Foods

Bran flakes, 3/4 cup (175 ml)	4
Bread, mixed grain, 1 slice	3
Oatmeal, cooked, 3/4 cup (175 ml)	4
Pasta, cooked, 1/2 cup (125 ml)	3
Pita pocket, whole-wheat, 1	6
Potato, baked, 1	3
Rice, long-grain, cooked, 1/2 cup (125 ml)	3
Fruit, 1 piece	1

Vegetable juice, 1 cup (250 ml)	2
Vegetables, 1/2 cup (125 ml)	2

Nutrition Supplements

Energy bar, high-carbohydrate (e.g., PowerBar, Clif)	7
Energy bar, 40/30/30 (e.g., Balance Bar, Zone Bar)	14–18
Energy bar, high-protein (e.g., Pure Protein, ProMax)	21–35
Soy protein powder, plain, 1 scoop (28 g)	25
Soy protein powder, flavoured, 1 scoop (28 g)	14–16
Whey protein powder, 1 scoop (32 g)	22–25

* 90 grams is the size of a deck of regular playing cards.

Source: *Nutrient Values of Some Common Foods,* table titled "Protein-Packed Foods," Health Canada (© 1999, reprint 2002). Reproduced with the permission of the Minister of Public Works and Government Services Canada, 2005.

You can see how these numbers add up, especially since most people eat more than a 3 ounce (90 gram) serving of meat or chicken in one sitting. It's estimated that the average North American male adult consumes 105 grams of protein each day, and female adults get roughly 65 grams. Here's what a typical food day looks like for my 13-year-old nephew, Alex. (Based on Alex's body weight, he needs 70 grams of protein each day).

PROTEIN IN ALEX'S DAILY FOOD INTAKE (GRAMS)

Breakfast

Cereal, 1 1/2 cups (375 ml)	8
Milk, 1 cup (250 ml)	8
Apple juice	0

Lunch

Whole-grain bread, 2 slices	6
Ham or turkey, 3 oz (90 g)	21
Crackers, 4	2
Apple juice, 1 cup (250 ml)	0
Water	0

After-School Snacks

English muffin with jam	4
1 apple or banana	0
Apple juice, 1 cup (250 ml)	0

Dinner

Chicken or meat, 4–6 oz (120–180 g)	28–42
Rice, 1 cup (250 ml)	4
Assorted vegetables, 1 cup (250 ml)	4
Milk, 2 cups (500 ml)	16
Daily Protein Intake	*101–115*

As you can see, Alex has no problem meeting his daily protein requirements. In fact, for most teenagers, eating too little protein is simply not an issue. Yes, it's true that teenagers do need more protein than adults, but they need more of everything—calories, vitamins, and minerals. As long as teenagers are meeting their calorie needs, there's little need to worry that they're missing out on protein. Even during growth spurts, it's likely that teenagers with a healthy appetite will eat more, thereby increasing their intake of calories and protein.

What Happens If Teens Don't Eat Enough Protein?

There are some cases in which teenagers might not be meeting their protein needs. Your child may be at risk of not getting enough protein if she

- is weight-conscious and restricting her food intake,
- fills up on high-carbohydrate foods that are low in protein (bagels, pasta, cereal bars, low-fat frozen dinners),
- is a vegetarian who avoids meat but does not incorporate enough high-quality vegetable protein into her diet, or
- engages in heavy exercise and is not meeting her daily calorie requirements.

Eating too little protein day after day, week after week, will hamper the body's ability to repair itself, slow down metabolism, and weaken the immune system. I have counselled many clients whose main concern was a lack of energy and catching one cold or flu bug after another. There was a common thread in all of their diets: they lacked a sufficient amount of protein. After a few months of following a higher-protein diet, these clients not only felt better, but they also reported being sick less often.

When it comes to teenage health, a diet that's chronically low in protein will have an impact on growth and development. The phenomenal growth that occurs during adolescence is second only to that in the first year of life, and it increases the body's demand for protein—along with energy and all other nutrients. Nutrition and physical growth are integrally related. A diet that's lacking sufficient protein (and calories) can slow or delay sexual maturation, slow linear growth (height), and compromise bone building.

Keep in mind that some of the best sources of protein can pack a punch when it comes to certain vitamins and minerals. Meat, for example, is an excellent source of iron, a mineral needed to carry oxygen to all body tissues. One's iron stores are also linked to the ability to concentrate. In addition to protein, milk products deliver a hefty dose of calcium and vitamin D, two nutrients critical for bone development. And dairy is a good source of zinc, which is important for sexual development. You can see that an ongoing shortage of protein-rich foods will not only impact growth and development but can also influence a number of other body functions that rely on the vitamins and minerals found in these foods.

If you suspect your teenager's diet is too low in protein, encourage her to eat more protein-rich foods. Scientists at the Mayo Clinic think that the amount of protein you eat when you are young may be an important predictor of your future bone density. (Much of our bone density is achieved by the time we are 18 years old). Their study found that higher intakes of dietary protein were linked to greater bone density in premenopausal women, but this relationship was not seen in older women.[1] Getting enough protein early on in life appears to be an important strategy for strong, healthy bones.

What Happens If Teens Eat Too Much Protein?

Eating extra amounts of protein doesn't simply do more of what the recommended amount does. Studies reveal that consuming more protein than you need may actually increase the risk of health problems, including high blood pressure, bone fracture, and certain cancers. The effect of excessive protein intakes on bone health is a concern for teens whose bones are developing during the adolescent years.

A number of studies have established a connection between excessive consumption of protein (animal protein in particular) and calcium loss. Epidemiological studies clearly show that populations that consume the most protein suffer the most osteoporosis, a bone-thinning disease that affects both women and men. In countries where protein intake is lower and most of it is plant-derived, rates of osteoporosis are considerably lower. Animal protein foods contain sulphur, which causes the kidneys to excrete calcium in the urine instead of reabsorbing it in the bloodstream.

If your teenager is a meat lover, he may be getting more than just an extra dose of protein. Some animal protein foods, such as cheese and meat, pack a hefty amount of saturated fat, the artery-clogging fat that raises blood cholesterol levels. Today we are seeing an increasing number of adolescents with high cholesterol levels. And elevated cholesterol levels increase your child's future risk of heart disease.

Top Protein Foods for Teenagers

There are a few top-notch protein foods that deserve a place on your family's weekly menu. Whether you eat meat or not, make a plan to add the following foods to your family's meals each week.

Fish

Fish is a great source of protein, without the high amounts of saturated fat found in fatty meats. We've known for years that populations that eat fish a few times each week have lower rates of heart disease. Special fats in fish, called omega-3 fats, can lower high levels of blood fats (triglycerides) and reduce the stickiness of platelets, the cells that form blood clots in arteries. For the best sources of omega-3 fats, choose oily fish—salmon, trout, sardines, anchovies, herring, and mackerel are good choices.

Aim to eat fish two to three times each week. You'll find plenty of tasty fish recipes in Part 4. Fish is an excellent source of high-quality protein, and I encourage you and your kids to eat it more often. But there are a few things you need to know about fish to help you make safe food choices.

Mercury and fish

The biggest concern with fish is mercury contamination in certain species of large fish. Mercury is a naturally occurring metal found in very low levels in the air, soil, lakes, streams, and oceans. But it can also make its way into the environment from industry— pulp and paper processing, mining operations, and burning garbage and fossil fuels all release mercury.

Once mercury enters a waterway, naturally occurring bacteria absorb it and convert it to a form called methylmercury. Mercury then works its way up the food chain as large fish consume contaminated smaller fish. Instead of dissolving or breaking down, mercury accumulates in these large fish. Predatory fish such as large tuna, swordfish, shark, and king mackerel can have mercury concentrations in their bodies that are 10,000 times higher than those of their surrounding habitat.

Eating fish is the main way that people are exposed to methylmercury. Each person's exposure depends on the amount of methylmercury in the fish they eat and how much and how often they eat that type of fish. While mercury can affect almost any organ in the body, the most sensitive organ is the brain.

In 2001, Health Canada issued an advisory recommending that Canadians limit their intake of swordfish, shark, king mackerel, and (fresh and frozen) tuna—the species of fish that accumulate high levels of mercury. The government advised women who are of child-bearing age, pregnant, or nursing, as well as teenagers younger than 15 to reduce their intake of these high-mercury fish to *no more than once per month*. Older teens should limit their consumption to no more than once per week. Health Canada is in the process of reviewing its evidence on fish and health, and it's possible that stricter consumption guidelines will be released in the future.

According to Health Canada, mercury is not an issue with canned tuna, since the tuna used for canning is young and hasn't had time to accumulate mercury. However, research conducted in the United States has revealed that white (albacore) tuna has a higher mercury content than light tuna (yellowfin, bluefin, and skipjack). If your teen eats tuna sandwiches frequently, I recommend that you buy light tuna (flake, chunk, or solid) instead of albacore.

Soy Foods

Tofu, tempeh, soy beverages, soybeans, veggie meats, soy nuts, and soy flour are a great source of protein. They also contain isoflavones, plant chemicals that may guard against a number of health problems. A growing body of research suggests that a regular intake of soy foods can protect the heart, lower elevated blood cholesterol levels, slow down bone loss, and perhaps even lower the odds of getting prostate or breast cancer.

When it comes to breast cancer prevention, it appears that getting soy at a young age—before puberty—offers protection. The Shanghai Breast Cancer Study found that soy food intake during adolescence was strongly associated with a reduced risk of breast cancer later in life.[2] This benefit persists even when Asian women immigrate to Western countries where soy is less likely to be a regular component of the diet. This suggests that early exposure to soy might be important for protection against breast cancer later in life. It's thought that isoflavones in soy foods enhance early breast cell development and maturation of mammary glands, making breast cells more resistant to cancer-causing substances. (Mammary glands develop primarily during the adolescent growth spurt.)

Consider adding the following soy protein to your teen's diet:

Soybeans Look for canned soybeans in your local grocery store. Just open the can, give the beans a rinse, and then add them to a soup, salad, casserole, chili, or curry. Or mash them up and add them to burgers. If you have the time, buy dried soybeans, soak them overnight, then simmer for one hour until they're cooked. Buying dried soybeans rather than canned means you'll avoid added sodium.

Soy beverages This is the most popular way to introduce soy. Buy soy beverages fresh or in tetra packs and use them just as you would milk—on cereal, in smoothies, in coffee, in lattes, in soups, and in cooking and baking. To get more calcium, vitamin D, and B12, choose a fortified product.

Soy flour Available in health food stores and some supermarkets, soy flour can be substituted for up to one-half of the all-purpose flour called for in bread, muffin, loaf, cookie, cake, and scone recipes.

Soy meats These ready-to-eat or frozen soy foods resemble meat and can be used in place of burgers, hot dogs, deli cold cuts, and ground meat. You'll find them in the freezer, deli, or produce sections of grocery stores.

Soy nuts These tasty roasted munchies have less fat and more fibre than other nuts, and come in plain, barbecue, and garlic flavours. Sprinkle on salads, stir into yogurt, or enjoy them on their own. Buy unsalted soy nuts.

Soy protein powder Make a morning power shake with one or two tablespoons (15 to 25 ml) soy protein powder made from isolated soy protein. Buy a product that's made with Solae brand soy protein. This extract of soy protein is manufactured by Protein Technologies International using a process that prevents isoflavone loss. It's also the soy protein isolate that's used in most of the scientific studies. Products that use Solae include Interactive SoyOne, Interactive JustSoy, Reliv, Twinlab Vege Fuel, and GNC Natural Brand Soy Protein.

Tempeh You'll find this soy food refrigerated or frozen in health food stores. Tempeh is a cake of fermented soybeans mixed with grain. It can be sliced and added to casseroles and stir-fries, or you can grill it in kebabs and burgers.

Texturized vegetable protein (TVP) Made from soy flour that's been defatted and dehydrated, TVP is sold in packages as granules. You can also buy TVP in the bulk section of the health food store, as flakes or chunks the size of croutons. Rehydrate TVP with an equal amount of water or broth, and then use it to replace ground meat in pasta sauces, lasagna, chili, and tacos.

Tofu Use soft tofu in smoothies, dips, lasagna, and cheesecakes. Firm or extra-firm tofu is best for grilling and stir-frying. Add cubes of firm tofu to homemade or canned soups for a vegetarian protein boost. Refrigerate unused portions immersed in water.

Legumes

Kidney beans, black beans, navy beans, chickpeas, and lentils are low in fat, high in fibre, and packed with important nutrients and protective plant chemicals. Legumes contain soluble fibre, the type of fibre that helps lower blood cholesterol and keep blood sugar levels stable. In fact, an American study linked eating beans at least four times per week with a 22% lower risk of heart disease.[3]

Eat a meatless meal that features beans at least once a week. Buy dried beans, or if time is an issue, buy them canned (that's what I do). Just drain and rinse them, then add them to your family's favourite dishes. Here are a few suggestions:

- Enjoy a mixed bean salad in a pita pocket for a high-protein vegetarian sandwich.

- Add black beans to tacos and burritos. Use half the amount of lean ground meat you usually would and make up the difference with beans.

- Make a vegetarian chili with kidney beans, black beans, and chickpeas.

- Sauté chickpeas with spinach and tomatoes; serve over pasta.

- Add white kidney beans to pasta sauce.

- Toss chickpeas or lentils into your salad.

- Add a can of lentils or your favourite beans to a vegetable soup (store-bought or homemade).

- Serve soup made from beans or peas—minestrone, split pea, black bean, or lentil.

- Use beans for vegetable dips or sandwich fillings.

- Explore your recipe books: try a new legume recipe more often.

Nuts

In addition to providing protein, nuts are rich sources of vitamin E, minerals, fibre, and essential fatty acids (read Chapter 4 for more information about dietary fats). Nuts also contain plant sterols, special compounds that have been linked to a number of beneficial effects in the body, especially cholesterol lowering.

So far, six large scientific studies suggest that a regular intake of nuts protects from heart disease. The Nurses' Health Study from Harvard University discovered that women who ate more than five ounces (142 grams) of nuts each week had a 35% lower risk of heart attack and death from heart disease compared with women who never ate nuts or ate them less than once a month.[4] A number of studies have found that almonds, peanuts, peanut butter, walnuts, pecans, pistachio, and macadamia nuts can lower LDL (bad) cholesterol levels. A few studies even suggest that nuts might protect from certain cancers.

Nuts may also help ward off type 2 diabetes, a condition that's now being diagnosed in overweight children and teenagers. The ongoing Nurses' Health Study found that compared with women who almost never ate nuts, those who consumed 1 ounce (28 grams) of nuts at least five times per week were 27% less likely to develop type 2 diabetes. Regular peanut butter eaters were 20% less likely to have the condition.[5]

Eat five to seven servings of nuts each week. To prevent taking in too many calories, keep portion size small—about 1 ounce (28 grams), or 1/4 cup (50 ml). Eating too many nuts each day can lead to weight gain, as 1 cup (250 ml) of nuts contains about 850 calories and 18 teaspoons (90 ml) of oil. Protein-packed nuts make great snacks for hungry teenagers. Replace sugary and refined snack foods with nuts. Nuts can also replace red or processed meats. Try these suggestions to add a small portion of nuts to your family's meals and snacks:

- Add sliced almonds to your morning bowl of cereal.

- Toss a handful of peanuts or cashews into an Asian-style stir-fry.

- Stir-fry collard greens with cashews, adding a teaspoon (5 ml) of sesame oil at the end of cooking.

- Add walnuts to a green or spinach salad.

- Mix sunflower seeds or pumpkin seeds into a bowl of hot cereal or yogurt.

- Add chopped pecans to your favourite low-fat muffin recipe.

- Snack on a small handful of almonds with dried apricots. Or try my recipes for homemade trail mix (pages 254–55), a tasty snack for all members of the family.

- Sprinkle casseroles with a handful of mixed nuts.

Leslie's Tips for Incorporating High-Quality Protein Foods into Your Teen's Diet

1. To meet protein requirements, your teen should eat at least two servings of high-protein foods per day. To meet these targets, each meal needs to contain a protein-rich food. A serving is considered 3 ounces (90 grams) of lean meat, poultry, or fish; 1 to 2 eggs (or 2 to 4 egg whites); 1/3 of a block of firm tofu; or 1/2 to 1 cup (125 to 250 ml) of cooked legumes. Higher-protein breakfast foods include low-fat milk or soy milk, yogurt, and cottage cheese.

2. Encourage your family to follow a plant-based diet. Incorporate more vegetarian protein foods into your weekly menu. More often, replace meat and poultry with soy foods, nuts, and beans.

3. Encourage vegetarian teens to add legumes, nuts, or soy products to each meal. Make sure they understand there's more to vegetarian eating than giving up meat.

4. Plan meals made from fish two or three times a week, or more often if you wish. For heart healthy omega-3 fats choose salmon, trout, sardines, herring, or mackerel.

5. To reduce exposure to mercury, limit your teenager's intake of swordfish, shark, and fresh or frozen tuna to no more than once per month if she's younger than 15, and to once per week if she's 15 or older. If your kids eat tuna sandwiches, buy canned light tuna instead of white (albacore).

6. Choose lower-fat animal protein foods for family meals. Lean cuts of beef (sirloin, flank steak, eye of the round, lean ground beef), pork tenderloin, poultry breast, and turkey all have less saturated fat and cholesterol than other cuts or types of meat. Avoid charring animal foods on the grill: blackened parts on meat contain chemicals called benzopyrenes, which are carcinogenic in animals.

7. If you and your family do eat meat, limit it to no more than a 3 ounce (90 gram) serving per day. Three ounces is the size of a deck of regular playing cards.

4

⎯⎯⎯∞⎯⎯⎯

The Facts on Fat

Are you concerned that your teen eats too many foods high in fat and cholesterol? It's not uncommon for teenagers to snack on cookies, muffins, chocolate bars, potato chips, and french fries. Unfortunately, the most popular snacks among teens tend to be loaded with bad fats—the types that raise blood cholesterol. Considering that signs of heart disease are showing up in teenagers, the time is *now* to help our kids learn to make healthier food choices.

More and more teens are eating their meals and snacks away from home, often at fast food restaurants. Many of these foods are higher in fat, especially saturated fat, and contain less fibre, vitamins, and minerals than foods prepared at home. We certainly know that a high-fat diet and sedentary lifestyle are contributing to the epidemic of obesity among teenagers.

However, it's not all bad news when it comes to fat. You might be surprised to learn that certain types of dietary fat have some positives. Some fats may actually help prevent heart disease, and others may ease the symptoms of inflammatory bowel disease, depression, and rheumatoid arthritis. It's only when we consume too little or too much fat that health problems arise.

So how are we doing? Unfortunately, we don't have a good handle on how much fat our teenagers are consuming each day. The most recent data collected for 1544 adults and 178 adolescents shows that, since 1970, Canadians have reduced their intake of total and saturated fat.[1] And according to the What's on Your Plate? High School Nutrition Survey, 55% of students said they were concerned about fat in their foods—in fact, fat was the highest ranked nutrient concern for teenagers.

It seems we are getting the message about fat and health. But we still need to be aware of the hidden sources of fat that creep unknowingly into our food supply. This chapter will arm you with information to get your whole family choosing the right fats—and limiting the bad fats—when at home.

Food Fat and Body Fat

Molecules of fat in food and in the body are called triglycerides. Each triglyceride is made up of individual building blocks called fatty acids. Once we eat fat in a meal (for example, in a greasy cheeseburger or a salad with dressing), digestive enzymes in our intestine break down food fats into their individual fatty acids. These fatty acids are then absorbed into the bloodstream, where they make their way to the liver.

In the liver, fatty acids are repackaged into larger triglyceride molecules so they can be transported to different tissues in the body. Every cell in your body has enzymes that dismantle these circulating triglycerides into their fatty acid building blocks. By doing so, fatty acids can enter your cells, where some will be used immediately for energy. Fatty acids that aren't needed right away are once again repackaged into triglycerides and stored as body fat. So yes, if you eat too much fat—no matter what type of fat—you can gain weight.

Fat has many important roles in the body. Stores of body fat provide an important source of energy for daily activity. In fact, about half of your daily energy requirements are supplied by stored fat. The small stores of fat in your muscles provide most of the fuel used during light exercise—walking or climbing a flight of stairs, for example.

Our ability to store fat is pretty much unlimited, since our fat cells can increase in size if we consume more food than we need. And we can always form new fat cells if we've filled up our existing ones to the point that they can't expand any more. And once new fat cells are formed, you can't get rid of them, you can only shrink them.

Your body fat serves another purpose: it acts as a layer of insulation protecting your major organs. Body fat comes in two varieties. There's subcutaneous fat, a noticeable layer of fat that lies just below the skin, and there's visceral fat, which is buried beneath the muscles. Although we do need a little body fat, storing too much fat around the abdomen can increase the risk of heart disease, diabetes, and certain cancers. Researchers are learning that fat is an organ that produces proteins and hormones that can adversely affect metabolism and health.

Visceral fat grows close to your kidneys and liver. Genes account for as much as 60% of the visceral fat you carry. But diet and exercise also play a role. Studies show that getting too little exercise and eating too much saturated fat can also contribute to how much visceral fat the body stores. Too much visceral fat potentially increases your risk of heart disease and diabetes. It's not yet clear why visceral fat is a hazard, but scientists believe it affects liver function, which could lead to higher levels of cholesterol in your blood.

Why Teens Need Fat in Their Diets

Believe it or not, we need a little fat in our foods. With all the talk about fat and the proliferation of low-fat products, some teens may decide to completely cut out fat from their diet. Bad idea. Some fat is needed for good health. Fat is necessary for developing bodies, especially during puberty, when the body grows very quickly. The body even needs some cholesterol from foods to help make important hormones.

So, it's not healthy to eliminate fat completely from your diet. Most of us agree that fat in foods enhances flavour, adds "mouth feel," and helps us feel satisfied after finishing a meal. That's because dietary fat empties from the stomach slowly, imparting satiety, or a feeling of fullness. From a health perspective, dietary fat supplies your body with fat-soluble vitamins A, D, E, and K, nutrients that you can't live without.

There's yet another reason why teenagers must include some fat in their diets. Consuming fat in your meals is the only way your body can get alpha-linolenic acid and linoleic acid, two essential fatty acids that form cell membranes, aid in immune function and vision, and produce immune compounds called eicosanoids. Without these essential fatty acids we would not be able to maintain good health.

How Much Fat Do Teens Need?

Teenagers experience impressive changes in growth and maturation. Girls begin the maturation process about two years earlier than boys. But boys go through a much more dramatic increase in size than do girls. Both muscle mass and bone width increase. That's why the calorie needs of adolescent males reach a lifetime high. But those extra calories shouldn't come from greasy fast foods and high-fat baked goods. Despite their higher calorie needs, teenagers still must moderate their fat intake. (See Chapter 1, page 15, for a list of how many calories teenagers need each day.) And that's particularly true of the types of fats that can raise blood cholesterol levels. A change in the level of blood cholesterol in teenage boys is considered to be a significant factor in future risk of heart disease. During the early teen years, adolescents should be gradually lowering their fat intakes.

Once linear (height) growth has stopped, teenagers should adopt the recommended fat target for adults. Based on years of scientific study investigating the link between dietary fat and disease, the recommendation for Canadians is that we get no more than 30% of a day's calories from fat. Right now, we're getting roughly 38% of our calories from fat. Here's how the 30% rule translates into grams of fat (fat content is always reported as grams of fat):

DAILY UPPER LIMIT OF FAT

Daily Calorie Intake	Daily Upper Limit (grams)
1600	53
1800	60
2000	65
2200	73
2500	80
2800	93
3200	106
3600	120

The average Canadian woman needs to cut about 20 grams of fat from her diet; the average man, about 30 grams. We don't have hard numbers for teens, but you can be sure that many need to cut their intake by at least this much.

The Problems with Getting Too Much Fat

While we all need some fat in our diets, eating too much is not a good thing. For starters, a diet that's packed with greasy fast foods and snacks can lead to weight problems in teenagers. Gram per gram, fat delivers double the calories of protein and carbohydrate. That means that fat calories add up fast. Fat can pack a lot of calories into even small portions of food. A typical side of french fries has 350 calories and 17 grams of fat. For the same amount of calories you can eat four apples, five slices of whole-wheat bread, or 1 1/2 cups (375 ml) of spaghetti with tomato sauce. You get a lot more volume for the same calories when you go low fat.

That's why cutting back on fat can help people lose weight—people who eat lower-fat diets can fill up on a larger quantity of food for fewer calories. If you skip the side of fries and have a baked potato with salsa instead, you'll save 130 calories. Or if you replace the fries with a green salad with 4 teaspoons (20 ml) of dressing, you'll save close to 300 calories. I'm sure you get the idea. Don't get me wrong; I am not saying that eating too much fat is the only reason we're witnessing an epidemic of overweight and obesity among Canadian youth. It's only part of the reason. But if you have an overweight teenager, cutting excess fat calories is a good place to start.

Eating too much fat, in particular saturated and trans fats, can raise blood cholesterol levels. And that puts teenagers at a higher risk for heart disease. A steady intake of trans fat may also increase the risk of type 2 diabetes. You'll read more about these so-called bad fats later on in this chapter. For now, let me just say that teenagers must become aware of these bad fats. Guess what's inside those muffins, cookies, and french fries sold in the high school cafeteria? You got it—trans fat.

A high-fat diet also increases the levels of estrogen and progesterone, two female sex hormones that may be associated with an increased risk for breast cancer later in life. Researchers at the Fox Chase Cancer Center in Philadelphia studied 286 teenage girls and found that those on a low-fat diet had significantly lower levels of sex hormones than girls on a higher-fat diet.[2] These findings suggest that even a small reduction in daily fat intake could lower the risk of breast cancer later in life.

Where's the Fat?

Where are we getting our fat? Here's a rough summary of where the fat in your diet comes from:

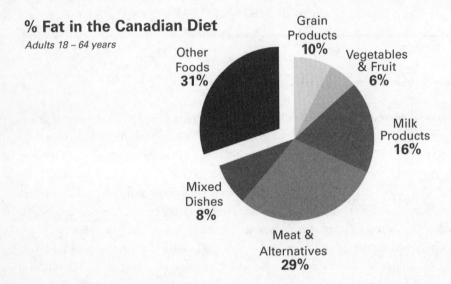

% Fat in the Canadian Diet
Adults 18 – 64 years

Grain Products **10%**
Vegetables & Fruit **6%**
Milk Products **16%**
Meat & Alternatives **29%**
Mixed Dishes **8%**
Other Foods **31%**

Source: *Food Habits of Canadians, 2001*
Beef Information Centre, A Matter of Fat, 2003. www.beefinfo.org

As you can see, almost one-third comes from meat and alternatives. This is not just the fat we can see on steaks and chops; it's also the hidden fat in foods such as sausages, meat pies, pâté, and salami. But the majority of fat in our diet comes from items in the Other Foods category, which includes added fats and oils, as well as high-fat desserts and snack foods. Added fats and oils are the visible fats that we add to our foods in the form of cooking oils; high-fat spreads such as mayonnaise, butter, and margarine; and salad dressings. But added fats and oils are also the hidden fats that are added to commercial foods during the manufacturing process. It's the hidden fats that are tricky—you can't see them, so you may not realize they are present in a food. For instance, many teenagers don't realize that the typical muffin sold in the school cafeteria contains 4 to 6 teaspoons' (20 to 30 ml) worth of oil. Here's a look at other sources of hidden fat in your teen's diet:

HIDDEN OIL AND FAT CONTENT OF SELECTED FOODS

	Teaspoons of Fat	Fat (grams)
Bread and Baked Goods		
Donut	3 tsp	12
Muffin, large store-bought	3 tsp	12
Whole-wheat toast, 1 slice, with 1 tsp (5 ml) butter	1 1/4 tsp	5
Whole-wheat toast, 1 slice, with 1 tbsp (15 ml) peanut butter	2 1/2 tsp	10
Poultry and Meat (3 1/2 oz or 100 g)		
Chicken breast, roasted, skinless	1/2 tsp	2
Chicken breast, roasted, with skin	2 1/4 tsp	9
Chicken drumsticks, breaded and fried	4 tsp	16
Chicken pot pie, 7 oz (200 g)	6 1/2 tsp	26
Meatloaf (lean ground beef)	2 tsp	8
Rib roast, trimmed, with 1/4 cup (50 ml) gravy	3 tsp	12
Sirloin steak, trimmed	1 1/2 tsp	6
Sirloin steak, untrimmed	2 3/4 tsp	11
Fast Foods		
Chicken nuggets, 6 pieces	4 1/4 tsp	17
Fish burger with tartar sauce	4 1/2 tsp	18
Hamburger, regular, single patty	2 tsp	8
Pizza, cheese, 2 slices	2 3/4 tsp	11
Pasta and Noodles (1 cup or 250 ml)		
Chow mein	3 3/4 tsp	15
Fettucini alfredo (homemade)	4 tsp	16
Macaroni and cheese	4 tsp	16
Pasta with tomato and meat sauce	1 3/4 tsp	7
Potatoes		
Baked, medium-sized, with 1 tsp (5 ml) butter	1 tsp	4
French fries (30 strips)	4 tsp	16
Poutine (30 strips)	10 tsp	40
Roasted, medium-sized, with olive oil and herbs	2 1/2 tsp	10

	Teaspoons of Fat	Fat (grams)
Salads (2 cups or 500 ml)		
Garden, with 1 tbsp (15 ml) Italian dressing	2 3/4 tsp	11
Garden, with vinegar or lemon juice, and herbs	0	0
Greek	3 tsp	12
Dairy Products		
Cheese, cheddar, 2 oz (50 g)	4 1/4 tsp	17
Cheese, mozzarella, 3 sticks, deep fried, 2 oz (50 g)	5 1/2 tsp	22
Cheese, part-skim mozzarella, 2 oz (50 g)	2 tsp	8
Cheese, processed, 2 slices, 1 1/2 oz (42 g)	2 tsp	8
Milk, skim, 1 cup (250 ml)	0	0
Milk, 1% white or chocolate, 1 cup (250 ml)	3/4 tsp	3
Milk, 2%, 1 cup (250 ml)	1 1/4 tsp	5
Milk, homogenized, 1 cup (250 ml)	2 1/4 tsp	9
Yogurt, fat-free or less than 1% MF*, 3/4 cup (175 g)	0	0
Yogurt, low-fat (1% to 2% MF), 3/4 cup (175 g)	3/4 tsp	3
Yogurt, 2.1% to 4% MF, 3/4 cup (175 g)	1 1/4 tsp	5
Yogurt, more than 4% MF, 3/4 cup (175 g)	2 1/2 tsp	10
Desserts (1/2 cup or 125 ml)		
Apple pie, 1/8 pie	3 1/2 tsp	14
Frozen yogurt	1 tsp	4
Ice milk	3/4 tsp	3
Ice cream, premium	3 1/4 tsp	13
Ice cream, regular	2 tsp	8
Snack Foods		
Beef jerky, 1 strip, 1 oz (20 g)	1 1/4 tsp	5
Chocolate bar, 2 oz (50 g)	3 3/4 tsp	15
Granola bar, 1 oz (28 g)	1 1/2 tsp	6
Peanuts, 1/4 cup (50 ml)	4 1/2 tsp	18
Popcorn, regular buttery microwave, 2 cups (500 ml)	3/4 tsp	3
Potato chips, 15	2 3/4 tsp	11
Pretzels, 10 small twists	1/2 tsp	2
Raisins, 1/2 cup (125 ml)	0	0

* milk fat

Note: Some foods that show 0 teaspoons of fat may have a trace amount.

Beef Information Centre, A Matter of Fat, 2003. www.beefinfo.org

Learning where fat lurks in foods is the first step to cutting back daily fat intake. To help you and your family consume no more than 30% fat calories, limit intake of visible added fats and oils to a daily total of 5 to 8 servings per day. If your teenager is trying to lose weight, he should stick to five servings per day. Some foods, such as avocados and olives, are high in fat and should be eaten in moderation. One fat serving is

- 1 tsp (5 ml) vegetable oil, margarine, or butter

- 2 tsp (10 ml) diet margarine

- 2 tsp (10 ml) regular mayonnaise

- 2 tsp (10 ml) salad dressing

- 1 tbsp (15 ml) nuts or seeds

- 1 1/2 tsp (7 ml) peanut or nut butter

- 1/8 of a medium-sized avocado

- 10 small or 5 large olives

The next step is learning where hidden fat lurks in foods. Most of us realize that greasy fast food is loaded with the stuff. A McDonald's Big Mac packs 32 grams of fat. Add the large fries and a large chocolate shake and you've hit (or exceeded) your fat quota for the day—a whopping 78 grams in just one meal!

Many other fast foods also deliver a lot of fat to your plate, despite their healthier sounding names. For instance, a typical taco salad from a Mexican fast food joint can pack as many as 900 calories and 12 teaspoons (60 ml) of hidden fat. The deep-fried shell that holds the salad and high-fat toppings such as cheese and sour cream are the culprits here. Even a chef's salad can be upward of 650 calories once the high-fat dressing is added. Some of those packets of creamy dressing served at fast food outlets are 400 calories alone—each one of those calories coming from fat.

Decoding Nutrition Labels

By the end of 2005, most prepackaged foods sold in Canada will carry a new and improved nutrition label. (See page 102 for an example of what it looks like.) Many companies have already added these labels to their products. Some foods, however, are exempt from this new label—alcoholic beverages, fresh fruit and vegetables, raw meat and poultry (except if ground), raw fish and seafood, foods sold only in retail establishments where they are prepared or processed, and individual servings of food intended for immediate consumption.

The table in the Nutrition Facts box gives you the information you need to make smart food choices and compare products. You can scan the table for calories, total fat, saturated and trans fats, cholesterol, sodium, carbohydrate, fibre, sugars, protein, calcium, iron, and vitamins A and C in one serving of the food.

To help you choose a lower-fat food, look at the grams of total fat per serving stated in the table. This information is listed after the calories per serving. For example, a 1 cup (264 g) serving of soup might provide 13 grams of fat. Do you usually eat one cup of the product or more? If you eat twice as much, you'll be consuming 26 grams of fat. That's a lot of fat from just one food. You can use this information on nutrition labels to choose among different brands. Where possible, choose a brand that provides no more than 3 grams of fat for every 100 calories (this means the product has no more than 30% fat calories).

You'll also see the total fat listed in the table, as well as the saturated plus trans fats, expressed as a percentage of a daily value (% DV). This tells you whether one serving of the food has a little or a lot of fat, and whether it has a little or a lot of saturated and trans fat, two types of fat I discuss in the next section. For a 2000-calorie diet (the calorie intake that nutrition labelling is based on), the recommended daily total fat intake is 65 grams, which includes 20 grams of saturated plus trans fat. (No more than 10 percent of our daily calories should come from these two fats.) A product with 16 grams of total fat would have a daily value of 25% (16 grams divided by 65 grams). Keep in mind that many active teenagers need more than 2000 calories per day, so the % DV may overestimate the contribution of a particular nutrient to a teen's daily intake. You'll learn more about the Nutrition Facts box in Chapter 6.

Of course, not all products you buy must be low in fat. For instance, salad dressings and margarines are very high in fat. But that's okay. As long as your fat intake balances out over the course of the day, there's no need to worry. It is a good idea to compare grams of fat for different brands of crackers, cookies, cereals, frozen dinners, soups, and snack foods.

If nutrition information is not available on a product's package, you can always read the ingredient list. Manufacturers are required to list all ingredients in a product, beginning with the ingredient that's present in the largest quantity. To search out hidden fat, look for the words "lard," "shortening," "palm oil," "coconut oil," "vegetable oil," "partially hydrogenated vegetable oil," "monoglycerides," "diglycerides," and "tallow."

As I said earlier, not all the foods teenagers eat have to be low in fat. Teens will undoubtedly splurge on a burger and fries, pepperoni pizza, or bowl of ice cream. It's the overall picture that counts. Teenagers can eat a high-fat meal as long as their usual meals are lower in fat. Every single food, or meal, does not need to conform to the 30% fat calorie rule. It's what is eaten over the course of a day that matters. But if teens are eating french fries, pizza, muffins, and cookies every day, they are likely eating too much fat.

Good Fats, Bad Fats: What's the Difference?

When it comes to weight control, all types of fat are considered equal. Whether it's from butter, lard, margarine, or olive oil, one gram of fat packs 9 calories. That's more than double the calories found in one gram of carbohydrate or protein (both of which have four calories per gram). Fat calories from any source add up fast and can quickly lead to weight gain. When it comes to health, however, not all fats are created equally. It is important that you reduce the total amount of fat you eat, but there are certain fats that you need to focus on when doing so.

To help you and your teen understand about the different types of fat, we need to start with a chemistry lesson. Fatty acids in food (fatty acids are the building blocks of triglycerides, or blood fats) consist of long chains of carbon molecules linked together, which in turn are attached to hydrogen atoms. Each fatty acid has a different chemical structure that determines how it will behave in the body. For instance, when a fatty acid is completely full of hydrogen atoms, it is considered a *saturated fatty acid*. Animal fat in meat, poultry, and dairy products contains mostly saturated fatty acids. Fatty acids that are not saturated with hydrogen atoms are called *unsaturated fats*. These include *monounsaturated* (found in olive and canola oils) or *polyunsaturated* (found in corn, sunflower, and safflower oils).

Fat in food almost always contains a mixture of saturated and unsaturated fatty acids. We classify fats as saturated, monounsaturated, or polyunsaturated based on what fatty acids are present in the greatest concentration.

Blood Cholesterol 101

Eating too much fat can raise blood cholesterol levels. In order to understand how different types of fat affect our cholesterol levels, we first need to know about blood cholesterol. Here's a short primer. You may have heard these terms used by your doctor but were never sure what they meant.

Cholesterol can't dissolve in your blood. Rather, it needs to be piggybacked on protein carriers throughout your bloodstream.

LDL cholesterol

This cholesterol is transported to the arteries on low-density lipoproteins. LDLs packed with cholesterol are referred to as "bad" cholesterol because they are directly linked to the process of hardening and narrowing of the arteries. The higher your level of LDL cholesterol, the greater your risk of heart disease. This type of cholesterol is influenced by diet—too much saturated and trans fats can raise LDL, while a regular intake of nuts, soy, and soluble fibre can help lower LDL.

HDL cholesterol

High-density lipoproteins carry cholesterol away from the arteries toward the liver for degradation. It prevents the accumulation of cholesterol on your artery walls. That's why it's referred to as "good" cholesterol. Regular exercise can raise HDL.

Triglycerides

These fat particles are made in the liver from the food you eat and are transported in your blood on very low-density lipoproteins. High levels of triglycerides are associated with a greater risk of heart disease. Being overweight and consuming too much sugar can raise triglycerides.

Saturated Fats

This type of fat is found in all animal foods—meat, poultry, eggs, and dairy products all have saturated fat. Some vegetable oils, including coconut, palm kernel, and palm, are also saturated. Diets that contain a lot of saturated fat raise your risk for heart disease by increasing your blood cholesterol level. Saturated fat raises your LDL (bad) cholesterol. A diet that's high in saturated fat blocks the ability of your cells to clear cholesterol from your bloodstream.

To make matters even more confusing, there are many different types of saturated fats in foods, and researchers are learning that they don't all influence our blood cholesterol to the same degree. For instance, the saturated fat in dairy products is more cholesterol-raising than the saturated fat found in meat. And the saturated fat in chocolate does not seem to raise blood cholesterol levels at all.

You certainly don't need to know the different types of saturated fats in foods. What's most important is to just eat less saturated fat. No more than 10% of your daily calories should come from saturated and trans fats. If your teenager eats 3000 calories per day, that means no more than 30 grams of saturated and trans fats combined. The table below compares the total fat and saturated fat of common foods.

TOTAL FAT AND SATURATED FAT OF SELECTED FOODS (GRAMS)

Food	Total Fat	Saturated Fat
Dairy Products		
Cheddar cheese, low-fat, 7% MF,* 1 oz (30 g)	2.0	1.2
Cheddar cheese, regular-fat, 31% MF, 1 oz (30 g)	9.4	6.0
Cottage cheese, 1% MF, 1/2 cup (125 ml)	1.1	0.8

Milk, homogenized, 3.3% MF, 1 cup (250 ml)	8.1	5.1
Milk, skim, 0.1% MF, 1 cup (250 ml)	0.5	0.3
Milk, 2% MF, 1 cup (250 ml)	4.7	2.9

Meat and Poultry

Beef, flank steak, broiled, 3 oz (90 g)	9.3	4.0
Beef, rib roast, roasted, 3 oz (90 g)	9.7	3.8
Beef, short ribs, simmered, 3 oz (90 g)	14.3	6.1
Beef, strip loin steak, broiled, 3 oz (90 g)	8.2	3.1
Chicken breast, skinless, cooked, 3 oz (90 g)	1.8	0.6
Ground beef patty, extra-lean, broiled, 3 oz (90 g)	12.2	5.2
Ground beef patty, lean, broiled, 3 oz (90 g)	14.7	6.0
Ground beef patty, medium, broiled, 3 oz (90 g)	17.2	7.3
Pork, back ribs, broiled, 3 oz (90 g)	13.5	5.0
Pork, side bacon, fried, 5 slices (32 g)	16	5.6
Pork tenderloin, roasted, 3 oz (90 g)	3.2	1.0

Desserts

Frozen yogurt, vanilla, 5.6% MF, 1/2 cup (125 ml)	4.0	2.5
Fruit ices, 1/2 cup (125 ml)	0	0
Ice cream, vanilla, 11% MF, 1/2 cup (125 ml)	7.3	4.5

Fats and Oils

Butter, 2 tsp (10 ml)	7.7	4.8
Margarine, soft tub, corn, 2 tsp (10 ml)	7.5	1.4

* milk fat

Source: *Nutrient Value of Some Common Foods,* table titled "Comparing Total Fat and Saturated Fat of Some Common Foods (grams)," Health Canada (© 1999, reprint 2002). Reproduced with permission of the Minister of Public Works and Government Services Canada, 2005.

Trans Fats

If you haven't heard of trans fat, you might have heard the term "hydrogenated fat." Trans fats are formed when vegetable oils are processed into margarine or shortening. This chemical process, called hydrogenation, adds hydrogen atoms to liquid vegetable oils, making them more solid and useful to food manufacturers. Cookies, crackers, pastries, and muffins made with hydrogenated vegetable oils are more palatable and have a longer shelf life. A margarine that's made by hydrogenating a vegetable oil is firmer, like butter.

Over the past 50 years, industry-produced trans fat has become a common ingredient in hundreds of popular foods. Roughly 90% of the trans fat in our food supply lurks in commercial baked goods, snack foods, fried fast foods, and margarines. Trans fat occurs naturally in beef and dairy products, but in tiny amounts.

Hydrogenation makes a fat become saturated *and* it forms a new type of fat called *trans fat*. Hydrogenation also destroys essential fatty acids that your body needs from unprocessed vegetable oils. A high intake of trans fat, like saturated fat found in meat and dairy, increases total and LDL cholesterol levels. But consuming too much trans fat, unlike saturated fat, can lower your HDL (good) cholesterol. Compared with saturated fats, trans fats are linked with a 2.5- to 10-fold higher risk of heart disease. The harmful effects of trans fats aren't limited to heart disease. Research also suggests that diets high in trans fat increase the risk of type 2 diabetes.

It's estimated that Canadians consume an average of 8.4 grams of trans fat per day, and some of us scarf back as much as 39 grams per day. It's easy to do when many snack foods—cookies, donuts, pastries, crackers, potato chips—contain up to 50% of their total fat as trans fat. Even foods marketed as low fat can harbour trans fat.

Food companies have until December 2005 to declare grams of trans fat on the nutrition labels of prepackaged foods. In the meantime, you can use the ingredient list to sleuth out trans fat. Choose products that do not contain partially hydrogenated vegetable oils or shortening.

If you eat margarine, choose one that's made with non-hydrogenated fat. Many brands state this on the label. If you don't see "non-hydrogenated" printed on the margarine tub, use the nutrition label to add the values for polyunsaturated and monounsaturated fats. They should add up to at least 6 grams per 2 teaspoon (10 gram) serving for a regular margarine; 3 grams for a light margarine. If the values are lower, that means there are more saturated and trans fats present than you should consume.

In September 2002 the National Academy of Sciences (a panel of Canadian and American experts) issued a report stating there is no safe level of trans fat. While it is impossible to avoid all trans fat, our intake should be as low as possible.

Many food companies are making this an easier task by eliminating trans fat from foods. The makers of Voortman cookies, Pepperidge Farm Goldfish crackers, Doritos chips, and New York Fries have already launched their "zero trans fat" products across Canada. To be labelled "free of trans fat" a product must contain less than 0.2 grams of trans fat per serving, and it must have no more than 2 grams of trans and saturated fat combined.

But just because a food is stamped "zero trans fat" doesn't mean that it's good for you. Potato chips deep-fried in corn oil may be better for your arteries, but they won't do your waistline any favours. A regular-sized order of New York Fries will still set you back 792 calories and 39 grams of fat. Sure, they contain sunflower oil rather than partially hydrogenated vegetable oil. But when it comes to weight control, fat calories are fat calories. And while trans fat–free Goldfish crackers are a healthier snack than they once were, their number-one ingredient remains refined white flour.

Polyunsaturated Fats

There are two types of polyunsaturated fats in foods—omega-6s and omega-3s. Omega-6 polyunsaturated fats are found in all vegetable oils—soybean, sunflower, safflower, corn, and sesame. We need omega-6 oils because they contain linoleic acid, an essential fatty acid that the body can't make on its own. The problem is that our modern diet is overwhelmed with linoleic acid from vegetable oils that are used in processed and fast foods. In the body, some of this linoleic acid is used to fuel agents that contribute to inflammation and pain.

Meanwhile, we're not eating enough of the healthy omega-3 fats. Omega-3 poly-unsaturated fats are plentiful in cold-water fish—salmon, sardines, trout, and mackerel. These omega-3 fats are called DHA (docosahexanaenoic acid) and EPA (eicosapentaenoic acid). And there's another type of omega-3 fat that's found in some plant foods, for example, soybeans, flaxseed, and walnuts. Canola oil also contains lots. It's called alpha-linolenic acid (ALA) and it's an essential fatty acid—that means we must get it from the foods we eat.

Eating polyunsaturated fats in place of saturated fats can help lower elevated LDL cholesterol levels. And there's growing evidence to indicate there are other reasons why your family should consume more omega-3 fats.

Omega-3 fats in fish

Plenty of studies show that eating more fatty fish can lower the risk of heart disease. Researchers have known for some time that populations who consume fish a few times per week (the Greenland Inuit and the Japanese among them) have lower rates of heart disease. Scientists in Seattle recently learned that eating one fatty-fish meal per week was linked with significant protection from having a first heart attack.[3]

A recent analysis of 11 studies involving 222,364 people with an average 12 years of follow-up found that, compared with those who never consumed fish or ate fish less than once per month, persons with a higher intake of fish had lower risk of dying from heart disease. Those who ate fish more than five times per week were 38% less likely to die from heart disease. Even eating fish just once per week was linked with heart protection.[4]

DHA and EPA, the two omega-3 fats in fish, can lower high levels of triglycerides and reduce the stickiness of platelets, the cells that form blood clots in arteries. Omega-3 fats in fish may also increase the flexibility of red blood cells so they can pass more readily through tiny blood vessels. Recent studies have found that omega-3 fats in fish lower the risk of heart rhythm disturbances, the cause of many sudden deaths from heart attack.

Omega-3 fats in fish may also protect from cancer, most notably breast, colon, and perhaps prostate cancer. Laboratory studies have shown fish oil can enhance the immune system and suppress cancer cell growth.

The type of fat you eat determines what kind of eicosanoids your body produces. Eicosanoids are powerful hormone-like compounds that regulate our blood, immune system, and hormones. For instance, omega-6 oils are used to synthesize so-called unfriendly eicosanoids that cause inflammation and pain. The omega-3 fats in fish, on the other hand, produce "friendly" eicosanoids that tend to decrease inflammation and improve circulation.

These omega-3 and omega-6 fats compete with each other for the same metabolic pathways. So if you eat a diet packed with processed and fried foods that contain primarily omega-6 oils, the unfriendly eicosanoids win out. On the other hand, if most of the fat you eat is rich in omega-3s, more health-enhancing eicosanoids will be formed. Eicosanoids derived from omega-3 fats are believed to help prevent cancer, ease the symptoms of rheumatoid arthritis, and prevent flare-ups of colitis.

The best way to get plenty of DHA and EPA is by eating cold-water fish, for example, salmon, trout, and sardines. The colder the water the fish live in, the more omega-3 oil they contain.

Alpha-linolenic acid (ALA)

There's another omega-3 fat called alpha-linolenic acid (ALA), which is found in plant foods. Research suggests that higher intakes of ALA are linked with protection from heart disease, but the data are less compelling than for DHA and EPA in fish.[5]

For those of you who don't like fish, this is a good way to get your omega-3s. You'll find alpha-linolenic acid in flaxseed oil, canola oil, nuts (especially walnuts), soybeans, tofu, omega-3 eggs (laid by hens fed a diet high in flaxseed), whole grains, and leafy greens. To prevent a deficiency, teenage boys aged 9 to 13 years need to consume 1.2 grams of ALA per day, while girls must get 1 gram from their diet. Older boys need 1.6 grams, and girls, 1.1 grams each day. Here's how certain foods contribute ALA to your teen's diet:

ALA CONTENT OF SELECTED FOODS (GRAMS)

Canola oil, 1 tbsp (15 ml)	1.3
Flax oil capsule, 1000 mg	0.5
Flaxseed oil, 1 tbsp (15 ml)	7.2
Flaxseeds, 1 tbsp (15 ml)	2.2
Omega-3 whole egg	0.4
Soybeans, cooked, 1/2 cup (125 ml)	0.5
Tofu, firm, 1/4 block (81 g)	0.12

Monounsaturated Fats

Chances are you already know these unsaturated fatty acids are considered to be healthy fats. After all, who doesn't think of heart health when they hear the words "olive oil"? Monounsaturated fats found in olive oil, canola oil, peanuts and peanut oil, avocado, and some nuts (filberts, almonds, pistachios, pecans, and cashews) are a large part of the Mediterranean diet, a pattern of eating that's associated with lower incidences of heart disease and cancer.

There's no one typical Mediterranean diet. At least 16 countries border the Mediterranean Sea, countries with different cultures, ethnic backgrounds, and dietary practices. But there is a common pattern to the Mediterranean diet, and it encompasses more than the use of olive oil. In the Mediterranean diet,

- Fruits, vegetables, grains, beans, nuts, and seeds are eaten daily.
- Extra-virgin olive oil is the predominant source of added fat.
- Dairy products, fish, and poultry are eaten in moderate amounts.
- Eggs are eaten zero to four times weekly.
- Red meat is seldom eaten.
- Wine is consumed with meals, in low to moderate amounts.

How can this pattern of eating—aside from drinking wine, which I don't recommend for teens—protect your teen's heart? In addition to it being high in plant foods that contain antioxidants and fibre, its monounsaturated fat content can take some credit. Research shows that when you substitute monounsaturated fat for saturated fat in your diet, you can lower high levels of blood cholesterol, in particular LDL cholesterol. Some studies suggest that extra-virgin olive oil helps prevent blood clots from forming and acts as an antioxidant to help protect from heart disease.

When buying olive oil, be sure to choose the highest quality extra-virgin olive oil you can find. It has been processed the least (that's why it's a dark green colour) and contains more protective compounds than regular or light olive oil. Oils that do not meet the criteria for being extra-virgin have been sent to a refinery, where defects in colour, taste, and aroma are removed by industrial processing.

Dietary Cholesterol

A discussion about dietary fat would not be complete without mentioning dietary cholesterol. This wax-like fatty substance is found in meat, poultry, eggs, dairy products, fish, and shellfish. It's particularly plentiful in shrimp, liver, and egg yolks. Despite its bad rap, we do need some cholesterol for good health. Teenagers need cholesterol to synthesize certain hormones and digestive compounds and to help build strong cell walls.

But we don't need a lot. There is evidence linking high-cholesterol diets with a higher risk of heart disease, since too much dietary cholesterol can contribute to an elevated blood cholesterol level. That's why experts recommend that we consume no more than 300 milligrams of cholesterol per day. Cholesterol is found in foods of animal origin. Choosing low-fat animal foods will automatically cut dietary cholesterol from your diet. Here's how foods stack up when it comes to cholesterol content:

CHOLESTEROL CONTENT OF SELECTED FOODS (MILLIGRAMS)

Meat, Poultry, Eggs, and Fish

Beef sirloin, lean, 3 oz (90 g)	64
Chicken breast, skinless, 3 oz (90 g)	73
Calf's liver, fried, 3 oz (90 g)	416
Egg white, 1 large	0
Egg, whole, 1 large	190
Pork loin, lean, 3 oz (90 g)	71
Salmon, 3 oz (90 g)	54
Shrimp, 3 oz (90 g)	135

Dairy Products

Butter, 2 tsp (10 ml)	10
Cheese, cheddar, 31% MF,* 1 oz (30 g)	31
Cheese, mozzarella, part-skim, 1 oz (30 g)	18
Cream, half and half, 12% MF, 2 tbsp (25 ml)	12
Milk, skim, 1 cup (250 ml)	5
Milk, 2% MF, 1 cup (250 ml)	19
Yogurt, 1.5% MF, 3/4 cup (175 g)	11

* milk fat

Source: *Nutrient Vaule of Common Foods,* table titled "Cholesterol Content of Selected Foods," Health Canada (© 1999, reprint 2002). Reproduced with the permission of the Minister of Public Works and Government Services Canada, 2005.

Leslie's Tips for Choosing Healthier Fats and Oils

To limit *added* fats and oils

In your kitchen

- Use added fats and oils sparingly. Use cooking methods that add little or no fat to foods. Grilling, broiling, baking, steaming, lightly stir-frying, and poaching are good choices.

- When sautéing or stir-frying, use vegetable or chicken stock or water instead of heaps of oil.

- Cook and bake food in non-stick pans.

- Use high-fat spreads such as butter, margarine, mayonnaise, and cream cheese sparingly. Choose fat-reduced versions when possible. Avoid doubling up on your spreads—do you really need both butter and peanut butter on your toast? Both margarine and mayonnaise on your sandwich?

- Replace oil in quick-bread recipes with an equal amount of applesauce or other puréed fruit.

- Top baked potatoes with plain, low-fat yogurt, low-fat sour cream, or 1% cottage cheese. Add a few tablespoons of salsa or a dash of chili powder for flavour.

When dining out

- Don't be shy—ask that foods be prepared without added oil or butter (did you realize that steakhouses often add butter to your steak?).

- Encourage your teenager to visit the website of her favourite fast food restaurants. Many post the grams of total fat and saturated fat in their menu items. Some restaurants even declare the grams of trans fat.

- At fast food restaurants, search the menu for grilled chicken sandwiches, veggie burgers, grilled chicken salad, and chili.

- Save french fries and other fried foods for special occasions; order a small portion or share with a friend.

- Order salad dressings on the side—and don't use all of it. With creamy dressings, use the fork method: dip your fork in the dressing, then grab a bite of salad. You'll enjoy great taste with every bite while using only a fraction of the dressing.

- Limit your intake of rich pasta dishes covered with cream sauce, pesto sauce, or olive oil. Order pastas in broth (al brodo) or tomato sauce more often.

At the grocery store

- Start reading nutrition labels. The % DV (daily value) will tell you whether one serving of a food product has a little or a lot of saturated and trans fat. The daily values are based on recommendations for a healthy diet and can be used as a benchmark.

- When buying packaged foods, read ingredient lists. Fat can be listed as lard, shortening, palm oil, coconut oil, vegetable oil, hydrogenated oil, monoglycerides, diglycerides, and tallow.

To eat *less* saturated fat

Meat and poultry

- Choose leaner cuts of meat and poultry: flank steak, inside round, sirloin, eye of the round, extra-lean ground beef, pork tenderloin, centre-cut pork chops, poultry breast, and lean ground chicken are all lower-fat choices.

- Trim all visible fat from meat and poultry before cooking.

- Limit your portion of meat or poultry to 3 ounces (90 grams). That's the size of a deck of regular playing cards.

- Limit your intake of high-fat processed meats such as bacon, sausage, salami, pepperoni, bologna, and other cold cuts. Lower-fat deli choices include turkey or chicken breast, lean ham, and roast beef.

- Cook vegetarian meals more often. Legumes (dried peas, beans, and lentils) and soy foods have very little saturated fat.

Dairy products

- When buying milk, choose skim or 1% milk fat (MF). If you're used to whole-milk products (3.5% fat), you may find it easier to switch to lower-fat versions if you do so slowly. Try 2% milk first, then, once you're accustomed to that, change to 1% low-fat milk. Soon you'll be able to switch to skim milk (fat free) with no trouble.

- Buy yogurt with less than 2% MF.

- Try lower-fat cheeses, those having less than 20% MF content.

- Replace full-fat sour cream with products containing 7% MF or less.

- Substitute evaporated 2% or evaporated skim milk for cream in your coffee.

- Choose low-fat frozen yogurt or sorbet instead of ice cream.

Fats and oils

- Choose vegetable oils rather than solid fats.

- If you use butter, use it sparingly.

To minimize trans fat

- Avoid foods that list partially hydrogenated vegetable oil or shortening on the ingredient list.

- Buy a margarine whose label says it is made from non-hydrogenated fat.

- Limit your intake of fried fast food, commercial bakery goods, packaged snack foods, and store-bought cookies and crackers. Most of these contain high amounts of trans fat.

To eat *more* healthy polyunsaturated fats

· Eat fatty fish two to three times per week. The best sources of omega-3 fat are salmon, trout, herring, mackerel, sardines, anchovies, and albacore tuna (remember to watch your consumption of canned albacore tuna, though, because of the high levels of mercury it may contain). Frozen and canned fish are good choices, too.

· Use canola oil when cooking and baking. Not only does this oil contain alpha-linolenic acid, but it's also better suited for high-heat cooking. And it's a source of heart healthy monounsaturated fat.

· For a boost of ALA, toss a little walnut oil into homemade salad dressings. For every tablespoon (15 ml) of extra-virgin olive oil you use, add 1 teaspoon (5 ml) of walnut oil. Or use flaxseed oil in salad dressings and dips. You shouldn't heat this oil, but you can add a little to hot foods once they've finished cooking. Store flaxseed and walnut oils in the fridge.

· Add ground flaxseed to hot cereal, yogurt, smoothies, applesauce, and baking recipes.

· Choose omega-3 eggs. These eggs are a good source of alpha-linolenic acid.

5

———∞———

Water and Other Fluids

Water is considered an essential nutrient—just like vitamins and minerals—because our bodies can't make enough of it on its own to meet daily requirements. While a deficiency of other nutrients can take weeks, months, or even years to develop, you can survive only a few days without water. Water is the most abundant compound in the human body: it makes up 50% to 80% of our body weight, yet we tend to take it for granted.

Water lives inside and around every single cell in the body. There is not one system in your body that does not rely on a steady supply of water. Water in saliva and digestive juices help break down the foods you eat into smaller nutrients that can be absorbed into the bloodstream. These nutrients are then transported to all cells and tissues via water in your blood. Fluid in the blood, urine, and stool also helps remove toxic waste products from your body.

By carrying nutrients to all body tissues and waste away from cells, water helps teenagers maintain a healthy complexion. And it's no secret that teens are very concerned with how their skin looks, since many teenagers are affected, at least occasionally, by acne.

An adequate intake of water also helps the body regulate its temperature. Teenagers lose water through sweat when they exercise. The fluid in sweat allows their muscles to release heat that builds up during exercise. Not drinking enough water can drain a teenager of physical and mental energy during sports.

The amount of water in the bloodstream also regulates blood pressure and heart function. And finally, water acts as the body's central lubricant. It cushions joints, moistens the eyes, and protects the brain and spinal cord.

How Much Water Do Teens Need Each Day?

It's clear that we need to drink a certain amount of water every day—just like we need a certain amount of vitamin C or calcium. We usually think of water, be it tap water or bottled water, as the main fluid that keeps us hydrated. It is true that drinking water satisfies much of our body's total water requirements. But fluids in different kinds of beverages and foods can contribute significantly to our daily total water requirements.

Here's how much total water teenagers need each day to prevent becoming dehydrated. Use the recommended intakes outlined below as a general guide.

DAILY RECOMMENDED WATER REQUIREMENTS FOR TEENAGERS

	Total Water	Drinking Water and Beverages
Boys, 9 to 13 years	9.6 cups (2.4 L)	8 cups (1.8 L)
Boys, 14 to 18 years	13.2 cups (3.3 L)	11 cups (2.6 L)
Boys, 19 years	15 cups (3.7 L)	13 cups (3.0 L)
Girls, 9 to 13 years	8.4 cups (2.1 L)	7 cups (1.6 L)
Girls, 14 to 18 years	9.2 cups (2.3 L)	8 cups (1.8 L)
Girls, 19 years	11 cups (2.7 L)	9 cups (2.2 L)

National Academy of Sciences, Institute of Medicine, Food and Nutrition Board. Dietary Reference Intakes for Water, Potassium, Sodium, Chloride, and Sulfate. The National Academy Press, Washington DC, 2004.

The first column in the table above gives the *total* daily water requirements for teenagers. This is the water that comes from foods, drinking water, and other beverages. About 26% of our water requirements are met by eating foods, such as fruits and vegetables, that have a high water content. Believe it or not, solid foods can actually provide teenagers with as much as 2 cups (0.5 litres) of water each day. Following you'll find a list of the water content of certain foods as a percentage of their weight. But if only roughly one-quarter of your daily fluid requirements are provided by foods in your diet, the rest must come from water and other beverages. You'll see the recommended amount of water and beverages listed in the second column of the table above.

WATER CONTENT OF SELECTED FOODS (PERCENTAGE)

Apple	86	Grapes	81
Banana	75	Iceberg lettuce	96
Bread, white	36	Milk	89
Broccoli, cooked	89	Orange	87
Cantaloupe	90	Peach	89
Carrots, raw	88	Peanuts	2
Cheddar cheese	37	Pickle	92
Chocolate cookies	4	Potato, baked	75
Corn flakes	3	Steak, cooked	50

USDA Nutrient Database for Standard Reference, Release 14. U.S. Department of Agriculture, Agriculture Research Services, 2001.

How much water teenagers need each day can vary depending on their body size, their diet (high-fibre diets increase fluid needs), their activity level, and the weather. High temperatures and low humidity increase fluid needs.

Exercise Increases Water Needs

When you exercise, your muscles generate heat. This heat must be released from your body as sweat or else your performance will be impaired. If you lose too much sweat during exercise and become dehydrated, the fluid in your bloodstream can't circulate efficiently to your working muscles and your skin. As a result, you'll produce less sweat, causing your muscles to build up heat. Dehydration is one of the most common causes of early fatigue during exercise. You'll find hydration tips for exercise in Chapter 10.

Illness Increases Water Needs

When you're sick, your body loses more fluid than usual. Vomiting and diarrhea drain your body of water and important electrolytes such as sodium, potassium, and chloride. When you have a fever, your body loses extra water through perspiration. In fact, any disruption to the body's normal state, such as trauma, shock, or emotional stress, can increase your risk of mild dehydration. It's important to drink extra fluids during these times.

During a typical day, however, there is little reason to worry that healthy teenagers aren't meeting their daily fluid requirements. Fluid intake, driven by thirst and the consumption of beverages at meals, keeps most teens well hydrated on a day-to-day basis.

What Happens If Teens Don't Drink Enough Fluids?

Dehydration can be acute, say, from a bout of heavy exercise, or it can be chronic, resulting from a poor fluid intake day after day. Dehydration is defined as losing at least 1% of your body weight from fluids. For a 170-pound (77-kilogram) teenage male, that means losing almost 2 pounds (1 kilogram) through fluid loss. It may not sound like a lot, but losing as little as 1% of your body weight can impair your physical performance and thinking ability.

Early symptoms of dehydration include headache, early fatigue during exercise, cramping, flushed skin, light-headedness, dizziness, dry mouth and eyes, nausea, and loss of appetite. If dehydration progresses, your teen may experience difficulty swallowing, clumsiness, shrivelled skin, painful urination, numb skin, muscle spasms, and delirium.

The simplest way for your teen to tell if she's replacing the water that her body loses is to check the colour and quantity of her urine. She's well hydrated if her urine is plentiful and its colour is very pale yellow or pale yellow. She's dehydrated if her urine is dark coloured and scanty. There is one exception to this: some multivitamin supplements can change the colour of urine to a bright, almost neon, yellow colour. This is caused by a B vitamin called riboflavin. In this case, it's better to judge your need for fluids by the quantity of urine you produce.

You can't always rely on thirst alone to tell you when it's time to drink fluids. By the time your thirst mechanism has kicked in and you feel parched, your body is already a little dehydrated. During illness and during exercise in warm weather or a hot room, your thirst mechanism doesn't work as well. In these situations, teenagers should pay particular attention to their daily fluid intake.

What Beverages Help Teens Meet Water Requirements?

As I mentioned earlier in this chapter, your body gets its daily fluid from three sources: foods, drinking water, and other beverages. What counts as other beverages? The answer: all beverages, with the exception of alcoholic ones. That's right, even coffee counts toward daily fluid intake. Although caffeine—found in coffee, tea, and colas, as well as in chocolate and some medications—causes the kidneys to excrete water, so far there's no evidence that shows habitual intakes cause a deficiency of body water over the course of a day. Higher caffeine intakes (more than one cup of coffee) do increase your urine output, but for only a short time. The latest recommendations, released in 2004, state that caffeinated beverages can contribute to your daily total water intake. (However, there are a few reasons why teenagers should limit their intake of caffeine, which I discuss later in the chapter.) Here are a few facts, and tips, to help choose beverages wisely:

Tap Water

Tap water is drawn from the surface water of lakes, reservoirs, and rivers. To eliminate disease causing bacteria and viruses, most drinking water supplies are disinfected with chlorine. Some cities use ozone to disinfect their water. But because ozone breaks down quickly, small amounts of chlorine must still be added. Our water supplies have been treated with chlorine for more than a century, ensuring our safety from the likes of cholera and typhoid fever.

It's not possible to remove all disinfection by-products from your tap water, but you can minimize your exposure to them by using a water treatment device at home (e.g., pitcher-type products with activated carbon filters). Not only will these devices remove a fair amount of chlorine and its by-products from drinking water, they also improve the taste and smell of the water.

Bottled Water

More and more teenagers are carrying bottled water with them to drink during class and sporting events. Many people think bottled water tastes better than tap water because it doesn't have that chlorine taste. Bottled water is also perceived as being safer and of higher quality than tap water.

Technically, bottled water is simply water that's sold in sealed containers. Some bottled water is mineral water or spring water, and will be labelled as such. If it's not, then technically it may be water from any source, including the municipal water supply, that's been treated to make it safe to drink.

Bottled water differs from tap water in three ways. Usually one main difference is the source of water. While tap water comes from the surface of lakes and rivers, most bottled waters originate from a protected underground source. Another difference relates to how these waters are distributed. Municipal water is pumped through miles of piping, whereas bottled water is processed in food plants and packaged in clean, sealed containers. And finally, bottled waters do not contain any chlorine or chlorine by-products.

Some people worry that bottled water can contain bacteria that cause illness. It's true that bacteria levels can increase quickly if bottled water is left at room temperature for six weeks. But since most bottled waters use some type of disinfection process, this is not usually an issue. Like most food products, bottled water contains very low levels of harmless bacteria.

What's most important is that you refrigerate an opened bottle of water in case any harmful bacteria have been introduced after it was opened. Ideally, refrigerate your bottled water as soon as you get it home from the store, and if you can't, keep it in a cool place away from heat and sunlight. Bottled water normally contains low numbers of harmless bacteria. However, if it is stored for prolonged periods at room temperature, these bacteria can multiply rapidly. Although manufacturers give bottled water a best-before date or shelf life of two years, Health Canada suggests you replace it after a year. When buying bottled water, check the bottling date and best-before date to ensure its freshness.

Milk, Soy, and Rice Beverages

Teens can help meet their fluid requirements and get important nutrients at the same time by drinking milk, soy, or rice beverages. Low-fat milk offers protein, calcium, vitamin D, B vitamins, and zinc. Lactose-reduced milk is a good option for those teens who are lactose intolerant; look for it in the dairy case of your grocery store. People who are lactose intolerant can't properly digest lactose, the natural sugar in cow's milk. Symptoms include bloating, gas, abdominal pain, and, sometimes, diarrhea. Soy and rice beverages are another option for teenagers who can't tolerate lactose and for those who follow vegetarian diets.

If your teen opts for soy or rice milk, be sure to buy a brand that has been fortified (enriched with calcium and other nutrients). Many fortified soy beverages provide the same amount of calcium; vitamins D, A, and B12; riboflavin; and zinc as milk. But read labels to be sure. The label should state "enriched" or "high in calcium." If you don't see these words, scan the Nutrition Facts table for the % daily values (% DV). Fortified brands will supply 27% to 30% DV for calcium, 40% to 45% DV for vitamin D, and 50% DV for vitamin B12, all-important nutrients for growing teenagers.

Unsweetened Fruit and Vegetables Juices

Whether you make your own or buy them at the grocery store, fruit and vegetable juices are another good hydration option. They provide your body fluid along with vitamins C and A and folate. And 1 cup (250 ml) of fruit or vegetable juice also supplies a fruit and vegetables serving. However, if your teen is watching her weight, I don't recommend that she fill up on fruit juice. Despite its nutritious qualities, the calories from natural fruit sugar still add up. Plain water is the better option to quench thirst.

When you buy fruit juice, choose unsweetened varieties, which don't have added sugars. Avoid fruit punches and fruit drinks (e.g., Fruitopia), which are made with mostly sugar and water.

Vegetable juices have far less sugar than fruit juice and pack a lot of vitamin C. Tomato-based juices are also a great way to get a boost of lycopene, a natural plant chemical that appears to lower the risk of prostate cancer. The only drawback to bottled or canned vegetable juice is the hefty sodium content in many. For instance, a single serving of commercial vegetable juice packs close to 700 milligrams of sodium—more than a quarter of the daily recommended intake. But if this is the only high-sodium food your teenager consumes for the day, he or she will still be well below the 2300-milligram upper limit for sodium. For teenagers watching their sodium intakes, sodium-reduced brands are available.

Soft Drinks, Iced Tea, and Fruit Drinks

As a nutritionist, I am reluctant to include these beverages as an option for getting your daily amount of fluids. They do provide your body with water, but they are the least healthy choices of all the beverages. Teenagers just don't need all the sugar these drinks provide. One 12 ounce (355 ml) can of pop provides 10 teaspoons (50 ml) of added sugars, not to mention plenty of chemical additives. The fruit drink Fruitopia might advertise added vitamin C, but look at the nutrition label and you'll see there are 60 grams (15 teaspoons or 75 ml) of sugar per 16 ounce (473 ml) bottle.

A little extra sugar never hurt anyone, but if teenagers are gulping these beverages regularly, excess calories can be an issue, especially if your teen is overweight. Larger-than-life serving sizes make matters worse. Today, the average medium-sized fast food soft drink delivers 220 calories and 17 ounces (495 ml) of sugary liquid. That translates into 14 teaspoons (70 ml) of sugar. And many bottled fruit drinks and iced teas, easily accessible in vending machines, the school cafeteria, and corner stores, provide much more than what is considered one beverage serving (1 cup or 250 ml). Read the Nutrition Facts box and you'll see the standard 16 ounce (473 ml) bottle contains as many as two and half servings. Let's face it: most teenagers don't share the bottle with a friend.

There's another reason why teenagers, especially females, should avoid soft drinks. Studies have found an association between drinking pop, both colas and non-colas, and the risk of bone fracture in teenage girls. A study of 460 girls in grades nine and ten found that drinking carbonated soft drinks was linked with a threefold higher risk of bone fractures. Among physically active girls who drank only cola drinks, the relationship with bone fractures was even stronger.[1]

Researchers don't know exactly why soft drinks are harmful to bones, but they have a few hunches. For starters, teenagers have doubled or tripled their intake of soft drinks over the past 30 years. It's estimated that North American teens have cut their consumption of milk by 40% and, as a result, are missing out on bone-building nutrients such as calcium and vitamin D. It's also possible that some ingredient in soft drinks has a detrimental effect on bones. Carbonated soft drinks contain phosphoric acid, and there is concern that high levels of phosphorus may upset the body's calcium balance. If teenagers do drink soft drinks, they should limit their intake as much as possible. They need to consider soft drinks as liquid candy.

Energy Drinks

Red Bull, SoBe Adrenalin Rush, and Mountain Dew Energy are three energy drinks advertised to Canadian youth, especially male teenagers. Energy drinks appeal to young people, especially, it seems, to those interested in extreme sports, video games, and hip hop. At $3 per 8 1/2 ounce (250 ml) can, these trendy brews are marketed as drinks that "improve muscle tone," "increase endurance," and "invigorate the mind and body." The stimulating effect of some energy drinks is due to a combination of ingredients such as caffeine, ginseng, and taurine (an amino acid). Energy drinks also contain a fair amount of sugar, although sugar-free versions are available.

I have had many parents express concern over their teen's consumption of energy drinks. Because of their high caffeine content, energy drinks should not be used by teenagers to meet fluid requirements. Among other ingredients, Red Bull contains 80 milligrams of caffeine—more than three times the amount that's in the same amount of Coke. Teenagers need to know that energy drinks are not the same as sports drinks (e.g., Gatorade), which replenish fluids. Products like Red Bull contain so much caffeine that they can actually dehydrate you. In fact, Red Bull is banned in Denmark, Norway, and France because of concerns over side effects of the drink's ingredients.

In Canada, Red Bull (and Mountain Dew Energy) cans carry a warning stating the beverage is not suitable for children or caffeine-sensitive persons and that it should not be mixed with alcohol. Yet the fact that energy drinks are sold in corner stores means that kids have no difficulty buying them.

If your teen uses energy drinks, make sure he realizes these beverages are not intended to be used as fluid replacements. They're sugary soft drinks with caffeine and other ingredients that have stimulant effects. Teenagers should also be warned about the potential hazards of mixing energy drinks with alcohol. Caffeine and alcohol are both diuretics, substances that cause the body to lose fluid. The effects of both could cause heart problems in some teens, particularly when consumed before, during, or after sports, when teens are losing fluid from sweat.

Caffeine and Teens

Caffeine occurs naturally in coffee beans, tea leaves, and chocolate. It's also added to soft drinks and some pain medications. While some teenagers get the majority of their caffeine from colas, others get their hit mainly from coffee, and yet others gulp a fair bit from energy drinks such as Red Bull.

Caffeine is defined as a drug because it jolts the central nervous system (the network that includes your nerves, spinal cord, and brain), causing increased heart rate and alertness.

Teenagers who are sensitive to caffeine may also feel a temporary increase in energy and elevation in mood. Like other stimulants, caffeine does most of its work in the brain, and you may feel its effects for up to six hours after consuming it.

Some teenagers are more sensitive to the effects of caffeine than others. Caffeine sensitivity—the amount that will produce an effect—varies from person to person. In general, the smaller the person, the less caffeine it takes to produce side effects in him or her. But teenagers of all sizes will become less sensitive to caffeine if they consume it daily. Bottom line: the more caffeine you consume, the more caffeine you'll need to feel its effects.

And more caffeine is not a good thing. Although caffeinated beverages do count toward daily fluid requirements, I certainly don't advocate that teenagers head to their local Starbucks to quench their thirst with coffee. That's because too much caffeine can affect bone development, sleep patterns, and recovery from exercise. Not to mention make teens feel anxious and tense. Here's what teenagers need to know about the effects of caffeine:

Caffeine and Bone Health

Caffeine causes your kidneys to excrete calcium in your urine. It is estimated that every 6 ounce (177 ml) cup of coffee leaches 48 milligrams of calcium from your body. The negative effects of caffeine on bone density are likely most detrimental for teenagers who are not getting enough calcium each day—and according to surveys, that might be a lot of teenagers. One study found that 400 milligrams of caffeine (about 3 small cups of coffee) caused calcium loss in women whose daily diet had less than 600 milligrams of calcium.[2] Another study from Tufts University in Boston found that women getting more than 450 milligrams of caffeine and less than 800 milligrams of calcium had significantly lower bone densities than women who consumed the same amount of caffeine but got more than 800 milligrams of calcium.[3]

Caffeine and Sleep

It's true that caffeine can boost your mental alertness because it stimulates your central nervous system. That's why coffee appeals to teenagers who need a jolt to stay up late to finish homework or study for an exam. But while one or two cups of coffee can give you a gentle lift, the fourth or fifth cup can overstimulate the body and cause insomnia. Studies have shown that as few as one or two cups of coffee in the morning can affect the quality of sleep that same night. Caffeine blocks the action of adenosine, a natural brain chemical that slows the body and signals your body that it's time to sleep. Caffeine keeps your brain's nerve cells running. Contrary to what some teenagers might think, caffeine doesn't give them more energy—it just keeps the body from getting the message that it's sleepy.

Caffeine and Mood

A lot of teenagers enjoy the way caffeine makes them feel. They like to feel wired and more focused in class. But too much caffeine can sometimes bring on feelings similar to an anxiety or panic attack—insomnia, nervousness, tremors, and an irregular heartbeat. Too much caffeine can also make teens feel irritable and jumpy.

Caffeine and Blood Pressure

If your teen has high blood pressure, it's a wise idea for him to limit or avoid coffee altogether. Studies have found that small doses of caffeine can cause temporary stiffening of the blood vessel walls. Researchers from Greece found that people with treated mild hypertension who took a pill containing 250 milligrams of caffeine—equivalent to the amount of caffeine in two cups of coffee—experienced a temporary increase in blood pressure and in the stiffness of the aorta, the main artery leaving the heart. In another study, a small group of people with normal blood pressure who were given a pill containing as much caffeine as one cup of coffee also experienced a temporary increase in the stiffening of arterial walls.[4] Scientists speculate that caffeine-induced stiffness of the artery walls may make high blood pressure worse.

More recently, American researchers studied 159 teenagers, aged 15 to 19 years. The teens in the study had height, weight, and blood pressure measurements taken. The researchers calculated how much caffeine teenagers were consuming each day and ranked them in one of three categories: low (0 to 50 milligrams caffeine), medium (50 to 100 milligrams), and high (more than 100 milligrams). As you'll see below, a 12 ounce (355 ml) can of cola contains 40 to 50 milligrams of caffeine. The researchers found that teenagers in the high-caffeine group had blood pressure readings higher than those who consumed caffeine in the middle caffeine group.[5]

How Much Caffeine Is Too Much for Teens?

Experts don't agree on what the upper caffeine limit should be for teenagers. Health Canada recommends that 10- to 12-year-olds not consume more than 85 milligrams, and 13- to 19-year-olds no more than 400 to 450 milligrams. However, many experts and paediatricians recommend that teenagers consume no more than 100 milligrams of caffeine per day, which is the amount in two to three 12 ounce (355 ml) cans of cola or one small cup of coffee (less than 6 ounces, or 177 ml). Getting more than 100 milligrams of caffeine per day can lead to addiction—the dependence on a chemical that is not naturally produced by the body. Here's a look at how little it takes for teenagers to reach the 100-milligram cut-off.

CAFFEINE CONTENT OF SELECTED BEVERAGES, FOODS, AND MEDICATIONS (MILLIGRAMS)

Beverage	
Coffee, brewed, 8 fluid oz (250 ml)	135
Coffee, decaffeinated, 8 fluid oz (250 ml)	5
Coffee, instant, 8 fluid oz (250 ml)	76–106
Coffee, Starbucks, 8 fluid oz (250 ml)	200
Cola, regular	36–46
Cola, diet	39-50
Espresso, 2 fluid oz (60 ml)	90–100

Tea, black, 8 fluid oz (250 ml)	43
Tea, green, 8 fluid oz (250 ml)	30

Chocolate	
Dark chocolate, 1 oz (28 g)	20
Milk chocolate, 1 oz (28 g)	7

Medication	
Anacin, 2 pills	64
Excedrin, 2 pills	130
Midol, 2 pills	64

Foods and drinks are not required to list how much caffeine they contain, so it can be challenging to gauge how much caffeine your kids are getting. Here are some of the less obvious caffeine culprits that can lurk in teenagers' diets:

SOURCES OF HIDDEN CAFFEINE (MILLIGRAMS)

Beverages	
Dr Pepper, 12 oz (355 ml)	42
Snapple Iced Tea, 16 oz (475 ml)	42
Barq's Root Beer, 12 oz (355 ml)	15
Red Bull Energy Drink, 8 1/2 oz (250 ml)	80
SoBe Energy Citrus, 12 oz (355 ml)	25
Mountain Dew Energy, 591 ml	91

Snacks	
Chocolate milk, 1 cup (250 ml)	8

Chocolate cake, 1 medium-sized slice	6
Chocolate pudding, 1/2 cup (125 ml)	9
Häagen-Dazs ice cream, coffee-flavoured, 1 cup (250 ml)	48
Hershey Bar, 1 1/2 oz (42 g)	31
Hot chocolate mix, 1 envelope	5
M&Ms, 1/4 cup (50 ml)	8
Danone yogurt, coffee-flavoured, 3/4 cup (175 g)	36

Think back to the upper limit of caffeine for a 12-year-old: 85 milligrams. That amount may not be hard to consume, even in a short time. A can of diet cola, two small scoops of coffee-flavoured ice cream, and a Hershey's chocolate bar total 125 milligrams of caffeine.

Reducing caffeine intake

How can teens tell if they are consuming too much caffeine? Simple: if they're having trouble sleeping or if they're anxious or irritable, they need to moderate their caffeine intake. Here are a few tips that will help teenagers cut back on caffeine:

- Skip free soft drink refills. Choose caffeine-free soft drinks such as Sprite, 7-Up, Mug Root Beer, and decaffeinated colas. Keep in mind that caffeine-free drinks still contain sugar—10 teaspoons of sugar per 12 ounce (355 ml) can.

- Order the smallest size. A 64-ounce (1.9 litre) super-sized Coke at 7-Eleven packs 185 milligrams of caffeine, more than twice as much as a 12-year-old should be getting.

- Order decaffeinated coffee or ask for half regular (with caffeine), half decaf.

- Limit intake of foods flavoured with coffee and chocolate.

- Limit caffeine gradually. Caffeine is addictive and may cause withdrawal symptoms for anyone who abruptly stops consuming it. These symptoms include headaches, muscle soreness, irritability, and temporary depression. If teenagers are getting too much caffeine, they should reduce their intake gradually over a period of three weeks.

Alcohol and Teens

We all know that it is illegal to buy or consume alcohol in Canada until the age of 19, with the exception of Quebec and Manitoba, where the legal drinking age is 18. Despite this, most teenagers are exposed to alcohol and have access to it. As a result, many teenagers will experiment with alcohol, and some may drink on a regular basis.

Adolescents, like adults, drink alcohol for many reasons. Curiosity, media advertisements, emotional pressures, and wanting to fit in with their peers are among the many reasons that teenagers are tempted to use alcohol. Teenagers are more likely to start experimenting with drinking if they have parents who drink, if they have friends who are also drinking, or if their parents don't give them clear messages about not drinking outside the house—teens may get mixed messages if they are allowed to drink some wine or beer at family gatherings.

Parents can have a strong influence on whether their child drinks alcohol. American surveys on teen drinking have found that students who drink alcohol report difficult family situations at home. Experts believe it's their way of rebelling against their parents. Children with supportive parents are more likely to act independently of their friends and not succumb to drinking.

Alcohol is a powerful drug that changes how you feel. Some of the initial sensations at lower blood alcohol levels are pleasant to teens. Feelings such as uninhibition, relaxation, or relief from emotional stress make some teenagers seek out alcohol.

How Alcohol Affects the Body

Alcohol is created naturally from grains, fruit, and vegetables when yeast and bacteria ferment their sugars. Grapes are fermented to make wine, beer can be made from barley, hops, or rye, and potatoes are often used to make vodka. Many teenagers think that beer has less alcohol than hard liquor, so it's okay to drink beer. But the fact is that one 12 ounce (355 ml) bottle of beer or a 5 ounce (150 ml) glass of wine has as much alcohol as a 1 1/2 ounce (45 ml) shot of liquor. Teenagers need to know that alcohol can make you drunk and cause problems no matter how you consume it.

From the moment alcohol enters your body, it gets treated as if it has special privileges. Unlike foods, which need to be digested, alcohol needs no digestion and is quickly absorbed. Roughly 20% gets absorbed directly through the walls of the stomach and can reach your brain within one minute. Drinking on an empty stomach will cause you to feel alcohol's effects much more quickly. Food in the stomach prevents some of the alcohol touching the stomach's wall and crossing into the bloodstream. The remaining alcohol is absorbed in the small intestine and goes directly to your liver for processing. Alcohol gets the red carpet treatment in the liver—it gets absorbed and broken down before most nutrients.

Alcohol affects every organ of the body, but it's most disruptive effects appear in the liver. Your liver cells normally prefer fatty acids (the building blocks of fats) as their energy source. Once they use some fatty acids for immediate fuel, the liver repackages the rest into fat particles (triglycerides) and ships them out to the rest of the body. But when alcohol arrives on the scene, your liver cells are forced to break down the alcohol first, while the fatty acids wait in line and build up. That's why heavy drinkers develop fatty livers.

Your liver can process only a certain amount of alcohol at a time—about one typical drink per hour. (A standard drink is 1 1/2 ounces/45 ml of liquor, 5 ounces/145 ml of wine, or 12 ounces/355 ml of regular beer.) This can vary slightly depending on a person's body size, drinking history, and food intake. If you drink at a faster rate than your liver can clear alcohol, the extra circulates in your body until your liver enzymes are ready to deal with it.

Alcohol has a profound effect on your brain. Many people think alcohol is a stimulant because it makes them feel (temporarily) happy and relaxed. But alcohol is actually a depressant, a downer—it sedates all of the cells in your central nervous system. People who become intoxicated with alcohol may stagger, lose their coordination, and slur their speech. Alcohol is responsible for most accidental deaths, including motor vehicle accidents. A teenager's impression may be that drinking alcohol makes him look cool, but the fact is it can make him look stupid, do embarrassing things, and engage in reckless and dangerous behaviours.

When large amounts of alcohol are consumed in a short period, alcohol poisoning can result. Alcohol poisoning is a serious, and sometimes deadly, result of drinking excessive amounts of alcohol. Binge drinking (drinking at least four to five drinks in a row), which is common on college and university campuses, can lead to alcohol poisoning. Signs and symptoms of alcohol poisoning include confusion, vomiting, seizures, slow or irregular breathing, blue-tinged skin or pale skin, and unconsciousness (passing out).

Why Teenagers Shouldn't Drink Alcohol

Teenagers' experimenting with drinking is considered by many to be normal behaviour. But what is often overlooked is that adolescents lack experience with alcohol, which may cause them to become intoxicated more easily than adults. Adolescents' immaturity and inability to recognize the cognitive or psychosocial effects of alcohol abuse adds to the dangers of using alcohol.

Deciding whether or not to drink is a decision that teenagers will ultimately make on their own. Here are a few sobering facts your teen should know:

Sexuality and drinking Researchers have linked drinking with early sexual activity and, as a result, with unintended teen pregnancies and sexually transmitted diseases. When teenagers mix sex with alcohol, those who average five or more drinks daily are nearly three times less likely to use condoms, thus placing themselves at greater risk for sexually transmitted diseases.[6] Alcohol use is also implicated in one- to two-thirds of sexual assault and acquaintance or date rape cases among teens and college students.

Academic performance According to American research, a clear relationship exists between alcohol use and grade point average among college students: students with grades of Ds or Fs drink three times as much as those who earn As.[7]

Alcoholism Youth who begin drinking before age 15 are four times more likely to develop alcohol dependence than those who begin drinking at age 21 (this research was conducted in the United States, where the legal drinking age is 21). More than 43% of teenagers who began drinking before age 14 later became alcoholics.[8] Alcohol abuse (using alcohol regularly) is usually just a step away from addiction—where teens depend on these substances just to feel good or get through their day. Here are a few of the early warning signs that your teenager may have a drinking problem (have your teen read this list of warning signs; it's also a way to tell if a friend has a problem):

- relying on alcohol to have fun, forget problems, or relax
- having blackouts when drinking or not being able to remember drinking
- drinking alone
- having frequent hangovers
- lying about how much alcohol was consumed
- withdrawing or keeping secrets from friends or family
- feeling run down, depressed, or even suicidal
- performing differently in school (grades dropping, skipping class)

- spending more and more money on alcohol

- building an increased tolerance to alcohol—gradually needing more and more to get the same feeling

A gateway to other drugs Alcohol consumption is often considered to lead to the use of illegal substances such as marijuana. Young people who drink are 7.5 times more likely to use other illicit drugs and 50 times more likely to use cocaine than young people who never drink.[9]

Health Alcohol used on its own, or in combination with other drugs, can retard the normal growth and development of young people.

Tips for Responsible Drinking

I think it's fair to say that many teenagers—but by no means all—will try alcohol at least once. Teenagers need to know that they should not feel obliged to drink just because alcohol is offered to them or just because others are drinking. Some teens find it easy to say no without giving an explanation. Others find it easier to offer explanations such as "I'm not into drinking" or "I have a big game tomorrow." Let your teen know that it's okay to put the blame on you for refusing alcohol. Excuses such as "I can't because my parents are coming to pick me up" or "I've already been caught once" might make it easier for some teenagers to say no to alcohol. Alcohol is easier to refuse than teenagers might think. They need to remember that the majority of their peers don't drink, so they'll be in good company if they too decline.

However, you need to come to terms with the fact that even once your teenager is made well aware of the dangers of drinking, to themselves and to the people around them, they may decide to drink anyway. For this reason, teenagers need sound advice on how to drink safely, and stay safe around friends who are drinking. Here are a few strategies for them to follow:

- Eat something before a party where alcohol will be present. Eating after you have started to drink won't help slow down alcohol absorption.

- Limit yourself to no more than one drink an hour. Since it takes an hour for your body to metabolize one alcoholic drink, drinking more often will result in a higher blood alcohol concentration. To slow your drinking pace, alternate alcoholic drinks with water, cranberry juice with soda water, or unsweetened fruit juice.

- Leave the driving to a parent or designated driver (someone who has not been drinking), or take a taxi or bus.

At the end of the day, teenagers who have high self-esteem are less likely to succumb to the peer pressures of drinking, or at least drinking regularly. All teens, though, need to know how drinking alcohol affects their bodies and the health risks it involves so that they can make an educated choice.

Part Two

————— ∞ —————

Making Healthy
Food Choices

6

———— ⦉⦊⦉ ————

Eating Healthy Foods at Home

Have you ever wished that your teenager would head straight to the kitchen after school and make himself a healthy snack instead of inhaling a handful of cookies or a bag of potato chips? Or perhaps you'd like him to lend a helping hand to get dinner on the table a few nights a week. Wouldn't it be great to come home from a long day at work to find a delicious and nutritious meal just waiting to be served?

Teenagers can be a big help in the kitchen, especially on days that are jam-packed with early evening music lessons, dance rehearsals, and team practices. And when busy schedules don't allow the whole family to enjoy a meal together, it's important that teenagers are able to whip up their own healthy meal before they rush out the door to study with friends or work at a part-time job. Teenagers who know their way around the kitchen are less likely to run out the door on an empty stomach and head straight for a burger or pizza slice.

The trick is helping your kids learn kitchen basics. If your teen is not active in the kitchen, it's not too late to get him more involved. Nor is it too late to get him interested in cooking. The information in this chapter will help teenagers get off on the right foot in the kitchen, navigate the aisles of the grocery store, decode nutrition labels on food packages, and choose smart snacks. These healthy eating skills will help prepare teenagers for cooking on their own or making healthy choices at the college or university dining hall. (You'll find plenty of tips for eating on campus in Chapter 7.)

Preparing healthy meals takes more than knowing that too much fat and sugar can pack on the pounds or that whole grains are better than refined. That's a great start.

The next step is putting that knowledge into action. And the first stop is in the grocery store. After all, you can't sit down to a nutritious snack or meal if the cupboards are bare.

To get your teenager started, ask him to plan a meal for the family one night. Have him scan your cookbooks and magazines for a recipe he'd like to try. Or better yet, have him choose one of the 65 healthy recipes in this book. Ask him to plan the whole meal—the main dish, side dishes, dessert, and even the beverage. Don't be concerned if the meal is higher in fat than you'd normally prepare. And don't worry if the side dishes don't go together. This exercise isn't about training a chef. At this point, the objective is to have your teen start to participate in the kitchen.

If your teen is already familiar with the inner workings of the kitchen and the grocery store, have him plan a meal with nutrition in mind. He may not know how to tell if a recipe is low in fat (not yet, anyway) and that's okay. Ask him to put together a balanced meal that includes foods from all the four food groups. Once the meal plan is set, it's almost time for your teenager to tackle the grocery store (with or without your help).

Before Grocery Shopping: Planning Meals

The grocery store is full of healthy foods. Determining which foods are healthier than others can be challenging, and I'll help you with that in a moment. First, you need to be organized before you head out the front door.

Make a grocery list to save time at the store and to prevent having to return for a forgotten item. Shopping from a list will also reduce the temptation to buy unhealthy foods that aren't on your list. There are a few different ways to organize your shopping list. Some people like to make a list that places similar items together. Others like to arrange the categories in their list around the order in which foods are found in the store. Your master list might have headings such as "canned goods," "dairy," "frozen foods," and so on. If it's your teenager's first time doing the grocery shopping on his own, this might not be the best approach, since it requires knowledge of the store's layout.

I recommend that teenagers make a grocery list based on the food groups of Canada's Food Guide. Not only will this give your son or daughter a chance to refresh their knowledge of the Food Guide, it will also help them put those nutrition principles in action. They'll be able to ensure that their meals are based on a mix of healthy foods from all food groups. Here's an example of what such a grocery list might look like:

- *Vegetables and Fruit:* apples, bananas, orange juice, Sun-Rype fruit bars, carrots, prepackaged salad, frozen peas

- *Grain Products:* 100% whole-wheat bread, bran flakes, instant oatmeal, low-fat granola bars, brown rice, whole-wheat penne pasta, rice cakes

- *Milk and Milk Products:* 1% milk, single-serving yogurts, soy milk, light sour cream, part-skim cheddar cheese

- *Meat and Alternatives:* ground turkey, firm tofu, canned black beans, peanut butter

- *Other Foods:* salad dressing, margarine, brown sugar, sorbet

You might want to add a few other categories for foods and items that don't fit anywhere, such as "condiments," "non-food items," and "health and beauty products." Do whatever keeps you organized. Once you've found a winning template, you might consider developing a master form on the computer. You can keep this form posted on the fridge and add to it during the week as needed.

Don't shop while hungry. Make sure your teenager has a meal or snack before heading off to the store. We all know what happens when we rush out to the store on an empty stomach—we come home with more food items than we planned, some of them not so healthy. Eating before grocery shopping will limit those impulse purchases.

Get familiar with the store's layout. Knowing how the grocery store is laid out can help you save time—and prevent unnecessary trips down the junk food aisle. The healthy foods—fresh fruit and vegetables, dairy products, and fresh meats and poultry—are usually placed around the perimeter of the store. Just stick to the outer aisles and you'll find plenty of nutritious foods. The unhealthy, processed foods are usually in the middle aisles. It's in these aisles that the cookies, potato chips, soft drinks, fruit drinks, and boxed pasta mixes are found. And beware of feature items at the end of shopping aisles. Often these foods are full of extra calories from fat or sugar.

Deciphering Nutrition Labels

Many prepackaged foods already carry nutrition labels to help you choose healthier foods. By the end of 2005, a new and improved nutrition label, designed by Health Canada, will be mandatory on most prepackaged foods. (Exemptions are alcoholic beverages, fresh fruit and vegetables, raw meat and poultry except if ground, raw fish and seafood, foods sold only in retail establishments where they are prepared or processed, and individual servings of food intended for immediate consumption.) Many food companies already have put a Nutrition Facts box on their packaging. The Nutrition Facts box is easy to locate and easy to read. To make healthy food choices while shopping, it's important to have a handle on all parts of the label. Let's get started.

By December 12, 2005, most prepackaged foods will have a Nutrition Facts table.

Nutrition Facts		
Per 1 cup (264 g)		
Amount	**% Daily Value**	
Calories 260		
Fat 13 g	20%	
Saturated Fat 3 g		
+ Trans Fat 2 g	25%	
Cholesterol 30 mg		
Sodium 660 mg	28%	
Carbohydrate 31 g	10%	
Fibre 0 g	0%	
Sugars 5 g		
Protein 5 g		
Vitamin A 4%	Vitamin C 2%	
Calcium 15%	Iron 4%	

The information is based on a specific amount of food.

The % Daily Value (DV) shows if there is a little or a lot of a nutrient.

A % DV of 5% or less is a low-fat choice.

The % DV is listed for saturated and trans fat together. A % DV of 10% or less would be low in these nutrients.

Serving Size

The information in the Nutrition Facts box is based on a specific amount of food. In this example, you'll notice that the nutrient content is given for a 1 cup (264 gram) serving of the food. When similar foods have similar serving sizes, product comparison is relatively easy. For example, if two brands of bottled pasta sauce list nutrient contents for a 1/2 cup (125 ml) serving, it's easy to compare and determine which one is lower in fat and sodium.

You can also compare this stated serving size with the portion you would actually eat in one sitting. For example, let's say your teenage son always eats a bowl of Quaker Corn Bran Squares as his bedtime snack. And because he's always hungry, he fills a large bowl with 2 cups (500 ml) of cereal, leaving just enough room to add milk. He wants to know how many calories and grams of fibre he's eating. The Nutrition Facts table lists 182 calories and 4.8 grams of fibre per 1 cup (30 g) serving of the cereal with 1/2 cup (125 ml) of milk. Since he's eating double that amount, that means your son's snack is providing him with 364 calories and 9.6 grams of fibre.

Nutrient List

The Nutrition Facts table will always show the calories, the amount of total fat, saturated and trans fats, cholesterol, sodium, carbohydrate, fibre, sugars, protein, calcium, iron, and vitamins A and C in a specified amount of food. These are the key nutrients important to health. Now that prepackaged foods must carry this standard Nutrition Facts box, it's much easier to choose foods that are lower in fat, sugar, or sodium. You can choose a product based on what nutrients are most important to your health.

Percent Daily Values (% DV)

In the Nutrition Facts table, vitamins and minerals are expressed as a percentage of a daily value (% DV). Fat, saturated plus trans fat, carbohydrate, and fibre are also expressed as a % DV. Daily values are generally based on Health Canada's recommendations for a healthy diet. They refer to both the recommended daily intakes for vitamins and minerals and to reference standards for other nutrients. The % DV is a simple benchmark that can be used for quickly evaluating the nutrient content of a food: use the % DV to determine whether there is a lot or a little of a nutrient in one serving of the food.

Here are a few examples of how the % DV might be used in choosing a food product. Let's say your daughter is shopping for a healthy frozen dinner to eat on those rushed evenings before swim practice. She wants to make sure it's lower in total fat, and in saturated plus trans fats. She now knows that it's recommended to get no more than 30% of daily calories from fat. For the 2000-calorie reference standard that's used for nutrition labels, that means 600 fat calories or 65 grams of fat (1 gram of fat has 9 calories). She picks up a package of frozen macaroni and cheese and reads that the daily value for fat is 53%. That means one serving of this product contributes 53% toward her recommended daily fat intake. A bit much for just one meal.

She puts the macaroni and cheese back into the freezer case and reaches for President's Choice Blue Menu Splendido Lasagna. It lists 14% beside the daily value for fat. Much better! She'll also notice that the % DV is listed for saturated and trans fats combined. We're advised to consume no more than 10 percent of our daily calories from these two fats, often referred to as the "bad fats." The PC Blue Menu Splendido Lasagna lists 24% DV for saturated and trans fats combined. Okay, it's lasagna after all—cheese does have saturated fat. She puts the lasagna back into the freezer case. One more try with PCs Blue Menu Ginger Glazed Chicken. With 2% DV listed for fat and 3% DV for saturated and trans fats, this one can be added to the shopping cart.

Once you get the hang of it, the % DV will allow you to quickly identify the strengths and weaknesses of a product. Here's what you need to know:

- A food that has a % DV of 5% or less for fat, sodium, or cholesterol will be low in these nutrients, and a healthy choice.

- A food that has a daily value of 10% or less for saturated plus trans fats will be low in these nutrients, and a healthy choice.

- A food that has a daily value of 15% or more for vitamin A, vitamin C, calcium, iron, or fibre will be high in these nutrients, and a good choice.

- A food that has a daily value of 25% or more for vitamin A, vitamin C, calcium, iron, or fibre will be an excellent source of these nutrients.

Ingredient Lists

The Nutrition Facts table isn't the only source of information about a food that you'll find on the packaging. In Canada, all packaged foods must have an ingredient list—whether it has a nutrition label or not. Ingredients in food are listed by weight, from most to least. That means that the product contains more of the first ingredient listed than of the ingredients that follow. A good rule of thumb is that the first five ingredients make up the bulk of the food.

Ingredient lists are very useful for people with food allergies or intolerances who need to avoid certain ingredients. Reading the ingredient list, for instance, is often the only way you can tell if breakfast cereals, breads, and crackers are made from healthy whole grains.

Here's the ingredient list for Kellogg's All-Bran Bars:

Flour, sugar/glucose-fructose, Kellogg's All-Bran cereal [Wheat bran, sugar/glucose-fructose, malt (corn flour, malted barley), salt, vitamins (thiamin hydrochloride, pyridoxine hydrochloride, folic acid, d-calcium pantothenate), iron], vegetable shortening (contains palm and palm kernel oils, TBHQ), oat hull fibre, blackstrap molasses, whole egg powder, milk ingredients, wheat bran, baking powder, soya lecithin, sodium bicarbonate, natural flavour, soya flour.

The first ingredient is white flour, a refined grain. That means there is more white flour in this product than any other ingredient. Next on the list is sugar. And then comes the All-Bran cereal, which adds four grams of fibre to each bar. You'll notice that this product contains wheat, egg, milk ingredients, and soy, so if your teenager has allergies to any of these foods, this product will not be appropriate.

Nutrition Claims

Some food companies often highlight a nutrition feature of a food by stating a claim on the front of the package. Making claims like "low in fat," "light," "sodium free," and "zero trans fat" helps manufacturers sell their products. Keep in mind that nutrition claims refer to one serving of the food as stated on the nutrition label. If you end up eating a box of low-fat cookies in one sitting, your snack might not be low in fat after all. To be able to carry a nutrition claim, products must meet certain criteria set out by Health Canada. Here are some of the more common nutrition claims and what they mean per serving:

- Free—an amount so small, health experts consider it nutritionally insignificant
- Sodium free—less than 5 milligrams of sodium

- Cholesterol free—less than 2 milligrams of cholesterol and low in saturated fat; cholesterol-free products are not necessarily low in total fat

- Low fat—3 grams or less of fat

- Low in saturated fat—2 grams or less of saturated and trans fat combined

- Trans fat–free—less than 0.2 grams trans fat and low in saturated fat

- Reduced—at least 25% less of a nutrient compared with the original product (e.g., reduced fat, reduced sodium)

- Calorie reduced—at least 25% fewer calories than the original product

- Light—when referring to a nutritional characteristic, this claim is allowed only on foods that are reduced in fat or reduced in calories. If referring to a sensory characteristic, such as taste or texture, there must be an explanation on the label (e.g., "light in colour").

- Source of fibre—at least 2 grams of fibre

- High in fibre—at least 4 grams of fibre

- Very high in fibre—at least 6 grams of fibre

- Good source of calcium—165 milligrams or more of calcium

Don't judge a food solely on the basis of a nutrition claim. You need to know the whole nutrition picture before you buy. That's why the Nutrition Facts box and ingredient list are useful. Just because a food is stamped "zero trans fat" doesn't necessarily mean that it's good for you. Better than before? Sure it is. Potato chips deep-fried in non-hydrogenated corn oil may be better for your arteries, but they won't do your waistline any favours. They're just as high in fat and calories as they were before. Goldfish crackers packaging says the crackers are made without trans fats. But read the ingredient list and you'll see that the number one ingredient is refined white flour. Packages of cookies that boast they are trans fat–free will still pack in the sugar and, often, fat. And just because a bottle of a sugary fruit drink claims its contents are high in a certain vitamin doesn't mean it's a healthy food. Get my point? Check out the Nutrition Facts box and ingredient list to know what you're buying.

Diet and Health Claims

For the first time in Canada, food companies are allowed to highlight a relationship between diet and disease on product packages. Diet-related health claims are allowed on all foods, prepackaged and non-prepackaged, no matter where they are sold. These claims are based on a strong body of scientific data between diet and the reduction of risk of a specific disease. You might see one of the following permitted claims on a food product:

- a diet low in saturated and trans fat reduces risk of heart disease
- a diet with adequate calcium and vitamin D, and regular physical activity, reduces risk of osteoporosis
- a diet rich in vegetables and fruit reduces risk of some types of cancer
- a diet low in sodium and high in potassium reduces risk of high blood pressure

Foods that carry a diet-related health claim must meet specific government regulations about nutrient content. For example, to make a health claim about calcium, vitamin D, and the link to osteoporosis prevention, the food must be high in calcium and vitamin D and must not have more phosphorus than calcium. To be allowed to make a health claim about fat and heart disease, the food must be low in (or free of) saturated and trans fat, must be limited in cholesterol and sodium, and must have a minimum amount of at least one vitamin or mineral.

Other Food Logos to Watch For

In an effort to help shoppers easily spot healthy foods, some food companies, including PepsiCo, Loblaws, and Kraft Foods, are stamping logos on healthier versions of their products. Walk down the aisles of the grocery store and you'll see PepsiCo's newly launched Smart Spot green symbol on Diet Pepsi, Gatorade, Baked Tostitos tortilla chips, Tropicana juices, and Quaker Oats. Enter a Loblaws grocery store and you'll see a product line called President's Choice Blue Menu. These products prominently display a blue menu icon that highlights a nutritional benefit of the product—low fat, low calorie, or high fibre, for example. And it's expected that Kraft Foods will bring its Sensible Solution labelling program to Canada by the end of 2005. The program was announced January 2005 in the United States.

The Heart and Stroke Foundation of Canada has been identifying healthy foods with its Health Check logo since 1999. Today more than 400 foods, from many food manufacturers, boast the red-and-white Health Check symbol—Ocean Spray cranberry juice, Astro BioBest yogurt, So Good soy beverage, and Becel margarine among them.

Symbols such as Smart Spot, Health Check, and Blue Menu help consumers easily identify a healthier version of a company's product. But buying a food based on the presence of a better-for-you logo should not be your only guide to good nutrition. These logos will help you choose *better* products, but not all identify *healthy* foods. That's because these programs use different criteria to evaluate their products. Here's what the symbols mean.

Heart and Stroke Foundation's Health Check Program Different food categories have different criteria based on Canada's Food Guide to Healthy Eating. To be eligible for the Health Check symbol, dairy products must be low in fat and a good source of calcium (165 milligrams or more), fresh meat and poultry must be lean (10% or less fat), breads must be low in fat (3 grams or less) and a source of fibre (2 grams or more), and margarines must be non-hydrogenated. Sodium levels are evaluated for all food categories.

President's Choice Blue Menu These products must contain no hydrogenated oils, no artificial colour or flavours, and no added MSG (monosodium glutamate) or flavour enhancers. Blue Menu foods also must meet one of the following nutrient criteria: (1) lower fat (at least 25% less fat than the original PC product in the category); (2) fewer calories (at least 25% fewer calories than the original version); or (3) high fibre (at least 4 grams of fibre per serving).

PepsiCo's Smart Spot Program Brands that display the Smart Choices Made Easy symbol must meet at least one of the following criteria: (1) the product is low in both total fat and saturated fat, and contains no trans fat, no more than 60 milligrams of cholesterol and 480 milligrams of sodium per 8 1/2 ounces (250 ml), and has no more than 25% of calories from added sugar (e.g., Tropicana juices, Quaker Instant Oatmeal); (2) the product delivers a benefit from natural or fortified ingredients and is proven to be effective (e.g., Gatorade); or (3) the product contains at least 25% fewer calories, fat, sugar, or sodium compared with the original version (e.g., Diet Pepsi, Baked Ruffles Potato Chips).

Some programs are stricter than others when it comes to their nutrient criteria. For instance, about 50% of PepsiCo's Smart Spot products would not meet the Heart and Stroke Foundation's Health Check criteria. You need to look past the logo to know why a particular food has earned its stripes. Read the company's explanation, usually printed right on the package. Read the Nutrition Facts box and the ingredient list. You can then decide if the product is a healthy choice for your diet.

Healthy Choices at the Grocery Store

Now it's time for your teen—with or without you—to walk down the aisles of the grocery store and fill the cart with healthy choices. Or, if you are doing the grocery shopping, have your teen accompany you and explain as you shop why you are making the healthy choices you are. Applying your nutrition knowledge of fats, sugars, whole grains, and sodium, along with your label-reading skills, it should be easier to sleuth out healthy foods.

The first stop in the supermarket will likely be the produce section. These foods don't have nutrition labels, but they're rich in nutrients such as vitamins A and C, folate, and potassium. And many are good sources of fibre. Of course, some of these tips will not apply, depending on what meal is planned.

Produce section

- Select a variety of colourful fruit and vegetables. Choose dark green and orange produce for a boost of beta-carotene.

- Avoid wilted vegetables and overripe fruit, even if they cost less. One exception is over-ripe bananas, which can be used in muffins, pancakes, and smoothies.

- Choose grapefruit and oranges that are heavy for their size; they'll be juicier.

- Check prepackaged produce carefully for quality; avoid produce that looks soggy or bruised.

- Prewashed, pre-cut fresh veggies—baby carrots, broccoli florets, cauliflower, shredded cabbage, grated carrot, cubed butternut squash, for example—and packaged salad greens may cost more, but they can save you time in the kitchen.

- Choose brands of frozen vegetables without salt; avoid those that are frozen in sauce.

- If possible, choose canned vegetables that are low in sodium.

- When buying canned fruit, choose brands that are packed in water or their own juice. Canned fruit in syrup has added sugar.

- Choose 100% unsweetened fruit juices; avoid fruit drinks and punches that have plenty of added sugar.

- Buy fresh fruit and veggies to wash and cut as soon as you get home. Store them in small containers or bags in the front of the fridge for easy-to-grab snacks.

- Look for tofu, veggie burgers, and soy slices in the produce section.

Dairy case

- Buy skim or 1% milk rather than 2%, whole milk (3.3% MF), or cream. You'll be getting less saturated fat and calories while still getting all the other nutrients. Look for the grams of total fat and saturated fat per serving as you compare similar products.

- When buying soy beverages, choose a brand that is calcium enriched. Check the Nutrition Facts box for the percentage of daily value (% DV) for calcium—the percentage should be between 27% and 30%.

- Buy evaporated skim milk for coffee instead of cream.

- Buy yogurt with a milk-fat (MF) content of less than 2%. Choose low-fat (7% MF) or fat-free sour cream over full-fat sour cream (14% MF).

- More often, choose cheese made from skim or part-skim milk. The label will state a milk-fat content of less than 20%. Choose 1% or fat-free cottage cheese.

- Butter is made from milk fat. It's high in saturated fat and contains dietary cholesterol, which can contribute to atherosclerosis (hardening of the arteries). If you use butter, do so sparingly.

- Margarine is made from vegetable oil. It is lower in saturated fat than butter and contains no cholesterol. Choose a soft tub brand that is made from non-hydrogenated vegetable oil.

- For dessert or snacks, choose ice milk, frozen or fruited low-fat or non-fat yogurt, sherbet, sorbet, or low-fat puddings.

- Don't buy foods past their expiration date. The sell-by date refers to the last date a grocery store can keep the product for sale on the shelf. You should buy the product before this date. However, the product is still safe and wholesome past this date if it has been properly stored. For example, if milk has been properly refrigerated at 40ºF (4ºC) or below, it generally stays fresh for up to three days after its sell-by date. The use-by date is intended to tell you how long you can keep the product at top eating quality in your home. A best-before date is recommended for best flavour and quality—it's not a purchase or safety date.

Meat and fish counters

- Buy lean cuts of meat and pork. Look for the words "round" or "loin" in the cut of beef, and "loin" or "leg" for pork. In Canada, all cuts of beef are lean (except for short ribs) when trimmed of visible fat. If buying ground meat, choose lean or extra-lean.

- Choose chicken and turkey breast, as they have less fat and fewer calories than other meats. Remove the skin before cooking.

- Read meat packages to determine how many servings you'll get. For instance, since the recommended serving size of meat is 90 grams (3 ounces), a package containing 1 pound (0.5 kilograms) of steak should serve five people.

- Buy fish filets to bread and bake at home. If you prefer the convenience of frozen fish sticks, look for products that are made without partially hydrogenated oils and have no more than 10 grams of fat and 500 milligrams of sodium per 85 to 113 gram serving. If the serving size is larger, sodium numbers can be slightly higher.

- If buying canned tuna, choose light or flaked tuna more often than white or albacore. Light tuna has less mercury, not to mention is less expensive.

- Canned salmon is a great source of omega-3 fats. Most canned salmon is wild, not farm-raised.

- Leaner deli meats include turkey, chicken breast, roast beef, and lean ham. Avoid fatty sausage, salami, and bologna.

Bread and cracker section

- Read the ingredient list. Look for the words "whole-wheat flour" or "whole-rye flour" or some other whole grain to be listed as the first ingredient. Whole grains include whole spelt flour, flaxseed, oats, kamut, quinoa, barley, and brown rice.

- When buying bread, don't be fooled by healthy sounding names such as 7 Grain, Multigrain, Prairie Bran, Oat and Honey, or Pumpernickel. When you look past the name at the ingredient list, you may find that the first ingredient is white flour (wheat flour).

- Choose bread that has at least 4 grams of fibre and less than 400 milligrams of sodium per two slices. Don't forget to check serving sizes here. For most people, a serving size of bread is two slices, yet some nutrition labels state the calories, fibre, and sodium per one slice.

- Pay attention to portion size. These days, loaves of bread are getting bigger and bigger. According to Canada's Food Guide, a slice of bread should be about 30 to 35 grams and provide roughly 65 to 85 calories. Some brands have slices that weigh in at 50 grams and have as many as 140 calories. Sometimes this is because of grains that have been added, other times it's because the slice is bigger.

- Read the Nutrition Facts table on boxes of crackers. Compare brands on fat and sodium.

Cereal aisle

- Choose a cereal that is made with whole grains, is low in fat, low in sugar, and high in fibre. Best bets have at least 4 to 5 grams of fibre and no more than 4 grams of fat and 8 grams of sugar per serving.

- Keep in mind that the sugar numbers on the nutrition label include both added sugars and naturally occurring sugar in fruit. Cereals with dried fruit will boost the sugar content, but it will also boost the fibre and nutrient content.

- High-fibre cereals may have more sugar than lower-fibre cereals, as sugar is added to make the cereal more palatable. It's more important to choose a cereal with more fibre than to choose a lower-fibre one just because it has fewer grams of sugar.

- When buying instant oatmeal, choose the plain, unflavoured version to cut added sugar. If you're hooked on flavoured hot cereal, try a sugar-reduced brand (these have half as much sugar as the original version).

Healthy choices in other aisles

- Buy whole-wheat, whole-spelt, or kamut pasta and brown rice to add whole grains to your menus.

- Stay clear of prepackaged pasta and rice mixes. These side dishes add a hefty dose of sodium, and often fat, to your meal. Ditto for instant potato mixes.

- Stock up on canned beans for quick vegetarian meals. Buy black beans, soy beans, chickpeas, kidney beans … the list goes on.

- Oils can go rancid quickly, so avoid the urge to buy an economy-sized bottle of vegetable oil. Buy small bottles and store them in a cool, dark cupboard (walnut, sesame, and flax oils should be stored in the fridge).

- Buy a non-stick cooking spray to use when baking and sautéing to cut down on added fat.

- If buying bottled salad dressings, choose those made from olive or canola oil. Read labels to compare amounts of sodium and sugar.

- Stop by the bulk food section to pick up dried fruit and unsalted nuts for snacks.

Cooking Tips for Teens

Cooking is a great way to get teenagers interested in nutrition. Have your kids choose recipes that aren't too complicated when starting out. There's nothing more frustrating than being overwhelmed by a recipe that calls for unusual ingredients or involves difficult steps. A good starting point might be a one- or two-pot meal such as a pasta, hearty soup, or casserole. Be sure to check out all the recipes in Part 4 of this book. Whether you're looking for breakfast ideas, interesting lunches, quick dinners, or snack ideas, there are plenty to choose from there. All are low in fat and can be made in 30 minutes or less. Here are a few tips to enhance success in the kitchen:

- Before beginning to cook, read the recipe from start to finish and make sure you have all the ingredients and cooking utensils.

- Check the clock. Do you have enough time to make the recipe? Most recipes state in the instructions the amount of preparation time. It's always a good idea to pad this with an extra 15 minutes.

- It saves time to be organized. Assemble all the ingredients in one place. Measure out each ingredient before you start.

It's also important to teach teenagers kitchen food safety. Teens need to know how to avoid spreading bacteria that can cause food poisoning. Bacteria are present everywhere—in the air, soil, water, and in people and animals. But if foods are not handled properly during food processing and meal preparation at home, these bugs can grow rapidly and cause illness. You can't see these micro-organisms, so there are no clues as to a harmful food. The only way to prevent food poisoning is to handle foods safely in the first place.

Whenever I visit my family in Vancouver, I'm delighted to see how helpful my nephews are in the kitchen. And thanks to helpful reminders from their dad, these teens are careful about how they handle foods. Here are tips to help teens practise safe food handling at home:

Keep It Clean

Even though the kitchen might look clean, hands, countertops, and utensils may contain bacteria that you can't even see. Here are some cleanliness tips to follow when in the kitchen:

- Wash hands (for 20 seconds), utensils, and cooking surfaces with soap and hot water before handling food, repeatedly while preparing food, and again once finished.

- Use paper towels to wipe counters or change dishcloths daily to avoid the spread of bacteria.

- Don't use sponges to clean kitchen surfaces; they're harder to keep clean.

- Before cutting, wash all fresh vegetables and fruit with cool running water to remove dirt and residue. Scrub fruits and vegetables that have firm surfaces or rinds such as carrots, oranges, melons, and potatoes.

- Cut away damaged or bruised areas on produce—bacteria can thrive in these places.

Avoid Cross-Contamination

Cross-contamination occurs when we transfer, usually unknowingly, bacteria from one object to another object, from one object to a person, or from person to person. We can cross-contaminate our food by failing to wash our hands before cooking and failing to use separate plates for cooked and raw food. Follow these tips to avoid cross-contamination:

- Separate raw meat, poultry, and seafood from other foods in the refrigerator.

- Store raw meat, poultry, and seafood in plastic bags or sealed containers on the lowest rack in the fridge to prevent juices from leaking onto other foods.

- Always wash your hands before you start cooking and again after touching raw meat, poultry, fish, and eggs.

- Keep separate cutting boards for raw meats and vegetables. Clean your cutting board thoroughly between uses.

- While you are cooking, use separate cooking utensils for vegetables and meat. Always wash cooking utensils that handled raw food before using them on other foods.

- Never put cooked food on a dish that previously held raw food and has not yet been washed.

- Don't use dressings that have been used to marinate raw meat on cooked foods. Boil leftover marinade if you plan to use it to baste cooked foods.

Cook It Right

Many teenagers I have counselled are responsible for cooking several of their own meals. Other teenagers aren't introduced to cooking until they leave home for college or university. It's important that teens know how to cook foods thoroughly and serve them immediately after cooking to prevent food poisoning. Foods should not be left to linger at temperatures where bacteria can flourish. Bacteria multiply in the danger zone, a temperature range of 40°F (4°C) and 140°F (60°C). To avoid keeping foods in this temperature zone, keep hot foods hot and cold foods cold.

- Use a digital instant-read meat thermometer to ensure meats are cooked to a safe temperature. Take the temperature from the thickest part of the meat, away from the bone, within 1 minute of removal from heat for thin meats and within 5 to 10 minutes for roasts. Leave the thermometer in the meat for at least 30 seconds.

- Cook fish until it's opaque and flakes easily with a fork.

- When cooking in the microwave, cook, stir, and rotate once or twice for even cooking, and to ensure there are no cold spots, where bacteria can survive.

- Eat any leftovers within three to five days or freeze them. Reheat leftovers until steaming hot, at 165°F (74°C).

- Salmonella bacteria can grow inside fresh unbroken eggs. Cook eggs until the yolks and whites are firm, not runny. Don't use recipes in which eggs remain raw or only partially cooked.

- Don't eat raw sprouts (alfalfa, broccoli, radish, clover). Instead, cook them in stir-fries or soups. Seeds used for sprouting are a likely source of salmonella contamination. Bacteria can lodge in tiny seed cracks and multiply during warm, humid sprouting conditions. Heating to high temperatures during cooking kills harmful bacteria.

Keep Foods Chilled

To keep your foods safe when they are being stored, the fridge should be set at 40°F (4°C) or colder and the freezer at 0°F (-18°C).

- Refrigerate or freeze prepared food (and leftovers) within two hours of cooking it.

- When batch cooking for the week ahead, divide large portions of hot food into small, shallow containers for refrigeration to ensure safe, rapid cooling.

- Don't overstuff the fridge. Cold air needs to circulate above and beneath the food to keep it properly chilled.

- When freezing leftovers, freeze them in one- or two-portion servings so they'll be easy to pull out of the freezer, defrost, and reheat. Eat frozen leftovers within two months.

- Don't defrost foods at room temperature. Instead, thaw them in the fridge or in cold water. Or use the defrost button on the microwave oven if cooking the food immediately after thawing.

Smart Snacking Strategies for Teens

Snacks are an important way for teenagers to meet their energy and nutrient needs. Teenagers often feel hungry because their bodies are growing and demand more calories, vitamins, and minerals. I'm sure you've witnessed on countless occasions your teenager searching the fridge and cupboards for something to munch on. It's important for teens to pay attention to what they're snacking on. Making smart snack choices will help manage teenagers' energy levels during the day and keep their appetites at bay until the next meal. The right snacks will prevent hunger and overeating at mealtime—an important strategy for overweight teenagers.

The best snacks provide carbohydrate for energy, protein, and a little fat for staying power, and ideally some calcium and iron. I also recommend snacks that have a low glycemic index value. (See Chapter 2, page 35, for a list of foods with a low glycemic index value.) These snacks get digested slowly, leading to a gradual rise in blood sugar. That means the energy from the snack lasts longer, and teens stay feeling full longer. Plenty of the snack foods that teenagers often eat—cereal bars, muffins, bagels, toast, low-fibre cereals, and pretzels—have a high glycemic index value. In other words, they get digested and absorbed into the bloodstream quickly. Choosing low glycemic snacks might also help overweight teenagers manage their weight. Studies of overweight boys suggest that eating high glycemic foods triggers overeating, whereas low glycemic foods put the brakes on one's appetite.

You'll notice I didn't walk you through the ever-expanding snack aisle of the grocery store (other than the cracker section, that is). There's nothing wrong with eating these packaged snacks every once in a while. But even those labelled low in fat or fat free are not necessarily the best snacks to be munching on. That's especially true if teens munch these snack foods mindlessly and endlessly. It's important for weight-conscious teenagers to know that low-fat cookies and baked potato chips often have just as many, and sometimes more, calories than the original version. That's because some fat-reduced snacks such as cookies and granola bars are packed with extra sugar.

Portion size needs to be considered, too. If you read the label on a package of Quaker Crispy Minis, you'll see that one serving of eight rice chips provides 62 calories and 1.7 grams of fat. Not bad at all. But not many teens sit down to a serving of just eight rice chips. Teenagers often devour the entire bag—and then look for more to eat. That's because high glycemic starchy foods don't fill you up.

Healthy Snack Ideas for Hungry Teens

Encourage the teenagers in your house to prepare healthy snacks ahead of time. Whether that means cutting up veggies, making a homemade trail mix, or baking low-fat, whole-grain muffins, teens who make their own snack foods have control over the ingredients and get to add what's good for them. It also means that healthy snacks are ready on demand when hunger calls. Check out the recipes in the Snack Attack! section of Part 4.

Here are a few suggestions for healthy snacks:

- Munch on fresh fruit paired with part-skim cheese or nut butter (including peanut butter).

- Try a handful of homemade trail mix—toss dried apricots, apples, prunes, and raisins with almonds, walnuts, and sunflower seeds; store in resealable snack bags. Try my recipes for Grab-a-Snack Mix, Hiker's Happy Trail Mix, and Hit-the-Road Mix. You'll find them in the snack section of Part 4.

- Snack on raw veggies (baby carrots, bell pepper strips, grape tomatoes, broccoli florets, cucumber slices) dipped in hummus.

- Stuff mini whole-wheat pita pockets with bean dip or tuna salad.

- Make mini pizzas. Top a whole-wheat pita or tortilla with pizza sauce and low-fat mozzarella cheese; toast or bake in the oven at a low setting until the cheese melts.

- Whip up a homemade smoothie or power shake in the blender—add low-fat milk or soy milk, yogurt, frozen berries, and a banana. Add wheat germ or ground flaxseed for a boost of whole grain. You'll find five tasty smoothie recipes in Part 4.

- Make a turkey wrap sandwich in a whole-wheat tortilla; spread with roasted red pepper dip.

- Heat up a bowl of hearty bean soup.

- Enjoy a bowl of whole-grain breakfast cereal topped with dried cranberries and low-fat milk or soy milk.

Because busy teenagers spend a lot of time away from home—at school, at practices, at work, babysitting or hanging out with friends—they should make a habit of carrying healthy snacks in their backpacks or workout bags. Having a healthy snack within reach will prevent your kids from grabbing a side of fries or slice of pizza to tame their appetite.

What about the snack food aisle? If you're buying potato chips, cookies, or granola bars, make sure you read labels. Choose products that do not contain partially hydrogenated oils (a source of trans fat). As much as 50 percent of the fat in commercial baked goods and snack foods can come from artery-clogging trans fat. Check the Nutrition Facts box on packages and compare brands for grams of fat, saturated fat, trans fat, and sugars.

Best bets in the snack aisle include fig bars, low-fat granola bars (with added fruit rather than chocolate), baked potato and tortilla chips, pretzels, brown-rice cakes and whole-grain crackers (add your own topping), and Sun-Rype fruit bars (FruitSource plus Veggie, Energy to Go). To boost the nutritional content (and fullness factor) of these snacks, pair them with a glass of low-fat milk, soy milk, or a serving of yogurt.

Besides snacks that are laced with partially hydrogenated oils, teenagers should avoid snacking on sugary pop and fruit drinks. Be cautious of the nutrition claims on products. "Organic" fruit punch and "natural" colas still have a good 10 teaspoons (50 ml) of sugar per 12 ounce (355 ml) can, regardless of the source of sugar.

Now that teens have a few tips for eating healthy at home, it's time they use their nutrition skills when eating away from home. Keep reading.

7

---∞∞∞---

Eating Healthy Away from Home

As teenagers gain independence, they often spend more and more time away from home. Whether they're at the school cafeteria, a fast food restaurant, or at the mall, teenagers are frequently faced with the task of making food choices on their own: according to the results of the What's on Your Plate? High School Nutrition Survey, students do grab meals away from home often. Take a look:

- 4 out of 10 teenagers buy lunch at the school cafeteria at least twice per week.

- 25% of students buy lunch at a fast food joint at least once per week.

- 33% of students buy snacks from the school vending machine at least once per week.

- Only half of the students surveyed said they eat dinner at home every day.

- One-third of teens report eating dinner at a restaurant or fast food place at least once or twice per week.

How do your teens compare? Does your daughter bring her lunch to school or does she line up for a muffin and diet Coke in the cafeteria? Are weeknights so hectic driving your son to and from team practices that dinner is often served through the drive-through window?

While a burger and fries once in a while won't do any harm, a steady diet of fast food can lead to problems. The most obvious problem is weight gain, a health issue that's increasing rapidly in teenagers. Overweight teens are at greater risk of developing type 2 diabetes, a disease that used to affect only adults. A regular intake of foods that are loaded with saturated and trans fats can also lead to high blood cholesterol levels.

Poor food choices outside the home can affect teenagers in other ways, too. A diet that's high in fat and sugar can rob teens of much-needed energy and slow down mental functioning. It's important to remember that the food we eat affects all aspects of how our body functions, and as a result, it will affect how we think and feel.

Eating healthy on the go is easier than you think. Today, restaurants—both family-style and fast food—offer healthy choices to cater to nutrition-conscious diners. As you'll read below, there are many items that teens can feel good about ordering—even at places known for greasy foods such as chicken fingers and fish and chips.

High school cafeterias are also improving their menus by adding salads and whole-grain choices. The food services industry is finally starting to realize that teenagers want to eat more than just french fries and chicken strips.

Eating Healthy in Restaurants

Ordering healthy meals requires teens to learn the language of restaurant menus. Menu items that are fried, basted, braised, au gratin, crispy, escalloped, pan fried, pan seared, sautéed, stewed, stuffed, and butter-brushed are usually high in fat and calories. For alternatives, look for words that indicate low-fat cooking techniques: baked, broiled, grilled, steamed, poached, roasted, and lightly sautéed or stir-fried. If you're uncertain about a dish, ask your server how it's prepared.

Sometimes healthier items are marked "light" or "heart healthy" on menus. If this is the case, the server should be able to provide nutritional information to back up the claims.

Even if there isn't a lower-fat item on a menu, teenagers might be able to choose a healthy meal if they read between the menu lines, so to speak. For example, if a menu features a creamy broccoli soup, there's a good chance it's possible to order a side of steamed broccoli even though it's not offered on the menu. In general, the higher the quality of the restaurant, the more likely the chef will cater to special requests.

Teenagers should keep nutrition in mind when ordering a meal; meals should contain a balance of lean protein (fish, chicken, tofu, or beans), fruit and vegetables, and grains. Encourage your teen to order foods made with whole grains—a sandwich made on whole-wheat bread or a stir-fry made with brown rice, for example.

The following strategies will help teens eat well in any restaurant:

Cut the Fat

Here are some tips to help you reduce the fat in your restaurant meal:

- When ordering grilled meat, fish, or chicken, ask that the food either be grilled without butter or oil, or prepared lightly with only a little oil or butter.

- Choose tomato-based pasta dishes rather than creamy ones. Tomato sauces are much lower in fat and calories than cream-based alfredo sauces. And a serving of tomato sauce counts as a vegetable serving, too.

- Ditto for soup—stick with broth-based soups such as vegetable, minestrone, lentil, or bean. Chowders, bisques, and cream-based soups are much higher in fat, especially saturated fat.

- Order sandwiches made with bread or pita pockets instead of high-fat croissants.

- If you have a choice of sides, order steamed veggies or salad instead of french fries.

- Ask for salsa with a baked potato instead of butter, sour cream, cheese, or bacon bits. Salsa is fat free and very low in calories.

- Order sandwiches without butter, mayonnaise, or "special sauce." Ask for mustard, which adds flavour with virtually no calories.

- Watch out for salads, even if they sound healthy. Salad entrees that come laden with cheese, bacon, nuts, and plenty of dressing can have more fat and calories than an all-dressed burger.

- Order salad dressings, sauces, and sour cream on the side. That way you can control how much you use.

Cut the Sugar

Here are some tips to help you reduce the sugar in your restaurant meal:

- Choose water, unsweetened iced tea, or milk to drink with your meal. Avoid unnecessary sugar calories in pop, fruit drinks, and fruit juices.

- If you're craving dessert, opt for something healthy—fresh berries or fruit, for example.

- If you really want the rich dessert, share it with a friend. Remember, half the dessert means half the sugar and half the calories (and half the fat, too).

Slim Down the Portion Size

These days it's hard to know what constitutes an appropriate serving size as restaurants dish out gargantuan portions on larger plates and fast food chains pour bucket-sized drinks into bigger takeout containers. For instance, some steak dinners that come with a baked potato, garlic bread, salad with ranch dressing, and french fries provide enough calories for two days! A regular fare of super-sized portions can contribute to super-sized teenagers.

A *portion size* is simply the amount of food someone eats at a sitting. A *serving size* is a unit of measure based on nutrition needs. For example, Canada's Food Guide to

Healthy Eating suggests a range of serving sizes from the four food groups based on an individual's calorie and nutrient needs. So, it's serving sizes that we should be paying attention to. But don't worry; you don't need to take measuring cups or a food scale to the restaurant. Below are some quick ways to visualize what an appropriate serving size is for common foods.

"EYEBALL" FOOD GUIDE SERVING SIZES FOR SELECTED FOODS

One serving of...	Looks like...
Bagel, 1/2	A hockey puck
Baked potato, 1 small	A computer mouse
Butter, margarine, or oil, 1 teaspoon (5 ml)	The tip of your thumb
Cheese, 1 1/2 oz (45 g)	Three dominos
Fruit, 1 medium-sized	A baseball
Meat, fish, or chicken, 3 oz (90 g)	A deck of regular playing cards
Muffin, 1 small	A large egg
Pasta or rice, cooked, 1/2 cup (125 ml)	Half a baseball
Salad greens, 1 cup (250 ml)	A baseball
Vegetables, cooked, 1/2 cup (125 ml)	Half a baseball or a small fist

And here are strategies that will help your son or daughter practise *portion* control when eating in restaurants:

- Don't eat it all—take half of your meal home. Ask the server to bring a doggie bag with your meal. When the meal is served, immediately portion off half and put it away. If you leave it sitting on your plate, you'll be more likely to eat it.

- Instead of a large entree, order two appetizers, or an appetizer and a salad, as your meal. Consider sharing an entree with a friend. Many steak dinners weigh in at 8 to 10 ounces/250 grams—a perfect share size.

- Cut down on starchy sides. Skip the bread basket if the meal comes with rice, potato, or pasta. Or ask for extra vegetables instead of the potatoes or rice.

- Don't want a huge bowl of pasta? Ask for a half portion.

- Slow down your pace. After every bite, put down your knife and fork and chew your food thoroughly. Stop eating when you feel full, not stuffed. Remember, it takes 20 minutes for your brain to get the signal that your stomach has had enough food.

Best Choices at Family-Style Restaurants

Family-style restaurants are popular with my clients because their menus offer something for everyone, including teens. Of course there are burgers, but there are also choices for nutrition-conscious teens—entree salads, stir-fries, veggie burgers, and grilled fish. And many of these restaurants are now making it easier for families to eat well. As part of a program of the Canadian Restaurant and Foodservices Association, many large restaurant chains, including Pickle Barrel, Kelsey's, East Side Mario's, and White Spot, have voluntarily agreed to make nutrition information available to patrons by the end of 2005.

At the time of writing, of family-style restaurants, only Swiss Chalet posted the nutrition facts of its menu items on its website. After scanning each restaurant's menu, I came up with a list of better choices to order at family-style restaurants. Keep in mind that all locations may not have the items listed below. As well, menus are subject to change and some of the choices below may be removed from the menu (and hopefully replaced with an equally healthy one).

Casey's Bar & Grill Best Choices

Starters: Chicken Noodle Soup, Chicken Quesadilla, Grilled Bruschetta Flatbread, Red Pepper and Tomato Soup
Sandwiches: Amazing Vegetarian Burger, Bison Burger, Grilled Chicken Wrap, Veggie Wrap
Entree salads: Casey's House Salad with a Chicken Breast, Cobb Salad, Honey Lime Chicken Salad
Entrees: Beef and Broccoli Stir-Fry, Cashew Chicken Stir-Fry, Centre Cut Sirloin (9 ounce/ 250 gram), Chicken Fajitas, Grilled Salmon (hold the herb butter), Salmon and Shrimp Bowtie Pasta

East Side Mario's Best Choices

Starters: Bruschetta, Grilled Shrimp Skewers, Hearty Italian Vegetable Soup, Steamed Mussels
Sandwiches and pizza: BBQ Chicken Pizza, Build Your Own Pizza (with veggies and roasted chicken or ham), Italian Roasted Vegetable Mariboli Wrap, Tuscan Turkey Club, Vegetarian Two Cheese Pizza
Entree salads: Chicken Garden Salad, Grilled Salmon Salad, Soho Chicken Salad
Entrees: Pasta By You (choose napoletana or arrabbiata sauce, chicken, shrimp, or veggies), Seafood Linguine

Jack Astor's Bar and Grill Best Choices

The lunch menu features a section called "A Little Lighter." Although these menu items may be smaller, you still need to use common sense to order healthfully.

"A Little Lighter" lunch: Chicken Quesadilla and Salad, 1/2 Blackened Chicken Pita and Salad

Starters: Grilled Chicken Quesadilla, House Salad

Sandwiches and pizza: Cajun Chicken Sandwich, Hand-Tossed Pizza (order chicken or veggies)

Entree salads: California Grilled Chicken Salad (ask for salad dressing on the side or for the salad to be lightly dressed), Jack's Greek Chicken Salad

Entrees: Baked Chicken Tortillas (skip the Creole rice), Bourbon-Glazed Salmon, Lemon Pepper Salmon, Teriyaki Chicken, Teriyaki Stir-Fry, Top Sirloin (split this 10 ounce/285 gram steak and forgo the butter-brushing)

The Keg Best Choices

Starters: Grilled Portabella Mushroom, House Salad, Shrimp Cocktail, Soup of the Day (if it's not cream based)

Sandwiches: Grilled Chicken Sandwich, Salmon Wrap

Entree salads: Sirloin Salad, Spicy Chicken Salad (hold the tortilla chips)

Entrees: Baked Salmon, Chicken Stirfry, Filet Mignon, Grilled Salmon, Grilled Sirloin, Grilled Tiger Shrimp, Mediterranean Chicken, Teriyaki Chicken, Teriyaki Sirloin

Sides: Portabella and Button Mushrooms, Steamed Asparagus

Kelsey's Best Choices

Starters: Kelsey's House Salad, Spinach Salad

Entree salads: Seafood Greek Salad, Sonoma Valley Salad

Sandwiches and pizza: Kelsey's Vegetable Burger, Roast Beef Focaccia, Vegetarian Gourmet Pizza

Entrees: Asian Chicken Stir-Fry, Balsamic Chicken (substitute a baked potato for the "mound of garlic mashed potatoes"), Blackened Salmon, Centre Cut Top Sirloin (8 ounce/225 gram), Chicken and Shrimp Jambalaya, Lemon Pepper Salmon, Steak and Chicken Fajita, Vegetable Fajita

Montana's Best Choices

Starters: Ancho Chicken Quesadilla, Chicken Noodle Soup, Grilled Bruschetta Flatbread

Sandwiches: Grilled Chicken Breast Sandwich, Smoked Turkey Clubhouse, Vegetable and Feta Burger

Entree salads: County Cobb Salad, Lodge House Salad with Grilled Chicken Breast, Spinach Salad with Grilled Chicken Breast
Entrees: Canyon Falls Top in Sirloin (8 ounce/225 gram), Chicken Fajitas, Chicken Stir Fry, Jack Daniel's Skillet Seared Wild Pacific Salmon

Red Lobster Best Choices

Starters: Fresh PEI Mussels, Jumbo Shrimp Cocktail, Lobster Pizza
Sandwiches: Grilled Chicken Sandwich
Entree salads: Apple Walnut Chicken Salad, Grilled Salmon Salad
Entrees: Broiled Fisherman's Feast, Broiled Fish Fillets, East Coast Seafood Pasta, Garlic Shrimp, Grilled Chicken, Steak (8 ounce/225 gram) and Broiled/Steamed Seafood, Ultimate Broiled Seafood Feast

Swiss Chalet Best Choices

Starters: Chalet Chicken Soup (only 97 calories and 2 grams of fat), Garden Salad, Greek Salad, Rotisserie Vegetable Salad
You definitely want to skip the chicken wings—an order of eight wings will cost you 954 calories and a whopping 50 grams of fat.
Sandwiches: Chicken on a Kaiser, Grilled Santa Fe Chicken Sandwich, Veggie Burger
Entree salads: Santa Fe Grilled Chicken Salad (only 274 calories.)
Entrees: Grilled Chicken Breast, Quarter Rotisserie Chicken (skinless), Vegetable Stir Fry
If you remove the skin from the Quarter Chicken White, you'll save 14 grams of fat. Order the Half Chicken skinless and you'll cut 21 grams of fat and 235 calories from your meal.
Sides: Baked Potato, Corn, Fresh Vegetables, Rotisserie Vegetables, Steamed Rice

White Spot Best Choices

Starters: Chipotle Chicken Quesadilla, Garden Salad
Sandwiches: Chargrilled Spot Veggie Burger, Chicken Caesar Wrap, Chipotle Chicken Wrap, Mediterranean Chicken Burger
Entree salads: Mediterranean Chicken Salad
Lifestyle choices: Chargrilled Chicken Burger, (calorie reduced) Pasta Primavera, Under 5g of Fat Chicken Dinner
Entrees: Blackened Cajun Chicken, Cajun Blackened Sirloin Steak, Canada AAA Sirloin Steak (8 ounce/225 gram), Spicy Cantonese Chicken Stir-Fry, Teriyaki Chicken, Teriyaki Chicken and Prawns, Tomato Basil Fettuccini

Healthy Choices at the Mall and Fast Food Restaurants

Most teenagers know that fast food isn't exactly good for them, but many can't quite break the habit. After all, it's quick, it's easy, and many (though not all) teenagers think fast food tastes good. In fact, consumption of high-fat fast food is increasing, in part because fast food restaurants are an inescapable part of life. You can grab a greasy burger at the mall's food court, at the drive-through, and even while you're shopping at Home Depot and Wal-Mart.

Besides fuelling an epidemic of obesity, fast food has other hidden dangers. According to Eric Schlosser, author of *Fast Food Nation: The Dark Side of the All-American Meal,* the fast food industry has radically transformed our diet, landscape, economy, and workforce, often in subtley destructive ways. He charges that fast food chains have indirectly changed the way cattle are fed, slaughtered, and processed, making meat-packing the most dangerous job in North America and increasing the risk of large-scale food poisoning. Not to mention the fact that the industry runs on labour usually supplied by overworked and underpaid teenagers. If you read the book, you might be tempted to ban fast food from your diet altogether.

I've talked with a number of teenagers who say they've outgrown greasy fast food—especially the food sold at burger joints such as McDonald's. Many teenagers say they don't like the taste ("it's fake food") or the smell ("it's really gross"). And some, after watching Morgan Spurlock's 2004 hit documentary *Super Size Me,* criticize fast food from a health perspective, saying it's fattening. It's hard to ignore the side effects of his fast food binge—the weight gain, high cholesterol, and fatty liver that Morgan experienced after eating breakfast, lunch, and dinner at McDonald's every day for one month. While no teenager I know eats three times a day at McDonald's, the movie does illustrate the point that a steady diet of grease and sugar can harm your health—and in a short time. These days, many teenagers are steering clear of burgers and fries in favour of subs, pizza, and Japanese and Greek foods.

But not all teenagers veto traditional fast food. Luckily, even at the burger joints, healthier fare can be found. The trick is deciding what to order ahead of time to avoid impulse buying. If you stand in line thinking about how much money you can save, you'll end up with some kind of high-fat, high-calorie combo meal. If you do order the combo or value meals, you can always substitute the fries for a side salad, and the pop for milk.

Whether your teen goes for stuffed pitas, sushi, chicken burritos, or cheeseburgers, here's what he or she needs to know about fast food:

Fast Food Losers and Winners

When it comes to calories, fat, saturated fat, trans fat, and sodium, fast food can be a nutritional nightmare. And let's not forget about the bucket-sized drinks that add as many as 14 teaspoons (70 ml) of sugar to a meal. Below I describe worst-possible fast food choices and give healthier alternatives for each. Okay, they may not all be winners. Let's just say they are the best of the worst. As you'll see, many of the leaner options still provide a hefty dose of sodium. Most fast food meals are processed, and that means lots of salt. Teenagers should consume no more than 2300 milligrams of sodium each day.

All-dressed burger

Fast food loser. The more meat, cheese, and bacon you pile between the bun, the more calorie, fat, and sodium numbers soar. For example, Burger King's Original Double Whopper with Cheese packs 1060 calories, 69 grams of fat (27 of them saturated), and 1540 milligrams of sodium. The average 14-year-old sedentary male needs 2090 calories and no more than 69 grams of fat, 23 grams of saturated fat, and 2300 milligrams of sodium per day. One Double Whopper supplies half his daily calories and sodium requirements and a whole day's worth of fat. Just imagine the numbers if he ordered fries with that burger.

Best bets for burgers: McDonald's Quarter Pounder without Cheese has 420 calories, 19 grams of fat (8 of them saturated), and 620 milligrams of sodium. Quite a departure from the all-dressed Double Whopper. Teenage girls would be better off ordering the plain hamburger (250 calories, 8 grams fat) since they need fewer calories than their male peers. Boring? Perhaps. But you can always spruce up your meal with a side salad, frozen yogurt, or fruit (Wendy's sells fresh fruit with yogurt dip).

Veggie burgers made from soybeans are also a good fast food choice. Harvey's Veggie Burger has 300 calories, 13 grams of fat (fewer than 5 of them saturated), and 452 milligrams of sodium. Burger King and McDonald's also sell veggie burgers.

Fish fillet sandwich

Fast food loser. Just because it's fish doesn't mean that it's healthy. Most of these sandwiches are breaded, fried, and smothered with tartar sauce. Order the Fish Filet Sandwich at Burger King and you'll scarf back 520 calories and 30 grams of fat. McDonald's Filet-O-Fish has 410 calories and 19 grams of fat.

Best bets for fish sandwiches: Hold the sauce. If you skip the tartar sauce when you order Burger King's BK Fish Filet Sandwich, you'll save 160 calories and 17 grams of fat. If you visit Harvey's, try the Grilled Salmon Burger. At 337 calories, this sandwich has only 8 grams of fat and 1.4 grams of saturated fat. The downside: a whopping 1159 milligrams of sodium. That represents one-half of a teen's daily upper limit for sodium (2300 milligrams).

Crispy chicken burgers and strips

Fast food losers. Stay clear of crispy, spicy, and home-style chicken sandwiches. These are usually breaded and fried. McDonald's McChicken Sandwich has 490 calories and 27 grams of fat. Not much different than a Big Mac at 530 calories and 28 grams of fat (of course, the beef burger has more saturated fat than the chicken sandwich). Wendy's Spicy Chicken Fillet Sandwich has 17 grams of fat—10 grams more than its grilled version. And anything that's fried is a potential source of artery-clogging trans fat. At the time of writing, most fast food restaurants are still frying their food in hydrogenated oils.

The same warning goes out for chicken nuggets, strips, and tenders. An order of three Crispy Strips from KFC supplies 400 calories and 24 grams of fat. That means 55% of the calories in this meal comes from fat. And don't be fooled by McDonald's White Meat Chicken McNuggets. They may be made from leaner breast meat, but they are still deep-fried. An order of 10 will set you back 520 calories and 32 grams of fat. But here's the real zinger: you also get 6 grams of trans fat with your order of white-meat chicken nuggets.

If you frequent KFC, stick with the Original Recipe and order chicken breast. The Extra Crispy recipe adds 80 calories and 10 grams of fat to each chicken breast. Of course, you'll cut even more fat if you ask for your chicken without skin and breading. Resist the temptation to order KFC's Chicken Pot Pie. It might sound like something from your own kitchen, but low fat it is not. At 770 calories, this little dish gets 47% of its calories from fat.

Best bets for chicken sandwiches: Order a grilled chicken sandwich. These sandwiches have much less fat than their deep-fried counterparts, and some restaurants even serve them on a whole-wheat bun. Wendy's Ultimate Chicken Grill Sandwich has 350 calories and has only 18% fat calories (7 grams of fat, including 1.5 grams of saturated fat, and 0 grams of trans fat). The nutrition numbers for Harvey's Grilled Chicken Sandwich and McDonald's Chicken McGrill are similar.

Deli-style sandwiches

Fast food losers. In my opinion, these sandwiches are really just greasy burgers in disguise. Among the 15 deli sandwiches offered at Arby's, only two provide less than 30% of their calories from fat. Most weigh in at around 400 to 500 calories and get 40% to 50% of their calories from fat. Arby's Market Fresh Sandwiches aren't any better for you. The best of the bunch is Arby's Turkey Ranch and Bacon, at 670 calories and 23 grams of fat. The worst is Arby's Ultimate BLT at 740 calories and 42 grams of fat (51% fat calories).

When you consider the nutrition facts on McDonald's deli sandwiches, you'll see they're a far cry from Jared's low-fat subs. Some of these deli sandwiches have more fat and calories than a Big Mac. Take the Leaning Tower Italian on Whole Wheat, for example. All dressed, it serves up 610 calories and 31 grams of fat—not to mention 2060 milligrams of sodium. If you skip the sauce and cheese, you're down to 490 calories, 21 grams of fat, and 1720 milligrams of sodium. Better, but still not great.

Best bets for deli-style sandwiches: Many teenagers I counsel say that Subway and Pita Pit are favourite places to grab a quick lower-fat meal. Wraps, pitas, and submarine sandwiches are better choices, but teens still need to order carefully. Fill a sandwich with lean meats (roast beef, chicken breast, turkey) and plenty of veggies. Tuna salad, seafood salad, salami, sausage, gyros, philly steak, and falafel fillings are often higher in fat and calories. For instance, Mr. Sub's regular Assorted Classic Sub has 664 calories, 20 grams of fat, 7 of which are saturated fat. By choosing turkey instead, you save 200 calories and 15 grams of fat. Consider skipping the processed cheese slice (too much sodium, not enough taste) in favour of feta cheese.

Keep the fat content of your sandwich low by going easy on the fatty sauces and spreads. Lower-fat sauces include honey mustard, regular mustard, vinaigrette dressing, horseradish, barbecue sauce, pizza sauce, Louisiana sauce (Mr. Sub), and low-fat mayonnaise. Consider skipping the sauce at Mega Wraps—a two tablespoon (25 ml) serving adds 210 calories and 19 grams of fat to your sandwich. Yikes.

If you're watching your waistline, consider how much bread you're getting with your order. A regular (12 inch) submarine bun is the equivalent of four slices of bread. That's great for hungry teenage boys, but too much for most teenage girls, unless they're very active. The six-inch size is the same as two slices of bread. At Mega Wraps, the regular wrap is about four to five slices' worth of bread; the junior wrap supplies about three and a half slices each. At Pita Pit, you're also getting the equivalent of three and a half slices of bread per pita.

Fast food salads

These fast food meals can be losers or winners depending on what you order. Some fast food salads offer as many calories and grams of fat as a deluxe burger. And a whole lot more sodium. That's what I learned after rating the nutritional content of 18 fast food entree salads (with accompanying dressing) from McDonalds, Arby's, Wendy's, and Subway.

The average salad weighed in at 540 calories, 33 grams of fat, including 9 grams of saturated fat, and 1550 milligrams of sodium. For example, McDonald's Bacon Ranch Salad with Warm Crispy Chicken delivers 516 calories, 34 grams of fat, 10 grams of cholesterol-raising saturated fat, and 1608 milligrams of sodium. The Quarter Pounder with Cheese looks pretty similar at 520 calories, 27 grams of fat, 13 grams of saturated fat, and 1099 milligrams of sodium.

The real loser was Arby's Santa Fe Salad, a medley of mixed greens, veggies, chopped chicken fingers, and shredded cheese. All dressed, this hefty salad serves up 845 calories, 60 grams of fat, and 1760 milligrams of sodium. Wendy's Chicken BLT Salad also didn't fare well, coming in at 710 calories and 48 grams of fat.

Best bets for fast food salads: Only two salads came out winners: McDonald's Chicken Oriental Salad and its Crispy Chicken Oriental Salad, both served with Newman's Own Low Fat Sesame Thai Dressing. They scored points for having no more than 30% of calories from total fat and 10% calories from saturated fat, and at least 3 grams of fibre. Runners up include Arby's Asian Sesame and Martha's Vineyard Salads, Wendy's Mandarin Chicken Salad, and McDonald's Fiesta Salad.

Many fast food salads are certainly a healthier choice than a burger and fries. Eating a salad is also a great way to boost your daily vegetable intake. Arby's even tosses chopped apples, orange segments, and dried cranberries into its salads. But you need to order your salad carefully. Ask for a fat-reduced dressing. If there isn't one available, use half the portion of the regular-fat dressing. Next, limit the fatty toppings. Deep-fried croutons, crispy noodles, tortilla chips, cheese, and bacon add up on the nutrition calculator. Order your salad with grilled chicken, not fried.

Burritos, tacos, nachos

Fast food losers, but there are a few exceptions. The high-fat cheese and sour cream prevent most Mexican fast food meals from being considered winners. And the crunchy, deep-fried taco shells and tortilla chips add trans fats to a meal. Taco Bell's Fiesta Taco Salad delivers 870 calories, 48 grams of fat, including 16 grams of saturated fat (Taco Bell doesn't give numbers for trans fat).

Best bets for Mexican fast food: Order burritos made with beans, chicken, or steak. Taco Bell's Chicken Fiesta Burrito has 370 calories and 12 grams of fat (29% fat calories). That's a whole lot better than the Beef Chalupa Supreme at 390 calories and 24 grams of fat (55% fat calories). At Taco Bell you can also order your meal fresco style, which means that any cheese or sauce will be replaced with fat-free salsa. The 15 fresco-style items each have less than 10 grams of fat.

French fries, onion rings, and poutine

Fast food losers. It's no surprise that these side dishes don't make the nutritional all-star list. A large order of fries will add 500 to 550 calories and 25 grams of fat (including 6 grams of trans fat) to your meal. And don't count onion rings as a vegetable serving! A large order of onion rings at Harvey's provides 430 calories and 30 grams of fat (including 10 grams of trans fat). And only a measly 8 grams of potassium.

Best bets for side dishes: Skip the fries and onion rings and order a side salad instead. Or try a baked potato topped with salsa. Or order a small chili to have with your meal. A small serving of Wendy's chili provides 5 grams of fibre and only 5 grams of fat. Or consider ordering a serving of vegetable soup at Harvey's. You might even skip the side and order a healthy dessert instead. Try the Fruit and Yogurt Parfait at McDonald's or the Fruit Cup at Wendy's.

Beverages

By now, I probably don't need to remind you about the sugar in pop and fruit drinks. Let's just say if you order a large (32 ounce) soft drink, you'll gulp 14 teaspoons (70 ml) of sugar with your meal. Who needs those extra sugar calories?

Best bets for beverages: You're better off quenching your thirst with calcium-rich, low-fat milk, unsweetened fruit juice, or water. Overweight teenagers should avoid fruit juice and stick with calorie-free water or, as a last choice, diet pop.

Fast food Chinese

Fast food loser. Dishes such as Beef and Broccoli and Lemon Chicken might sound healthy, but don't be fooled. Unless you order your menu items steamed, you're getting plenty of fat from the oil used for stir-frying or deep-frying. Lemon Chicken, Sweet and Sour Chicken Balls, and many other Chinese dishes are breaded and fried. Here's a look at how a combo meal at Manchu Wok might break down.

	Calories	Fat (grams)	% Fat Calories	Sodium (milligrams)
Orange chicken	279	15	48	184
Beef and broccoli	271	23	76	620
Fried rice	310	14	39	957
Total for meal	*860*	*52*	*54*	*1761*

That burger is looking better, isn't it?

Best bets for Asian fast food: If you're partial to Chinese cuisine, order your veggies and rice and noodles steamed. That's about the best you can do at the mall food court. You're better off switching to Japanese fast food. Edo Japan, Made in Japan Teriyaki Experience, and other Japanese fast food restaurants offer dishes that are grilled in water, not oil. The Chicken Teriyaki Meal at Made in Japan has 523 calories and only 2.5 grams of fat. Edo Japan's Seafood Grill has 497 calories and 7.8 grams of fat. Chicken, shrimp, seafood, and tofu are your best bets. Tofu is a little higher in fat than chicken and seafood, but it's healthy unsaturated fat. Sushi (rice and fish) is also a low-fat choice.

To reduce your sodium intake, don't add soy sauce to your meal; try a dash of hot sauce instead. You can also request that teriyaki sauce not be used to prepare your meal.

Pizza

Who doesn't love pizza? It's fast, it's portable, it's social, and it tastes great. Even nutritionists like me have a tough time finding fault with pizza. You can cover all the food groups of Canada's Food Guide just by eating a slice or two. Although it's not a low-fat food, a slice of pizza does have considerably fewer calories, and less fat and sodium than a burger with fries. And unlike french fries and chicken nuggets, pizza is not deep-fried in a vat of partially hydrogenated vegetable oil (a source of trans fat). Another plus—you get calcium from the cheese and vitamins A and C from the tomato sauce.

But think twice before you place your next order. A pizza meal can be healthier than other fast food options, but that depends on what you order and how many slices you eat. Cheese-laden, meat-heavy pizzas such as Domino's Meatzza Feast and Little Caesars' Supreme can be minefields of sodium and fat, especially artery-clogging saturated fat. For instance, the individual-sized Bacon Double Cheeseburger pizza at Boston Pizza delivers 1210 calories, 56 grams of fat, and 2170 milligrams of sodium. (By comparison, a Big Mac and large order of fries from McDonald's has 880 calories, 45 grams of fat, and 1450 milligrams of sodium.)

Or consider Pizza Hut's Pepperoni Lover's pan pizza. Two slices from a large pie will set you back 500 calories, 22 grams of fat (10 of them saturated), and 1476 milligrams of sodium—almost two-thirds of a teen's daily sodium allowance (2300 milligrams).

The good news is that not all pizzas pile on a day's worth of fat and sodium. Here are a few tips to make your next pizza a healthy fast food choice:

- Start by ordering a whole-wheat crust if it's available.

- To save calories, skip the greasy, deep-dish pan crusts and ask instead for thin crust. Compared with their thin-crust cousins, most pan crusts add about one teaspoon (5 ml) of oil per slice. If you order thin crust instead of the classic hand-tossed at Domino's, you'll save 100 calories and 24 grams of carbohydrate (about a slice and a half of bread) per two slices of a medium pizza.

- To cut back on saturated fat and salt, ask for only half the cheese. You probably won't find this option on the menu, but all outlets will oblige. Or top your pizza with goat or feta cheese. Compared with full-fat mozzarella, you'll get less fat and more flavour.

- Choose your toppings wisely. Skip the fatty sausage and bacon. Leaner choices include chicken and ham. Avoid multi-meat toppings that send the fat and sodium numbers through the roof. Ask for double veggies to boost fibre and vitamins.

- Don't sit down to a pizza-only meal, unless you want to overeat. To avoid devouring the whole pie, eat your pizza with a salad. You can order a side salad at most pizza joints. Or serve your pizza with raw veggies or sliced fresh fruit.

- Stay clear of dipping sauces. Depending on the flavour, you'll add as much 35 grams of fat (and 315 calories) to your meal. That's more fat than you'll get in two slices of all-dressed pizza.

PIZZA PIE CHART: BEST BETS AT NATIONAL CHAINS

Numbers are for two slices from a large pizza unless indicated otherwise.

	Calories	Fat (g)	Saturated Fat (g)	Sodium (mg)
Boston Pizza's Californian	360	5.0	n/a	700
Boston Pizza's Vegetarian	440	10	n/a	700
Boston Pizza's BBQ Chicken	474	14	n/a	818
Boston Pizza's Zorba the Greek	540	18	n/a	1220
Pizza Hut's Thin 'N Crispy Veggie Lover's	342	12.0	6.0	816
Pizza Hut's Thin 'N Crispy Hawaiian	408	16	8.0	1132
Pizza Pizza's Sweet Chili Chicken	380	9.0	n/a	860
Pizza Pizza's Vegetarian	400	10	n/a	960
Pizza Pizza's BBQ Chicken	440	10	n/a	1100
Pizza Pizza's Mediterranean Vegetarian	440	14	n/a	1220
Pizza Pizza's Pesto Amore Whole Wheat Thin Crust	400	16	n/a	620
Pizza Pizza's Four Seasons	400	18	n/a	880
Domino's Hand Tossed Hawaiian Feast, 1/4 medium	450	15	7.0	1102
Domino's Hand Tossed Vegi Feast, 1/4 medium	439	16	7.0	987
Domino's Thin Crust Cheese, 1/4 large	382	16	7.0	1171
Little Caesars' Hawaiian	440	14	6.0	780
Little Caesars' Thin Crust Cheese	340	16	7.0	420
Little Caesars' Veggie	460	8.0	7.0	1380
Little Caesars' Thin Crust Pepperoni	400	18	8.0	600

Get Informed About Fast Food

If you're a frequent patron at a fast food restaurant, check out that restaurant's website. Nutrition-minded companies will post the nutrient breakdown of their menu items. In February 2005, the Canadian Restaurant and Foodservices Association announced the launch of a national voluntary program that will make it easier for consumers to make informed food choices when dining out. Participating restaurants will provide diners with the calorie, fat, cholesterol, carbohydrate, protein, and sodium content of standard menu items. Some restaurants may also identify the top ten allergens in their foods. This information will be presented in brochures and on company websites. Notices on menu boards or menus will tell consumers that this nutrition information is available.

At the time of writing, the company websites below provide nutrition information for fast food menu items. Other restaurant chains that plan to make nutrition information available include Casey's Bar & Grill, De Dutch Pannekoek House, Jack Astor's Bar and Grill, East Side Mario's, IKEA Canada, Kelsey's, Shoeless Joe's, and White Spot.

Burgers, Chicken, and Mexican

www.arbys.com
www.bk.com
www.dairyqueen.com
www.harveys.ca
www.kfc.com
www.mcdonalds.ca
www.tacobell.com
www.wendys.com

Sandwiches and Wraps

www.subway.com
www.mrsub.ca
www.pitapit.com
www.megawraps.com

Asian Food

www.edojapan.com
www.teriyakiexperience.com
www.manchuwok.com

Pizza

www.pizzahut.com
www.pizzapizza.ca
www.bostonpizza.com

Eating Healthy Ethnic Foods

In an effort to eat healthy, many teenagers opt for ethnic foods. But not all ethnic dishes are good choices for teens trying to watch their intake of fat. Many versions of popular ethnic dishes are high in fat and calories, especially fried items or recipes made with cheese, cream, or butter. That said, many ethnic dishes are composed of extremely nutritious foods, such as beans, nuts, whole grains, fresh vegetables, and lean meats. Here are a few strategies to help your teen dine healthy on foods from around the world:

Chinese Cuisine

Dishes at a typical Chinese restaurant are filled with vegetables, rice, and noodles, making healthy eating an easy task, especially for vegetarian teens. They also give you the opportunity to eat a variety of vegetables you probably don't get very often, such as snow peas, water chestnuts, bamboo shoots, bok choy, and lotus root. Traditional Chinese dishes tend to be high in fibre, vitamins, and minerals. What's more, many Chinese dishes are made to order, so it's possible to make special requests. The key is knowing where fat and sodium lurk.

- Beware of lemon and orange chicken and beef dishes, which are often breaded and fried and therefore high in fat. General Tsao's Chicken is another high-fat item.

- Look for the words "steamed," "boiled," "jum" (poached), "kow" (roasted), and "shu" (barbecued) for healthier cooking methods.

- Limit items that are deep-fried, crispy, batter-dipped, breaded, and fried.

- Choose dishes made with small portions of beef, chicken, or pork. Ask for dishes to be prepared with extra veggies. Chicken wings, duck, and spare ribs are high in fat.

- Opt for seafood, fish, and tofu dishes to reduce your intake of saturated fat.

- Ask for brown rice instead of white.

- Order clear soups instead of egg drop soup.

- Use chopsticks to slow down your eating. Chopsticks also help you eat less of the sauce that you might eat when using a fork.

- Keep in mind that most Chinese dishes are made with high-sodium soy sauce, so avoid using soy sauce at the table or ask for low-sodium soy sauce.

- If you're sensitive to MSG (monosodium glutamate), a flavour enhancer used by many Chinese restaurants, ask that your meal be prepared without it.

Italian Cuisine

Italian food is the most popular type of food ordered in restaurants in North America. And you'll find plenty of heart healthy dishes to choose from—leafy green salads, bean soups, pastas with tomato sauce, and grilled fish. But there are a few things to know to curb your calorie and fat intake:

- Beware of larger-than-life pasta portions. At some restaurants, a serving of pasta can easily yield 4 cups (1000 ml), which is the equivalent of eight slices of bread. Consider ordering a half portion of pasta.

- Choose plain bread or bruschetta instead of garlic-buttered or cheese-topped breads.

- Best bets for soup include lentil, bean, vegetable, and minestrone.

- Best bets for salads include misto (mixed), arugula, and spinach. Caprese and Caesar salads are higher in fat and calories. Consider ordering salad dressing on the side.

- Watch how much extra-virgin olive oil you use for dipping bread. Unlike butter that's full of saturated fat, olive oil contains heart healthy monounsaturated fat. But it is still 100% fat and full of calories.

- Choose lower-fat tomato-based sauces such as marinara, primavera, arrabbiata, and puttanesca.

- Limit your intake of high-fat dishes made with rich cream sauces such as alfredo, carbonara, rosé, and vodka.

- Choose dishes with grilled chicken, seafood, and fish. Mussels or clams in a tomato-based broth are excellent choices. Veal is also lean, especially if you choose a dish that is baked, not fried.

- Avoid dishes with sausage, excessive amounts of cheese, and breaded meats.

- Order thin-crust pizza with veggies and chicken. Ask for part-skim mozzarella—some restaurants may have it.

Mexican Cuisine

It can be tricky to choose lower-fat dishes at a Mexican restaurant, but not impossible. The fact that many menu items are deep-fried or contain generous portions of cheese and sour cream means you'll have to scan the menu carefully. Here are a few pointers to help you dine on healthy Mexican cuisine:

- Detour the basket of deep-fried tortilla chips. Instead, request plain, fresh tortillas for dipping in salsa.

- If available, order corn tortillas instead of ones made from wheat flour. Corn tortillas are lower in fat and calories.

- Best bets for starters include ceviche (raw fish marinated in lemon juice) and gazpacho, black bean, and vegetable soups.

- Best bets for entrees include chicken or black bean burritos, soft tacos, fajitas, and stuffed and baked tamales (corn tortilla).

- Load your tacos, burritos, or fajitas with salsa instead of sour cream.

- Ask for black beans instead of refried beans, which are fried in lard or some other type of fat.

- Limit higher-fat items such as nachos and cheese, taco salad, and deep-fried tortilla dishes such as chimichanga and taquitos.

- Go heavy on the rice, black beans, and veggies, all of which add fibre to your meal.

Thai Cuisine

Like Chinese cuisine, Thai cuisine offers something for everyone. You'll find dishes at Thai restaurants that offer plenty of vegetables, tofu, seafood, nuts, noodles, and rice. The emphasis on vegetables and grains means that meat portions are small. By planning ahead and watching how much you eat, it's entirely possible to enjoy a healthy, lower-fat Thai meal:

- Choose the lighter, stir-fried dishes over dishes made with coconut milk, peanuts, cashews, and peanut sauce.

- Ask that cooking be done with vegetable oil rather than coconut or palm kernel oil, both sources of saturated fat.

- Instead of fried spring rolls, order cold, fresh salad rolls.

- Best bets for starters include clear soups such as tom yam goong (hot and sour shrimp soup). Tom kha gai and tom yam hed soup are higher in fat because they're made with coconut milk. Green mango salad and seafood salad are also good choices.

- Avoid dishes with fried noodles (mee grob, radnar talay) and fried rice.

- Healthier dishes include satay, grilled or sautéed chicken, fish, lean meat, and sautéed tofu.

- To limit the saturated fat and boost your intake of omega-3 fats, look for seafood as your main protein source.

- Use chopsticks to slow your eating pace.

- For dessert, order lychees (a small, round fruit) instead of deep-fried ice cream or banana fritters.

Japanese Cuisine

It's hard to go wrong with Japanese cuisine. It highlights rice and vegetables and relies on preparation methods that require little or no added oil. Most of the fat you consume comes directly from the foods you choose, be it shellfish, fish, or soybeans. Portions of food are often smaller, too.

- Best bets for starters include seaweed salad, edamame (boiled or steamed soybeans), clear soups (miso and suimono), and tofu in broth.

- Sashimi (raw fish), sushi (raw fish and rice), udon and soba (buckwheat) noodles in broth are low-fat choices.

- Best bets for entrees include grilled (yakimono) dishes such as yakitori, teriyaki chicken, and salmon.

- Higher-fat menu items include tempura (shrimps and vegetables deep-fried in a light batter), shabu-shabu (thinly sliced prime rib cooked in broth and served with dipping sauce), and tonkatsu (deep-fried breaded pork cutlet).

- If you're trying to lower your sodium intake, ask for your food to be prepared without high-sodium marinades, sauces, and salt.

Indian Cuisine

On the plus side, many Indian dishes feature legumes, vegetables, and rice and de-emphasize animal protein foods. But many foods are prepared with ghee (clarified butter) or are fried or sautéed. That means many Indian dishes are high in fat and calories.

- Best bets for starters include lentil soup, mulligatawny soup, and raita (sliced cucumber in yogurt).

- Avoid fried appetizers such as samosas and pakoras.

- Opt for roti, chapati (thin, dry whole-wheat bread) or naan (leavened, baked bread) instead of fried and stuffed breads. Roasted papads (thin, crispy lentil wafers, also called papadams) are also good choices. If you're not sure whether the papads are roasted or deep-fried, ask your server.

- Lower-fat dishes include dhal (lentils), chicken or fish tandoori (marinated in spices and cooked in a clay oven), chicken or beef tikka (roasted with mild spices), kebabs, and chicken or vegetable biryani (rice dishes with spices).

- Ask for curry dishes that are made with a yogurt base. Limit curries made with coconut milk or cream.

Greek Cuisine

Although some people may think that Greek food is synonymous with heart health, it all depends on what you order. Traditional Mediterranean consists largely of vegetables, grains, and olive oil, and only a smattering of meat and cheese. But it's the other way around at many Greek restaurants in North America.

- Ask for dishes to be prepared with less olive oil. Ask for salad dressing, olives, and feta cheese to be served on the side. That way you'll be able to control how much fat and sodium you add to your Greek salad.

- Best bets for starters include dolmades (grape leaves stuffed with rice and served cold), octopus (grilled or marinated and served cold), steamed mussels and pita with hummus (chickpea dip) and tzatziki (yogurt dip).

- Appetizers to avoid include spanakopita or spinach pie (layers of phyllo dough that have been brushed with butter and filled with cheese, oil, and egg) and crispy calamari that's been breaded and deep-fried.

- The best bet for an entree is souvlaki—chicken, pork, or lamb. With the exception of extra salt from the marinade, shish kebabs are the healthiest items on a Greek menu. Other good choices include grilled chicken, lamb, and fish.

- Stay clear of moussaka (casserole that layers ground meat and fried eggplant and covers it with a buttery sauce). If you really must order this high-fat meal, consider sharing it with a friend and ordering extra vegetables and steamed rice to supplement your meal.

- Instead of a higher-fat gyro sandwich, order a souvlaki-stuffed pita. Gyro consists of a mixture of minced meat, bread crumbs, and onions that's moulded onto a vertical spit and then roasted.

- For dessert, you're best off ordering fruit. Many Greek pastries, including baklava, are made with buttery phyllo dough and plenty of sugar. A good-sized portion can set you back 550 calories, 21 grams of fat, and 8 teaspoons (40 ml) of sugar. If you want to splurge, split this treat with a friend.

Eating Healthy at the High School Cafeteria

The tips I've provided for eating at restaurants and fast food places apply to cafeteria food as well. First and foremost, teenagers should choose foods that will give them a balanced meal. Eating a lunch that consists of only french fries or a muffin is not balanced, nor is it nutritious. Besides getting more fat than they need (and trans fat), these teenagers are missing out on protein, vitamins, and minerals.

My research shows that the top five sellers in the high school cafeteria are (1) sugary drinks; (2) dairy products; (3) bottled water; (4) sweets and desserts (cookies, candy, chocolate bars, ice cream); and (5) french fries, potato chips, and nachos and cheese. These are the foods that students line up for at least three times per week.

The least popular menu items in the cafeteria include chicken burgers and nuggets; burgers, hot dogs, and pizza; hot pasta meals; unsweetened fruit juice; and sandwiches, subs, and wraps. Are burgers and chicken nuggets unpopular because teenagers are more interested in healthy foods? Maybe so. Among the 1046 students I surveyed, more than half (57%) said they would eat in the cafeteria more often if it offered more healthy choices. And 77% said they would buy lunch more often if a wider variety of foods was offered. Clearly, teenagers don't want the foods they indulged in as children.

If teenagers are nutrition conscious, why aren't wraps, subs, salads, and fruit on the list of cafeteria bestsellers? My study didn't ask this question, but the answer could be quite simple. Perhaps teenagers aren't buying these foods because the cafeteria offerings of these items are slim. Or maybe what is sold is unappealing to teenagers. Who wants to buy a bruised apple or a soggy prewrapped egg sandwich—even if it is made on whole-grain bread?

Fortunately, many high school cafeterias are in the midst of changing their menus, with pressure from parents and school boards. Chartwells School Dining Services, a member of Compass Group Canada that holds the market share in contracted high school food service, is committed to bringing healthy foods to the forefront. The company has added more healthy options to the menu—whole-grain wraps, salads made to order, stir-fries, and grab-and-go veggies—and it's promoting water and milk as beverage choices in their combo meals rather than sugary pop.

If you're concerned that your teen isn't eating well at school, discuss the cafeteria menu with her. Find out how often she eats french fries, potato chips, soft drinks, candy, and ice cream. Recommend items that are healthier, but realize your child will still buy junk food. Most importantly, encourage your teenager to pack her own lunch more often, or at least bring a few healthy foods from home to supplement the cafeteria offerings. By doing so, teenagers can control their portion size as well as their calorie and fat intake. And they get to eat the foods they like, rather than settling for whatever appeals the most that day in the cafeteria.

Brown-bag lunches don't have to consist of a boring sandwich. Try pitas or wrap sandwiches stuffed with grilled chicken and veggies. Try soups, chili, pastas, and salads. Last night's leftovers can also make a healthy and interesting school lunch.

If your teen relies solely on her school cafeteria for lunch, her meal should provide lean protein, grains (preferably whole grains), and vegetables. Healthy cafeteria meals include:

- Sandwich with turkey, chicken, ham, or veggies on whole-grain bread or a whole-wheat tortilla or pita
- Pasta with tomato sauce and a side salad (skip the garlic bread and watch portion sizes)
- Grilled chicken or veggie burger with side salad
- Veggie and chicken stir-fry with steamed rice
- Salad with grilled chicken or turkey breast

- Salad bar—choose beans and lentils for protein
- Bean soup or a vegetarian chili with a whole-grain roll and a salad

If the meal is shy on fruit and veggies, pick up a piece of fresh fruit, a fresh-fruit cup or kebab, or veggie sticks. Instead of a soft drink, try vegetable or tomato juice with lunch. To boost calcium and protein, buy a carton of 1% milk, soy milk, or low-fat yogurt.

If your teenager can't find a selection of healthy meals in the cafeteria, encourage her to speak to the food service manager. If done in a positive and supportive manner, requests for healthier lunch items can go a long way.

Eating Healthy at University: How to Beat the Freshman 15

University will broaden your teen's mind, but it might also broaden his waistline if he's not careful. And that's especially true for first-year students. It seems the long-rumoured "freshman 15"—in which entering students gain 15 pounds (7 kilograms) during their first year—is indeed a reality. Recent studies south of the border reveal that first-year students do pile on the pounds.

Researchers at Cornell University learned that freshmen students gained about one-third of a pound (0.15 kilogram) each week—an average of 4.2 pounds (1.9 kilograms) during the first three months at school. That may not sound like much, but it's roughly 11 times the weight gain expected for an 18-year-old.

It's surprising that first-year students gain excess weight considering that our awareness of nutrition is at an all-time high. My recent survey of Canadian high school students reveals that almost 8 out of 10 teenagers rate nutrition as important when deciding what to eat.

Healthy meal options are certainly available on university campuses—vegetable-packed stir-fries, pita sandwiches, salad bars, and soy burgers can be found on many menus. So where are college students going wrong? The first year away at university means freedom for teenagers—freedom to eat what they want, when they want, and often, as much as they want.

It's easy to dismiss the calories in an extra cookie eaten while studying or the two pints of beer at pub night. How could a single cookie (or two) do harm? Yet, those extra calories add up fast. It's the cumulative effect of a little extra here and a little extra there that shows up around the middle. If you scarf back an additional 500 calories each day—a bag of chips and a chocolate bar—you'll gain one pound (0.5 kilogram) per week if you don't up the exercise to compensate for extra nibbles. The Cornell students consumed a surplus of only

174 calories each day—fewer calories than one small chocolate bar—to gain their four pounds (1.8 kilograms) by December exam time.

For many first-year students, mealtime means dining halls that serve up hefty portions of fatty, starchy foods. Others eat meals at fast food courts, where burgers, fries, and pizza can tempt even the most health conscious of eaters. Late-night eating—snacking on sugary or salty foods to fuel study sessions or grabbing a slice of pizza after a beer party—is another culprit. Many first-year students also find they have less time to exercise because of their heavy course loads and the hours needed for study.

There is good news: college weight gain is not inevitable. The best way to combat the freshman 15 is to prevent it altogether. Here are a few tips for teenagers who are heading off to university:

- Stick to a regular eating schedule. Eat breakfast, lunch, a mid-day snack, and dinner to prevent hunger and overeating. Examine your class schedule and determine when and where you'll fit in meals.

- If meals at the campus dining hall are buffet style, resist the all-you-can eat mentality. Cruise the line to scope out healthy options first. If you're not sure what's in the mystery dish, stick with broiled meat, chicken, or fish.

- Moderate portion size of starchy side dishes. If you choose pasta, skip the bread. Instead of greasy potatoes or noodles, ask for a double serving of vegetables or salad.

- Don't add dessert to your tray on your first trip past the buffet. Finish your meal first— you'll be more likely to give sweets a pass.

- Don't linger: the longer you're there, the more you'll eat. This is great for active guys playing rugby or football, but not so great for freshman females watching their waistlines.

- For food court–style campus dining, stick with lower-fat options such as chicken or tofu stir-fries, pita sandwiches, salad with grilled chicken, veggie pizza, or pasta with tomato sauce. If you order a burger, substitute a side salad or vegetable soup for the fries. On many campuses today you'll find quick-service restaurants that allow you to customize your order—build-your-own-pizza joints, Mongolian grill and barbecue restaurants, cereal bars, and smoothie stations.

- Best bets for beverages include water, low-fat milk, and soy beverages. Keep your intake of sugary fruit juice to 1 cup (250 ml) per day. Save soda pop for a weekly treat.

- Avoid late-night eating. If you must snack while studying, keep healthy choices within reach: fruit and veggie bars, fresh fruit, almonds, low-fat granola bars, whole-grain crackers, mini cans of tuna.

- Never snack out of the box or bag. Measure out one serving of snack food and put it on a plate. It's too easy to lose track of how much you're munching when you're stressed out about exams.

- Instead of snacking on cookies or potato chips, sip while you study. Try a mug of herbal or flavoured black tea to fill the gap—you'll boost your fluid intake without adding calories.

- Stock up on healthy snacks. Most dining halls will let you take fruit with you. Consider getting a small fridge for your dorm room so you can keep cold snacks such as yogurt, baby carrots, hummus, and part-skim cheese strings handy.

- Practice party control. Eat a healthy meal before you go so you don't arrive famished and likely to overeat. Have a plan to limit your intake of alcoholic beverages. Just because the label says it's light or low-carb doesn't mean beer is calorie free.

- Make time for exercise to curb weight gain. Aim for 30 minutes of moderate exercise every day. Sneak in a power walk between or after classes to de-stress and combat extra calories. Or check out what the campus gym has to offer in terms of exercise classes and workout equipment.

With a little planning, organization, and nutrition know-how, your kids will gain knowledge at university, not pounds.

Food Safety Tips for Eating Outdoors

If your teen enjoys hiking and camping with friends, he needs to be extra vigilant about safe food handling. And not only when he's camping—food safety is paramount at picnics and outdoor barbecues, too. That's because the bacteria that cause food poisoning grow faster in hot temperatures and humid, moist weather. And when you cook outdoors, the safety controls of your kitchen—thermostat-controlled cooking, refrigeration, and washing facilities—are not always available. Here's what your teen needs to know:

- Pack foods in a well-insulated cooler with plenty of ice or ice packs to keep the temperature below (40°F) 4°C.

- Put the cooler in the coolest part of the car. If it's a hot day, forget about the trunk. Instead, transport the cooler in the back seat and turn the air-conditioning on. Keep the cooler out of the sun, and cover it with a blanket or tarp at the campsite. Keep the lid of the cooler closed as much as possible.

- Bring some hand soap and water for washing your hands. If you don't have soap and water, use disposable wipes or hand sanitizer.

- Remove from the cooler only the amount of raw meat that will fit on the grill.

- Defrost meat, poultry, and seafood before putting them on the grill.

- In hot weather (90°F/32°C), don't leave foods sitting out for more than one hour. If they have been left out longer than one hour, throw them away. For temperatures that aren't quite as hot, don't keep foods out for more than two hours.

Drink bottled water or tap water from a safe source. Water from lakes or streams must be purified even if the water looks clean. To purify, first let suspended particles settle or strain the water through a paper towel. Then bring the water to a boil and continue to boil for 3 to 5 minutes. Boil the water for 5 to 10 minutes if you're in the mountains or high altitudes. (Water boils at a lower temperature at high altitudes, where the air is thinner, so you need more time to kill any harmful bacteria.) You could also use water purification tablets and water filters, available in stores that sell camping gear and outdoor sporting goods.

Part Three

—⊗—

Nutrition for Health and Fitness

8

Nutrition Advice
for Vegetarian Teens

If the teenager in your family has made the decision to go meat-free, she's not alone. If you ask your teen, chances are she'll tell you that vegetarianism is becoming increasingly popular among her peers. In a recent national survey, 3% of 10- to 14-year-olds and 8% of 15- to 18-year-olds reported being vegetarian.[1] And it seems that the majority of vegetarian teenagers are female. Recent data from Ontario grade nine students reveal that almost 9% of females avoid meat.[2] The What's on Your Plate? High School Nutrition Survey I conducted in 2004 revealed that 7% of students followed a vegetarian diet, with the vast majority (78%) being female.

Many of the teens I've talked with in my nutrition counselling practice say "going veggie" was an idea that had been bubbling at the back of their minds for a number of years. It began as an experiment, then, after a month or so, their new diets stuck. Many of these kids say the impetus to embrace vegetarianism was a long-standing dislike for the taste of meat. Other teens turn to a meat-free lifestyle for ethical reasons, not wanting to harm animals or the environment. Still others go the vegetarian route because they view it as healthier, or in some cases, as a way to lose weight. Some teenagers follow a vegetarian diet because of parental preferences or religious beliefs.

If your teenager has announced she's going to follow a completely different menu from the rest of the family, it's going to have an impact on whoever does the cooking and shopping—most likely you. You may be totally supportive, or you may have your doubts. Is this just a phase? What foods will she eat? Will she get ill? It's normal to react this way. Your child has made an important decision, which, if followed sensibly, can enable her to develop valuable life skills. And another positive—it's a great opportunity for the whole family to enjoy a few plant-based meals each week.

Vegetarian eating covers a wide range of eating styles. *Semi-vegetarians* avoid only red meat; they eat poultry, fish, eggs, and dairy products. *Lacto-vegetarians* eat dairy products but avoid meat, poultry, fish, and eggs. *Lacto-ovo vegetarians* include dairy and eggs, but no meat, poultry, or fish. *Pesco-vegetarians* eat fish, dairy products, and eggs, but avoid meat and poultry. *Vegan* diets are the strictest. They contain only plant foods and shun *all* animal products—including honey and gelatin (gelatin is made from animal by-products). Vegans need to plan their diets carefully to get enough protein, iron, calcium, vitamin D, vitamin B12, and zinc.

Are Vegetarian Diets Healthy for Teens?

Many parents worry that their vegetarian teenager won't get all the nutrients he or she needs for good health. Depending on the type of vegetarian diet your child follows, there may be cause for concern. The growing teenage body demands more energy, iron, zinc, and calcium than at any other age, yet a number of studies show that vegetarian teens don't meet their daily targets for calories, protein, iron, zinc, and calcium. If your teenager follows a vegan diet, it's a good idea to talk to a registered dietitian. He or she can help your child develop a meal plan that includes adequate protein, vitamins, and minerals. Over the years, many concerned parents have asked me to consult with their teen about healthy vegetarian meal planning.

There's another reason to keep a watchful eye on your vegetarian teenager's diet. Vegetarianism in girls can sometimes be the first sign of an eating disorder: research has shown that some girls use a vegetarian diet as a way to hide an eating disorder. You'll learn more about the signs and symptoms of eating disorders in Chapter 11.

Despite these facts, there is good news. Vegetarian diets can provide adolescents with all the nutrients their bodies need if they are properly planned. In fact, the Dietitians of Canada and the American Dietetic Association have officially endorsed vegetarianism, stating that appropriately planned vegetarian diets are healthy and nutritionally adequate for teenagers. A plant-based diet might also protect your child's future health. Large studies suggest that, compared with their meat-eating peers, vegetarians have a lower risk of type 2 diabetes, heart attack, high blood pressure, gallstones, and certain cancers.

Researchers from Loma Linda University in California have been busy studying almost 35,000 Seventh-Day Adventists. Most Seventh-Day Adventists don't smoke or drink alcohol, and many are vegetarians. Compared with meat-eating men, vegetarian men had a significantly lower risk of heart disease, colon cancer, and prostate cancer.[3]

The fact that vegetarians enjoy unusually good health is also evident in the Oxford Vegetarian Study, an investigation of 6000 vegetarians and 5000 non-vegetarians living in the United Kingdom. After 12 years of study, the researchers found that compared with non-vegetarians, vegetarians experienced a 28% reduced risk of heart disease and 39% lower risk of certain cancers.[4]

These findings raise three important questions: (1) Are vegetarians healthier because they have a healthier lifestyle (e.g., they don't smoke cigarettes and they exercise more)? (2) Do vegetarians suffer from chronic diseases less often because they avoid unhealthy foods and food components (e.g., meat, saturated fat)? and (3) Do vegetarians experience better health because they include more healthy foods and food components in their diet (e.g., fruits, vegetables, nuts, antioxidants)?

Evidence indicates that the answer to each question is a resounding yes. While giving up red meat may have something to do with lower rates of heart disease and cancer, it's not the whole story. A steady diet of whole grains, nuts, vegetables, fruit, beans, and soy foods is low in fat and offers plenty of protective plant chemicals, antioxidants, and fibre.

Nutrients That Need Attention—and How to Get More

The keys to a nutritionally complete vegetarian diet are planning and variety. Here's what you and your teenager need to know:

Calories and Fat

That vegetarian diets tend to be lower in calories and fat than meat-based diets is good news for teenagers who need to lose weight or lower their cholesterol. But it's not so great for teenagers who are still growing and those who are already at a healthy weight. The real concern lies with strict vegan diets. Vegan diets can be high in fibre, which dilutes the calorie content of foods and contributes to the feeling of fullness. As a result, teenagers who eat vegan meals might feel full sooner and stop eating before they've consumed enough calories to keep their bodies healthy and strong. Avocados, nuts, seeds, dried fruits, and soy products can help boost the calorie and fat content of vegan diets.

Consulting a registered dietitian can help you and your child plan a vegan diet that provides adequate calories for growth and development. To find out how many calories your son or daughter needs each day, turn to Chapter 1, page 15. Daily calorie requirements are listed for males and females, by age and activity level. Later in this chapter, you'll find a Vegetarian Food Guide to help your teen get all the foods needed for proper growth and development.

Omega-3 fats

These special fats may protect from heart disease and possibly aid in weight control. Omega-3 fats are found in fish, seafood, flaxseed and flax oil, walnuts and walnut oil, canola oil, soybeans, and tofu. Vegetarians who don't eat fish need to get small amounts of omega-3 fats from plant sources.

Protein

This nutrient is needed to build and repair all body tissues, including muscles, bones, skin, hair, and even nails. New protein is also needed to form enzymes, hormones, and antibodies. Many teenagers think that a vegetarian diet is one that avoids animal foods such as meat and chicken. That's true, but it's only half the story. Vegetarian diets are ones that derive their protein foods from plant sources—namely legumes and tofu and other soy products. Too often I've met teenagers who forget this point and follow a diet that lacks sufficient high-quality protein. A steady intake of pasta and tomato sauce, vegetable stir-fry, and bagels with cream cheese won't supply teenagers with the protein they need.

Vegetarians get protein from four main sources: dairy and eggs; beans, peas, lentils, and soy meats; nuts and seeds; and grains and cereals. Lacto and lacto-ovo vegetarians can consume dairy and eggs to supply some high-quality protein, while vegans must rely solely on plant foods.

Protein-rich foods supply the body with 20 amino acids, all of which are needed for good health. Eleven of these can be manufactured by your body and are called non-essential amino acids. The remaining 9, however, must be supplied by your diet because your body can't synthesize them on its own. They are called essential amino acids.

Anyone who explores a vegetarian diet will inevitably hear the terms "complete protein," "incomplete protein," and "complementary proteins." Animal foods such as meat, eggs, and dairy contain all nine essential amino acids and are therefore considered complete. Plant protein foods such as beans, nuts, and grains are missing or are low in one or more of the essential amino acids and are considered—as you probably guessed—incomplete. An exception to this is soy. Soybeans are unique because they contain all the amino acids needed to make a complete protein.

When two or more vegetarian protein foods are combined so that the essential amino acid missing from one is supplied by another, they are called complementary proteins. Here's a look at some good combinations:

COMPLEMENTARY VEGETARIAN PROTEINS

Food	Limiting Amino Acids	Food to Combine	Complete Protein Meal Ideas
Legumes and soybeans	Methionine	Grains, nuts, seeds	Tofu and brown rice stir-fry
Grains	Lysine, threonine	Legumes	Pasta with white kidney beans
Nuts and seeds	Lysine	Legumes	Hummus with tahini (sesame seed paste)
Vegetables	Methionine	Grains, nuts, seeds	Bok choy with cashews
Corn	Lysine, tryptophan	Legumes	Black bean and corn salad

Seems complicated, doesn't it? Fear not. There's no need to plan vegetarian meals with amino acid tables. We used to think that strict vegetarians needed to combine different plant proteins at meals so that the essential amino acid missing from one was supplied by another. Now we know that amino acids that don't form a complete protein survive in the body for 12 hours. As long as a variety of protein foods are eaten over the course of the day, there's no need to worry about combining different protein foods at every single meal.

So, when it comes to protein, vegetarian teens must ensure they are eating a protein-rich food at every meal. And variety is the key. A common mistake made by lacto-ovo vegetarian teenagers is relying on cheese as their protein food. These vegetarians miss out on important nutrients found in plant protein foods and they also consume too much saturated fat. Use the Vegetarian Food Guide on page 153 to plan protein-rich meals.

Vitamin B12

This vitamin plays a role in cell division, the nervous system, and the production of red blood cells. Here's the concern with vegetarian diets and B12: the vitamin is found only in animal foods (eggs, dairy, meat, poultry, fish) and fortified soy and rice beverages. That means that vegan teenagers must take extra care to ensure they are getting adequate vitamin B12. Vegetarians need to include three of the following sources in their daily diet: fortified soy or rice beverage (1/2 cup or 125 ml), nutritional yeast (1 tablespoon or 15 ml), fortified breakfast cereal (30 grams), fortified soy analog (soy-based "meat," such as TVP and veggie burgers) (1 1/2 ounces or 42 grams), milk (1/2 cup or 125 ml), yogurt (3/4 cup or 175 grams), or one large egg.

Vitamin D

Also called the sunshine vitamin (because our skin can make vitamin D when it's exposed to sunlight), this nutrient helps the body absorb more calcium from foods and deposit it in bones. The best food sources are fluid milk and many soy and rice beverages, as they're fortified with the vitamin (yogurt and cheese are not fortified with vitamin D). One cup (250 ml) of milk or enriched soy or rice beverage provides 100 international units of vitamin D—one-half of a teenager's daily recommended intake. Vitamin D is also added to margarine, but in very small amounts. Oily fish, egg yolks, and butter contain vitamin D naturally.

Lacto and lacto-ovo vegetarians can drink milk to get vitamin D. Vegans must get adequate vitamin D from daily sun exposure (not possible during the long winter in Canada), fortified foods, or a multivitamin supplement.

Calcium

This mineral is vital for building strong bones and teeth. And because most peak bone mass is achieved by the age of 18, teenagers have high daily calcium requirements (1300 milligrams per day). Getting too little calcium during the teen years can increase the risk of osteoporosis later in life. Calcium also helps muscles contract and relax, supports nerve function and blood clotting, and helps maintain healthy blood pressure. As well, research suggests that meeting daily calcium needs can help reduce many symptoms of premenstrual syndrome.

Vegetarian teens who eat dairy foods get calcium from milk, yogurt, and cheese. To meet the daily calcium target of 1300 milligrams, teenagers need to consume four dairy servings each day (1 cup/250 ml milk, 3/4 cup/175 grams yogurt, or 1 1/2 ounces/45 grams cheese equals one serving). Other calcium sources, which vegans rely on, include fortified soy or rice beverages, fortified fruit juice, almonds, soybeans, tofu, bok choy, broccoli, Swiss chard, kale, and figs.

You'll notice a calcium-rich food group in the Vegetarian Food Guide that appears later in the chapter. One serving from this food group supplies 100 to 150 milligrams of calcium. Vegetarian teens need at least 10 servings each day. Servings from the calcium food group also count toward servings from other food groups. For instance, 1/4 cup (50 ml) of almonds counts as a calcium serving and as a protein-rich food serving. One cup (250 ml) of calcium-enriched orange juice counts as two calcium-rich servings and two fruit servings.

Iron

This important mineral is needed to maintain the body's supply of hemoglobin, the component of red blood cells that carries oxygen to all body tissues. It's also used to make brain chemicals that help regulate the ability to concentrate and pay attention. In fact, studies have shown that adolescents who are iron deficient do not perform as well as those with adequate iron stores when tested on memory, math, and verbal learning. Iron is especially important for teenage girls, who need more of the mineral than boys because of menstruation. Iron deficiency may occur in up to 39% of teenage girls in Canada according to a recent review of Canadian data.[5]

How much iron do teenagers need each day? Here are the recommended dietary intakes (RDAs). The first entry in each age group is for teens with a non-vegetarian diet.

Age	RDA for Iron (milligrams)
Boys and girls, 9 to 13 years	8
Vegetarians	14
Boys, 14 to 18 years, non-vegetarian	11
Boys, 14 to 18, vegetarian	20
Boys, 19 years, non-vegetarian	8
Boys, 19 years, vegetarian	14
Girls, 14 to 18 years, non-vegetarian	15
Girls, 14 to 18 years, vegetarian	27
Girls, 19 years, non-vegetarian	18
Girls, 19 years, vegetarian	32

Here's a look at how foods contribute to your teen's daily iron intake:

IRON CONTENT OF SELECTED FOODS (MILLIGRAMS)

Food	mg	Food	mg
Apricots, dried, 6	2.8	Just Right, Kellogg's, 1 cup (250 ml)	6.0
All-Bran, Kellogg's, 1/2 cup (125 ml)	4.7	Kidney beans, 1/2 cup (125 ml)	2.5
All-Bran Buds, Kellogg's, 1/2 cup (125 ml)	5.9	Oatmeal, instant, 1 pouch	3.8
Beans in tomato sauce, 1 cup (250 ml)	5.0	Prune juice, 1/2 cup (125 ml)	5.0
Beef, lean, cooked, 3 oz (90 g)	3.0	Raisin Bran, 3/4 cup (175 ml)	5.5
Blackstrap molasses, 1 tbsp (15ml)	3.2	Shreddies, 3/4 cup (175 ml)	5.9
Bran flakes, 3/4 cup (175 ml)	4.9	Spinach, cooked, 1 cup (250 ml)	4.0
		Wheat germ, 1 tbsp (15 ml)	2.5

Source: *Nutrient Value of Some Common Foods*, table titled "Iron Content of Selected Foods," Health Canada (© 1999, reprint 2002). Reproduced with permission of the Minister of Public Works and Government Services Canada, 2005.

There are two types of iron in foods. Animal foods—meat, poultry, fish, and eggs—contain heme iron, a form that's well absorbed by the body. Semi-vegetarians, pesco-vegetarians, and lacto-ovo vegetarians will get a little heme iron from their diets. But vegetarians also rely on plant sources of iron, called non-heme iron. Vegans rely solely on foods that contain non-heme iron. Vegetarian sources of iron include legumes (chickpeas, black beans, kidney beans, baked beans, lentils), soybeans and tofu, soy meats (veggie burgers, veggie ground round, veggie dogs), nuts, seeds, leafy green vegetables, whole grains, enriched ready-to-eat breakfast cereals, raisins, figs, and blackstrap molasses.

Unfortunately, non-heme iron is not absorbed nearly as well as heme iron. It is for this reason that vegetarian teenagers have higher daily iron requirements than their meat-eating peers. The iron requirements of vegetarians are increased by a factor of 1.8 to ensure they get an adequate amount of iron from plant foods. The good news is that vegetarians can enhance the amount of iron that is absorbed from plant foods by eating iron-rich foods with vitamin C-rich foods. For example, eating dried apricots, a source of iron, with a glass of orange juice will boost iron intake. Vegetarians should include citrus fruits and juices, tomato, red pepper, and broccoli with meals to boost their body's iron uptake.

Cooked vegetables also provide more iron than their raw counterparts. That's because phytic acid (phytate), a naturally occurring compound in plant foods, binds to iron and prevents its absorption. Cooking vegetables releases some of the iron that's bound to these compounds.

Zinc

This mineral is essential for growth, sexual maturation, wound healing, and a healthy immune system. Vegans get zinc from nuts, legumes, whole grains, breakfast cereals, tofu, and soy meats. Lacto-ovo vegetarians get additional zinc from milk, yogurt, cheese, and eggs.

A Vegetarian Food Guide

Published in 2003, this food guide meets the nutrient needs of most people following different types of vegetarian diets. It has been modified to meet the protein and calcium needs of growing teenagers. The number of food servings in each food group is for minimum daily intakes. Physically active teenagers may choose more foods from any of the groups to meet their increased energy needs.

Food Group	Servings	Serving Size	Calcium-rich foods
			(10 servings per day)
Grains	6	Bagel, 1/4 Bread, 1 slice Cereal, cold flake, 3/4 cup (175 ml) Cereal, hot, 1/2 cup (125 ml) Corn, 1/2 cup (125 ml) Grains (e.g., rice, quinoa, bulgur), cooked, 1/2 cup (125 ml) Pasta, cooked, 1/2 cup (125 ml) Pita pocket, 1/2 Roll, large, 1/2	Calcium-fortified breakfast cereal (28 g)
Legumes, nuts, and other protein-rich foods	6	Egg, 1 Fish, 1 oz (28 g) Legumes, cooked, 1/2 cup (125 ml) Meat analog, 1 oz (28 g) Nut or seed butter, 2 tbsp (25 ml) Nuts, 1/4 cup (50 ml) Tofu or tempeh, 1/2 cup (125 ml)	Almond butter, 2 tbsp (25 ml) Almonds, 1/4 cup (50 ml) Cheese, 3/4 oz (21 g) Cow's milk or yogurt, 1/2 cup (125 ml) Soybeans, cooked, 1/2 cup (125 ml) Soy nuts, 1/4 cup (50 ml) Tahini, 2 tbsp (25 ml) Tempeh, 1/2 cup (125 ml) Tofu, calcium-set, 1/2 cup (125 ml)
Vegetables	4	Vegetable juice, 1/2 cup (125 ml) Veggies, cooked, 1/2 cup (125 ml) Veggies, raw, 1 cup (250 ml)	Bok choy, broccoli, collards, Chinese cabbage, kale, mustard greens, or okra, 1 cup cooked or 2 cups raw
Fruit	2	Fruit, cooked, 1/2 cup (125 ml) Fruit, diced, 1/2 cup (125 ml) Fruit, dried, 1/4 cup (50 ml) Fruit juice, 1/2 cup (125 ml)	Figs, 5 Fortified fruit juice, 1/2 cup (125 ml)
Fats	2	Avocado, 1/8 of medium-sized Margarine, soft, 1 tsp (5 ml) Mayonnaise, 1 tsp (5 ml) Olives, 5 large or 10 small Salad dressing, 2 tsp (10 ml) Vegetable oil, 1 tsp (5 ml)	

V. Messina, V. Melina, and A.R. Mangels. "A New Food Guide for North American Vegetarians." *Canadian Journal of Dietetic Practice and Research* 2003; 64(2): 82–86.

Do Vegetarian Teens Need Vitamin Supplements?

I strongly recommend that all vegetarian teenagers take a daily multivitamin and mineral supplement to help them meet the recommended intakes for B vitamins, vitamin D, iron, and zinc. (In fact, I recommend a multivitamin and mineral supplement for all teenagers, vegetarian or not.)

A multivitamin and mineral supplement won't provide all the iron and calcium teenagers need, and many won't provide a full day's zinc. Vegetarian females who are menstruating should look for a product that provides 15 to 18 milligrams of iron. In general, these are multivitamin and mineral supplements that are sold as women's formulas. Some women's multivitamins have extra calcium added, often at the expense of other nutrients. You can find a complete woman's multivitamin and mineral that contains all vitamins and minerals. Read labels carefully.

Teenagers who don't consume enough calcium-rich foods should take a separate calcium supplement with vitamin D added. Supplements made from calcium carbonate generally provide 500 milligrams of calcium and should be taken with meals; those made from calcium citrate offer 300 milligrams and can be taken anytime, even on an empty stomach. Since all calcium supplements are not 100% absorbed, higher doses should be divided over two or three meals. If your vegetarian daughter needs to supplement her diet with 1000 milligrams of calcium, have her take one 500-milligram calcium tablet with breakfast and another with dinner. Absorption from supplements is best in doses of 500 milligrams or less, as the percentage of calcium your body absorbs decreases as the amount in the supplement increases.

If teenagers don't eat three servings of vitamin B12 foods each day, they should take a daily B12 supplement of 5 to 10 micrograms, or a weekly B12 supplement of 2000 micrograms. Many multivitamin products contain 10 to 25 micrograms of vitamin B12, so it should not be hard for teenagers to get their B12 from a multivitamin.

Supplements definitely help vegetarian teenagers meet their daily nutrient needs. But thoughtful food choices remain essential to a healthy vegetarian diet.

Meal Planning Tips for Vegetarians

If teens want to take vegetarianism seriously, they need to share some of the responsibility for their new diet. Take them grocery shopping, read through vegetarian cookbooks together, and allow them to participate in cooking. Have your teens plan and prepare a weekly vegetarian dinner for the whole family.

It's not difficult to prepare meat-free meals. I'll bet some of the popular dishes you serve are already vegetarian. Others are easy to modify by replacing meat or chicken with beans, tofu, or soy meats. Just try not to rely too much on cheese. It does have protein and calcium, but it's high in saturated fat.

Quick Meal Ideas for Vegetarians

You'll find plenty of recipes for vegetarian breakfasts, lunches, dinners, and snacks in Part 4. In fact, I've highlighted the vegetarian and vegan dishes in the table of contents to the recipes. These recipes come from the Canadian Living Test Kitchen, so they're guaranteed to taste great. And they all take no more than 30 minutes to make. Here are a few more very quick meal ideas for busy teenagers on the fly:

- Baked potato topped with veggie chili or beans and cheese. For a boost of beta-carotene, use sweet potatoes. Vegans can use soy cheese in place of cheese made from cow's milk. Most brands provide four grams of protein and 40 milligrams of calcium per 3/4 ounce (21 grams).

- Pasta with tomato sauce and veggie ground round or veggie "meatballs." Some of my favourite soy products are made by Yves Veggie Cuisine. Try Yves Veggie Meatballs—a 2 ounce (60 gram) serving packs 13 grams of protein and only 2 grams of fat.

- Vegetable soup with added lentils or tofu for protein. One of my favourite meals is Soup's On Hot and Sour Soup (you'll find this company's soups sold in mason jars in the refrigerated section of your supermarket). I add chopped firm tofu and kale for a nutrient- and protein-packed meal.

- Black bean tacos. This is really simple. Just drain a can of black beans, put in a saucepan along with a teaspoon of chili powder and a dash of cumin (or use sodium-reduced taco seasoning mix if you prefer), and heat. Serve on soft whole-wheat or corn tortillas along with chopped tomatoes and green pepper, grated cheese, and salsa.

- Baked beans on whole-grain toast. Open a can of beans and tomato sauce, put in a saucepan, and heat. Serve on toast with grated cheese or a slice of soy cheese.

- Green or spinach salad topped with cooked lentils (buy canned lentils for convenience). Or add chopped cold tofu with added herbs for protein. Add a few walnuts for omega-3 fats and dress with oil and vinegar. Serve with a whole-grain roll or pita pocket.

- Omelette with tomatoes, roasted red peppers, and feta or soy cheese. Use omega-3 whole eggs to get more ALA (alpha-linolenic acid), an essential fatty acid (see Chapter 4). As a breakfast meal, serve with Yves Veggie Breakfast Patties.

- Veggie sandwich fillings: veggie cheese and tomato, egg salad with spinach leaves, peanut or almond butter with sliced pear or banana, hummus with coarsely chopped nuts, veggie soy slices and Romaine lettuce, mashed tofu with low-fat mayonnaise and chopped fresh parsley, avocado mashed with curry powder and lettuce, cream cheese with grated carrots and raisins.

Vegetarian Recipe Modifications

Vegan teenagers who like to cook may need to modify recipes and find alternatives to dairy, eggs, and meat-based products. Here are a few suggestions.

Instead of …	Use …
Butter	In baked goods, use canola oil
	When sautéing, use water, vegetable broth, or non-fat cooking spray
Buttermilk	Add 2 teaspoons (10 ml) of lemon juice per 1 cup (250 ml) of soy milk
Cheese	Soy cheese or nutritional yeast flakes
Cottage cheese	Crumbled tofu
Eggs	In baked goods, use 1 tablespoon (15 ml) ground flaxseed plus 3 tablespoons (50 ml) of water to replace one egg
Gelatin	Agar-agar, arrowroot, ground nuts and seeds
Mayonnaise	Tofu mayonnaise
Meat, chicken, or seafood stock	Apple, cranberry, or orange juice; miso diluted with water; vegetable stock; vegetable bouillon cubes; water in which pasta or beans have been cooked
Milk	Fortified soy milk, rice milk, or almond milk

Snack Ideas for Vegetarians

Hungry teenagers need to snack, and vegetarians are no exception. In Part 4, you'll find 18 ideas for healthy snacks. All are vegetarian, and some are vegan. Here are a few more:

- Chopped raw vegetables and tzatziki

- Breadsticks or mini pita pockets with hummus

- Baked tortilla chips with bean dip (try my recipe for Bean Spread on page 228)

- Dried apricots and almonds, peanuts, or walnuts

- Homemade trail mix—you'll find three recipes on pages 254–55

- Homemade smoothie or power shake. Make your own concoction from milk or soy milk, or use one of the recipes in this book.

- Tofu hot dog wrapped in a whole-wheat tortilla

- Low-fat muffins, cookies, or loaves. The recipes in this book can be made ahead and frozen. They're easy to throw in a backpack or defrost at home after school.

- Soy puddings, soy yogurts, soy shakes. Sold in the dairy case at the grocery stores, these are a convenient way to add extra protein and calories to a snack. Enjoy them on their own or eat them with a piece of fruit.

Eating at the School Cafeteria

Variety, planning, and support at home will help your teenager embark on a healthy vegetarian diet. But vegetarian teens also need support at school. And unfortunately, vegetarian meal options in the cafeteria are woefully lacking. Sure there's cheese pizza and macaroni and cheese. Aside from these being meals unsuitable for vegans, they are loaded with high-fat cheese, something other vegetarians don't need a steady intake of. And yes, there's pasta and tomato sauce served with a green salad, but where's the vegetarian protein? Where's the tofu and beans or soy-based veggie burgers?

I've talked with a number of vegetarian teenagers who agree it's a challenge to find healthy vegetarian lunches at school. When I ask teenage girls what they buy to eat, most say a slice of pizza, french fries, or a muffin. Others say they don't bother to eat in the cafeteria. Instead, they leave the school grounds to pick up a veggie sub or Chinese food at a local restaurant.

Ask your daughter what her lunch options are in the school cafeteria or the university dining hall. If the pickings are slim, encourage her to speak to the cafeteria food service director to make suggestions for more veggie meals. Most food service managers are happy to expand their offerings as long as they know students will eat what they serve. Students may need to educate the food services manager about appropriate meal ideas and food companies that supply vegetarian foods, such as soy products.

Giving up meat can be healthy for teenagers if it's done with guidance and care. Moving toward a vegetarian diet presents teenagers with the opportunity to develop lifelong healthy eating habits. Encourage your son or daughter to learn more about vegetarianism. The websites listed in the Resources section of this book will help get him started.

Leslie's Tips for Vegetarian Teens

1. Teenagers who follow a vegan diet must ensure they consume adequate calories each day by adding foods such as avocado, nuts, seeds, and dried fruit to their diet.

2. Vegetarian teens should include a protein-rich food at each meal. Good choices include beans; tofu, tempeh, and other soy products; and nuts and seeds (as well as fish, dairy, and eggs for non-vegans).

3. To ensure adequate calcium intake, vegetarian teens should consume 10 servings of calcium-rich foods per day. Teens who don't get enough calcium from their diets need to take a calcium supplement with vitamin D added.

4. To boost iron intake from plant foods, vegetarians should include a source of vitamin C at meals—citrus fruit and juices, tomato juice, kiwi, strawberries, broccoli, cabbage, or bell peppers are good options.

5. To ensure an adequate intake of vitamin B12, vegan teens must include fortified soy or rice beverages (1 3/4 cups or 375 ml), nutritional yeast (1 tablespoon or 15 ml), or fortified cereal (1 ounce or 30 grams) in their daily diets. Other vegetarians will get B12 from dairy products and eggs.

6. To get healthy omega-3 fats, vegetarian teenagers must include fish and seafood, flax oil, canola oil, walnuts, soybeans, or tofu in their diets.

7. Consult the Vegetarian Food Guide on page 153 to help plan nutritious and balanced meals.

8. Vegetarian teenagers should supplement their diet with a daily multivitamin and mineral to help meet nutrient needs.

9. If vegetarian meals are missing in the school cafeteria or university dining hall, encourage your teen to discuss meals options with the food services manager.

10. Consult a registered dietitian (www.dieitians.ca) to help your son or daughter learn about vegetarian nutrition and plan balanced meals.

9

—⚬⚬⚬—

Weight Control Strategies
for Teens

I f you're concerned about your child's weight, you're not alone. Over the past 20 years, the prevalence of overweight and obesity in youth has risen dramatically. Today it's estimated that one-third of Canadian kids aged 9 to 13 years are overweight and 10% are obese. In 1981, only 11% of boys and 13% of girls were considered overweight, and 2% of boys and girls were obese.[1]

There's good reason to be concerned if your teenager has a weight problem. Being overweight increases the risk of a number of health problems, and teenagers are no exception. These days, we're constantly bombarded with news stories about the increase in high blood pressure, high cholesterol, type-2 diabetes, and sleep apnea among over-weight and obese children. What's more, obese kids are more likely to turn into obese adults.

Many experts feel that the most significant consequences of obesity in youth are the social and psychological problems it creates. Being overweight generates stress for teenagers, lowers their self-esteem, and affects their relationships with peers. Teenagers are extremely reliant on their peers for support, identity, and self-esteem. Being picked on or ridiculed because of his or her weight can be destructive to a teenager's social development. A recent study of 5746 Canadian adolescents found that overweight teens were more likely to be bullies or victims of bullying.[2]

Encourage your teen to assess her body weight by calculating her body mass index (BMI) and then plotting it on a growth chart. You'll find the tools you need to do this in Chapter 1, pages 23–24. The BMI-for-age will tell your teen if she is underweight, overweight, or at risk of becoming overweight.

So what's a concerned parent to do with an overweight teenager? Weight loss is a tricky topic. Teenagers are sensitive about their appearance. Being overweight is hard for kids and can make them feel lonely, an outcast among their peers. The last thing that overweight teens want to hear is their parents nagging them to lose weight, even though it's only natural for parents to worry and want to do something to help their teen be fit and healthy. This chapter offers plenty of strategies to help teenagers successfully manage their weight over the long term. You'll also find advice for parents to promote healthy attitudes about food and fitness in kids.

Should Overweight Teens Go on a Diet?

Dieting to lose weight is common among teenagers. The desire to be thin or have well-toned muscles is widespread among teens, just like it is among adults. While dieting is more common among girls, recent evidence suggests that weight concerns are increasing among boys.

If your teenage son or daughter is overweight, embarking on a restrictive diet to lose excess pounds is *not* recommended. In fact, it may even be counterproductive, causing teenagers to gain more weight over time. The Growing Up Today Study followed 15,000 American girls and boys, aged 9 to 14, for two years. Over the course of the study, the researchers found that the preteens and teens who dieted frequently actually gained more weight than kids who didn't diet.[3] Another study from the University of Texas followed 692 teenage girls for four years and found that the dieters were three times more likely to become overweight than the non-dieters.[4]

There are three reasons why dieting might lead to overweight. For starters, drastically cutting back on the number of calories you consume can result in a slower resting metabolism (the amount of calories a person burns at rest). Over time, people who diet may require fewer calories to maintain their weight because their bodies burn off fewer calories to maintain vital body functions such as heart rate, brain function, and breathing. People on restrictive diets often lose muscle along with body fat. Since muscle burns more calories than fat, a sluggish metabolism can result.

Weight gain may also be the result of a restrictive diet that's impossible to follow for an extended period. Feeling deprived can lead to bouts of overeating and binge eating. Studies show that dieters are more likely than non-dieters to binge eat. Repeated cycles of dieting and overeating can definitely lead to weight gain. Finally, the composition of a diet can also lead to greater weight gain. Low-fat diets that contain plenty of refined, processed carbo-hydrate foods—bagels, cereal bars, fat-free muffins, and so on—can trigger hunger, making a person more likely to overeat.

There are other reasons why teenagers should not follow a restrictive eating plan to lose weight. Low-calorie diets can rob growing teenagers of the energy and nutrients they need to stay healthy and energetic. For instance, low-carb weight loss plans that eliminate entire food groups deprive teenagers of iron and calcium, increasing the risk for anemia and osteoporosis later in life. Restricting food and nutrient intake for an extended time during the teen years can also stunt growth. Crash diets followed over a long period can delay breast development in females and muscle growth in males. Restrictive diets can also lead to irregular menstrual periods in teenage girls.

Dieting can make teenagers feel tired, moody, and anxious. And worse, it can cause low self-esteem. Self-esteem is defined, in part, by successes and failures. Unsuccessful dieting can negatively impact a teenager's self-worth. One of the more worrisome issues of teenage dieting is its relationship to disordered eating and eating disorders. Studies show that dieting is associated with a 5- to 18-fold increased risk of developing an eating disorder.[5] Whether the process of dieting causes the illness or represents the first stage of an eating disorder is not yet clear. But studies do show that many high school students who diet to control their weight adopt unsafe practices, including vomiting, using laxatives, and taking supplements.[6]

Popular Fad Diets

Many teenagers will try to follow a diet at least once. That goes for both teenagers who are overweight and those who are at a healthy weight. With the media's constant focus on dieting and diet books, it's only natural that some teens will wonder whether they need to go on a diet themselves. Not surprisingly, females tend to be more worried about fat and calories than their male counterparts. When I asked 1046 Canadian high school students if they had been on a diet to lose weight in the past year, 26% of teens said yes, and among the dieters, almost 75% were girls. Interestingly, only 6% said they had tried a fad diet—be it Atkins, South Beach, or the Zone.

Here's what you and your teenager need to know about popular diets before embarking on any program.

Dr. Atkins' New Diet Revolution

This plan, developed by Robert C. Atkins, M.D., restricts carbohydrates (e.g., starchy foods, fruits, and dairy products) and focuses on eating mostly protein and fats, and taking vitamin and mineral supplements. The premise is that following a low-carb diet will reduce your appetite and lower your blood sugar and insulin levels, thereby helping your body burn more fat for energy.

Does it help you lose weight permanently? So far, two studies have shown that Atkins dieters experience greater weight loss in the first six months, compared with a traditional low-fat, calorie-reduced diet. But after one year, there was no difference in weight loss between the two diets. Is it healthy? No. The diet includes foods that are high in saturated fat—butter, cream, cheese, and fatty meats. It drastically limits healthier foods, including whole grains, fruits, vegetables, and calcium-rich dairy products. We don't know about its long-term health effects beyond one year.

The low-carb craze is waning in popularity, but many adults still follow such weight-loss diets. When a parent follows a special diet, it can have an impact on other family members. Some of my teenage clients have told me they tried a low-carb diet after noticing how much weight a parent had lost. Teenagers should not be following a low-carb diet. The Atkins diet can be unhealthy for growing teens, even for those who are overweight. Teenagers have higher nutrient needs than do adults and these diets are just too restrictive.

Growing teenagers need more calcium than adults and their tissues need vitamins and minerals that come from fruits, vegetables, and grains. It's impossible for teens to meet their daily nutrient requirements on a diet that eliminates entire food groups such as fruit, grains, and dairy products. The bottom line is this: following a low-carb diet can affect a teenager's growth and development.

Following a low-carb diet might also hinder a teen's academic performance. Besides robbing the body of key nutrients, low-carb eating plans can impact thinking ability. When the body does not get carbohydrate, it draws its energy from ketones, a by-product that results from breaking down body fat. Ketones have a dulling effect on the brain and reduce alertness.

The South Beach Diet

Like the Atkins diet, this plan, devised by Arthur Agaston, M.D., eliminates foods that increase blood sugar. It consists of three phases, the first being a restrictive two-week phase that bans starches, fruits, sweet vegetables, and dairy products. The second phase reintroduces good carbs, those that have a low glycemic index value (see Chapter 2) and cause blood sugar levels to rise gradually instead of quickly. The third phase is less restrictive, allowing you to eat pretty much anything in moderation. The rationale is that by avoiding foods that quickly elevate your blood sugar, you'll lose weight, reduce your appetite, and lower your risk of heart disease.

Does it work over the long term? No studies have been done to show that this diet helps people keep the weight off once they've lost it. Is it healthy? It does score points for emphasizing protein foods that are low in saturated fat. It also promotes whole grains over refined starchy foods. The first phase is very restrictive, but the foods allowed in phase two and three are healthy. However, because of the restrictive nature of phase one, the South Beach diet, like the Atkins diet, can be unhealthy for growing teens, even for those who are overweight. Again, teenagers should *not* be following a low-carb diet.

The GI (Glycemic Index) Diet

This diet, designed by Rick Gallop, promises weight loss by eating low glycemic index (GI) foods, called green light foods, and avoiding high GI foods (red light foods). The theory? In short, high GI foods—white rice, white bread, sugary desserts, and so on—are rapidly digested and converted to blood sugar. This speedy process leads to fat storage, low energy levels, and hunger. The plan emphasizes meat, poultry, and dairy products that are lower in fat and starchy foods made from whole grains. Is it effective for weight loss?

There is some research to suggest that a diet based on low GI foods can help overweight teenagers eat less food. But so far there's no evidence that a diet based on low GI foods can cause permanent weight loss. That said, this diet is based on healthy foods and it is simple to follow—no measuring cups or calorie counters needed.

The Zone

This plan by Barry Sears, Ph.D., promotes a "balanced" approach, advocating that meals and snacks consist of 40% protein, 30% carbohydrate, and 30% fat. By eating the right amount of protein, carbohydrate, and fat "blocks" at meals, followers will burn more body fat, increase mental energy, and perform at their physical peak (a.k.a. the Zone).

Does it help lose pounds? Sure it does. But like most diets, weight loss is likely to do with eating fewer calories rather than with some magic combination of protein, carbohydrate, and fat. Is it healthy? The Zone diet promotes healthy foods: low-fat protein, whole grains, fruits, vegetables, and healthy fats. But it's too low in calories and calcium for growing teenagers. And this plan is complicated to follow. Most teenagers won't want to be bothered constantly measuring portions of food and counting "blocks."

"The Ultimate Weight Loss Solution for Teens: The 7 Keys to Weight Freedom"

This plan by Jay McGraw, outlined in the book of the same name, is a softer version of Dr. Phil's *Ultimate Weight Loss Solution* (Dr. Phil is Jay's dad). It's based on the notion that there are seven keys to achieve permanent weight loss, including right thinking, healing feelings, and mastery over impulse eating. McGraw divides foods into two categories:

low-response, low-yield foods and high-response, high-yield foods. The diet advice encourages what the author calls high-response, high-yield nutrition, foods that are nutrient-packed and take more time to prepare and eat. It's no surprise what these foods are—namely fruits and vegetables, legumes, low-fat meats, poultry, and whole grains.

Does it work to help weight loss? It's difficult to say. Although the foods emphasized are generally healthy, the book provides little concrete advice on how to actually implement the nutrition information. Perhaps most valuable are its behaviour modification strategies. However, some have criticized the book for using recycled tips that have been around for decades and offering unrealistically simplistic solutions to tackle overweight and obesity.

10 Weight Loss Strategies for Teens

As you can see, few of today's popular diets offer a long-term solution for teenagers who need to lose weight. Indeed, several shortchange growing teenagers of important nutrients and energy. And some cause kids to become preoccupied with foods by tracking calories or counting grams of carbohydrate or fat. Weight management is about long-term success. It's about losing weight at a safe pace and keeping the pounds off for good. Weight loss will be more successful and lasting if teenagers make permanent changes to their food and exercise habits.

In my private practice, I have helped many overweight teenagers lose weight. The advice I offer teenagers is not much different from what I tell adults. Current dietary guidelines such as "reduce saturated and trans fats" and "consume more fibre" are relevant for both adolescents and adults. There are, of course, a few exceptions, since teenage eating habits are usually quite different from those of their parents. When it comes to developing a food plan for my teenage clients, the difference lies in translating those nutrition strategies into a meal plan that's practical for teenage life and one that contains all the energy, calcium, and iron that growing teens need.

The following strategies will help overweight teenagers manage their weight. Some may be more relevant than others, depending on your son or daughter's eating habits. Start with strategies that are likely to make the biggest impact with the least effort. The secret to weight loss success is to make changes gradually—indeed, some changes may be barely noticeable.

1. Set Goals and Track Progress: Keep a Food and Fitness Diary

A common characteristic of highly successful people is that they are goal-oriented. Successful people know what they want to achieve in life, and they have a clear plan to get there. And most often, these goals are written down on paper. Written goals provide focus, clarity, and direction; enhance motivation; and bolster self-confidence. As teenagers observe the progress they are making toward achieving their goals, they'll be more confident in their ability to do so.

Goals need to be realistic, specific, and measurable. Encourage your teen to write down three nutrition or fitness goals that he or she would like to achieve. It's important that goals be written in positive terms. Goals should tell you what you are going to do, instead of what you're not going to do. Rather than saying, "I'm not going to eat cookies while watching television," express the goal in a positive way, for example, "I am going to eat a piece of fruit or a serving of yogurt if I feel like snacking."

A realistic goal for weight loss is losing one to two pounds (0.5 to 1 kilogram) per week. Some teenagers prefer to set goals that don't involve the bathroom scale; for example, going down one pant size in three months. Small and realistic goals are easier to achieve and, as a result, they're more motivating.

After your teenager has written his list of goals, he should choose one goal to work on first. Once he feels that he has mastered that one, he can move on to his next goal. Trying to tackle too much too soon can be overwhelming, so set small goals, which are more easily accomplished.

As your teen transforms his eating habits, I strongly recommend that he keep a food and fitness diary to track his progress. Many studies have shown that keeping a food diary is linked to weight loss success. Teenagers should document what times they eat, the foods eaten and approximate portion sizes, and their hunger level before eating. It's also a good idea for teens to use a food diary to monitor how they're feeling before they eat—bored, stressed, depressed, happy, or neutral. Teens should also track their daily exercise—gym class at school, team sport practices and games, bike rides, and other workouts.

A food diary helps keep people focused on and committed to their goals. It highlights in black and white the foods they are eating and the foods they are not eating. Writing down what you eat will make you think twice about going back for seconds at dinner or eating a bag of potato chips with lunch. Often, the extra calories we consume are from mindless eating. We don't pay attention to what we are putting in our mouths because we are always in a hurry or we're distracted. A food diary can provide a huge amount of self-awareness. It may highlight that your teenager doesn't eat enough fruit or vegetables or skips breakfast. It may also reveal emotions or behaviours that trigger overeating.

The best way for teenagers to track their progress is to review their food and fitness diary. If they are doing all the right things, weight loss will follow. But teenagers may also track their progress by weighing themselves once every one or two weeks. They should also measure their height every few months. Just because the number on the scale doesn't change doesn't mean the teen has not lost body fat. I have counselled many teenage boys who have grown a good few inches during a short period. It's motivating to see that they're getting taller and their weight has not changed. This means they are getting taller and slimmer. Teenagers should also record their body measurements once per month, especially their waist size. It's extremely encouraging to see these numbers change over time.

2. Eat Four to Five Times Per Day, Starting with Breakfast

The next step is for your teen to eat regularly during the day to fuel his brain and muscles. Eating at regular intervals also prevents overeating at meals. Skipping meals in an effort to save calories and lose weight almost always backfires because inevitably, you end up overeating at the next meal. The amount of calories you eat in one sitting relates to the amount of time that has elapsed since you last ate. The best way to control appetite in an effort to eat less is to eat more often during the day. Believe it or not, you'll consume fewer calories if you *don't* skip meals. Instead of devouring three big meals, people who have successfully lost weight eat more often. Spreading out their food keeps their stomach always partly full and prevents overeating at any one time.

Researchers believe that our bodies' sugar-clearing hormone, insulin, is somehow responsible for appetite control. Eating smaller quantities of food more often results in a prolonged elevated, but not maximal, insulin level, and this seems to reduce appetite.

Eating more often during the day is also associated with a steady metabolism, whereas stockpiling a day's worth of calories into two meals may cause the body to store more food as energy. Studies show that animals that gorge and eat periodic loads of foods absorb more carbohydrate from a meal, make more fat from glucose, produce more cholesterol in the liver, and store more body fat.

We've known since the 1960s that a strong relationship exists between eating frequency and body weight. Studies conducted in men and school-aged children found that infrequent eaters were more likely to be overweight and have more body fat.[7] Since then, a few studies have linked eating frequently with leanness. Japanese researchers gave 12 competitive boxers a 1200-calorie weight loss diet either as two meals per day or six meals per day. After two weeks, they found that while there was no difference in the amount of weight lost between the two groups, the frequent eaters lost more body fat and preserved more muscle mass.[8]

And there's another benefit to starting the day with breakfast. Studies have demonstrated that eating breakfast improves thinking power later in the morning. It certainly seems that breakfast skippers are at a disadvantage when it comes to mental performance. Studies show that compared with their peers who eat breakfast, teenagers who skip the morning meal make more errors and have slower memory recall on psychological tests.[9] Breakfast foods such as cereal, whole-grain bread, fruit, and milk are full of carbohydrates that supply glucose, or energy, to the brain. A steady supply of glucose is critical for mental tasks that require memory.

Teenagers should eat three meals plus two snacks daily, starting with breakfast. Breakfast should always include whole grains, a source of calcium (milk, yogurt, fortified soy milk), and fruit. These foods will boost a teenager's intake of fibre, iron, B vitamins, and, of course, calcium. Breakfast can also contain a little bit of protein or fat. A hardboiled egg, cottage cheese, or a tablespoon of peanut butter all give the carbohydrate eaten at breakfast additional staying power.

BEST BREAKFASTS

Whole-grain cereal with low-fat milk or calcium-fortified soy milk, 1 piece of fruit

Whole-grain toast, 1 tbsp (15 ml) nut butter, 1 apple, 3/4 cup (175 grams) low-fat yogurt

Small homemade low-fat bran muffin, 1 ounce (30 grams) low-fat cheese, 1 piece of fruit

Two slices whole-grain toast, 1 poached egg, 1 small skim or 1% milk latte, 1 fruit serving

Oatmeal with raisins, low-fat milk or calcium-fortified soy milk, 6 almonds

WORST BREAKFASTS

Fast food sandwiches (McDonald's Bacon, Egg and Cheese McGriddle packs 550 calories and 21 grams of fat)

Fatty sweets such as store-bought muffins, Danish pastries, cinnamon buns, scones, donuts, and coffee cake. (Most muffins and donuts pack 4 teaspoons' [20 ml] worth of fat, much of it artery-clogging trans fat. And large cinnamon buns can tip the scale at 700 calories. Even a Starbucks scone provides 500 calories.)

Kellogg's Nutri-Grain Bar. (Sure these are low in fat, and they do have some vitamins and minerals. But they lack fibre and real fruit, and they'll leave you feeling still hungry.)

Bagel with cream cheese. (Yes, it's one of the easiest breakfasts to grab on the go. The problem is that bagels are large. One bagel equals four to six slices of bread. And the generous portion of cream cheese that the bagel is usually topped with offers little calcium and is loaded with saturated fat.)

No breakfast at all.

Often breakfast is eaten on the run, or grabbed on the way out the door. Here are some ideas for breakfast on the go:

- 2 tablespoons (25 ml) of hummus or 1 tablespoon (15 ml) of peanut butter on half a whole-grain bagel

- Half a whole-wheat pita pocket stuffed with cottage cheese and fruit

- Smoothie made with low-fat milk or soy milk, frozen berries, and half a banana

- 3/4 cup (175 grams) low-fat yogurt, a piece of fruit, and a low-fat granola bar or Kellogg's All-Bran Bar

- Homemade trail mix—spoon-sized shredded wheat, whole-grain flakes, raisins, dried cranberries, and nuts. Plus a yogurt or small latte for calcium.

- 1 tablespoon (15 ml) of nut butter or tahini spread on a whole-wheat tortilla and then wrapped around a small banana

For optimal energy levels, teenagers should aim to eat every three to four hours. For most teens, this means planning for at least one midday snack. If your child eats breakfast at 7:30 a.m. and doesn't sit down to lunch until noon, he needs a snack around 10:00 a.m. And, unless he eats a late lunch (e.g., 2:00 p.m.), he definitely needs an after-school snack (between 3:30 and 4:30 p.m.). For teenagers who exercise after school, snacks provide a source of fuel for working muscles.

There are a few simple guidelines to remember when choosing snacks. First, plan ahead. Snacks eaten on impulse tend to be high in fat and sugar. Teenagers should bring snacks to school or eat something as soon as they get home in the afternoon. Second, snacks should provide carbohydrate for an immediate source of energy for the brain, protein to help maintain blood sugar level for a longer time, and a little fat to slow digestion and absorption of carbohydrate, giving the snack more staying power. Choose snacks with a low glycemic index value (see Chapter 2). This means the carbohydrate in the snack gets digested slowly, leading to a gradual rise in blood sugar. The energy from the snack lasts longer, making you feel full and satisfied longer. A snack also should provide 150 to 200 calories for girls and 200 to 250 calories for boys. And finally, pay particular attention to fruit, vegetables, and calcium-rich snacks: these are the foods and nutrients that many teens are lacking in meals; including them as snacks helps boost their intake.

Six Power Snacks for Teenagers

Power snacks are snacks that include carbohydrate for energy, plus a little protein and fat to help regulate, or release, that energy. They also include important nutrients such as iron and calcium that growing teenagers need. For this reason, they make great between-meal snacks.

Energy bars When it comes to snacks, many energy bars do have an edge over candy because they're lower in fat and sugar. Research has also shown that certain types of energy bars can help keep blood sugar levels stable, something candy can't do. Most energy bars provide 200 to 250 calories and they have added vitamins and minerals. However, energy bars are not all created equal. Avoid bars containing palm kernel oil and partially hydrogenated vegetables oil. Instead, choose a bar with 180 to 225 calories, 20 to 25 grams carbohydrate, and 10 to 15 grams protein.

Instant bean soup Instant bean soups are great—they take only five minutes to make. All you need to do is fill the kettle with water and plug it in. Bean soups offer low glycemic carbohydrate, protein, and plenty of fibre, so that teens feel satiated. Try PC Blue Menu Instant Black Bean Soup, at 240 calories, 45 grams carbohydrate, 10 grams protein, and 1 gram fat.

Whole-grain cereal and milk What teenager doesn't like cereal? And it's a healthy snack provided that teens limit their portion size and choose the right cereal. You've got carbohydrate and fibre from whole grains, plus protein and more carbohydrate from the low-fat milk. The milk also helps replace fluids. As well, the fibre content of cereal can keep a teenager's blood sugar level on an even keel, helping him feel full longer. Choose a cereal with at least 4 to 5 grams of fibre per serving (Rice Krispies would not be a good choice). A 3/4 cup (175 ml) serving of whole-grain cereal plus 1 cup (250 ml) 1% milk provide 200 to 250 calories, 30 to 45 grams carbohydrates, 12 grams protein, and 3.4 grams fat.

Hummus and baby carrots Legumes are low GI foods, releasing their energy slowly and keeping energy levels stable. Legumes also supply energy-boosting carbohydrate and protein. The chickpeas in hummus are part of a great power snack: 2 tablespoons (25 ml) hummus plus 10 baby carrots provide 105 calories, 14 grams carbohydrate, 3 grams protein, and 3.5 grams fat. Teenage boys can double the serving size.

Plain almonds and V8 juice Here you get the carbohydrate from vegetable juice, and the protein and fat from almonds. Almonds are a low GI food that provide a source of healthy monounsaturated fat, which can help lower cholesterol levels. Snack on 12 ounces (355 ml) of V8 juice plus 15 plain, unsalted almonds to get 174 calories, 20 grams carbohydrates, 6 grams protein, 9 grams fat. Teenage girls should stick to 10 almonds.

Cheese string (part-skim) and a piece of fruit This snack is portable and portion controlled. The low-fat cheese string provides protein and a little fat, and fruit—an apple, pear or orange, for example—provides low glycemic carbohydrates. An alternative would be a piece of fruit with a 3/4 cup (175 gram) container of low-fat yogurt or a small skim-milk latte. One medium-sized apple plus two low-fat cheese strings (42 grams) provide 190 calories, 20 grams carbohydrates, 6 grams protein, and 4 grams fat. Teenage girls should have only one cheese string, rather than two.

3. Eat More Meals Prepared at Home, and Choose Healthier Fast Food Options

Today teenagers are busier than ever. School, sports, extracurricular activities, and part-time jobs mean that they will often miss meals at home. But if teens are heading to fast food joints for their meals, weight control can be challenging. Researchers from the Children's Hospital in Boston and the University of Minnesota studied 26 over-weight teens and 28 healthy-weight teens, aged 13 to 17 years. As part of the study, teens visited a food court, where they were served an extra-large fast food meal, and were told they could eat as much as they wanted in a one-hour period. The researchers then calculated how many calories the teenagers ate. The teenagers were also telephoned four times, on different days, and asked to recall their food intake and exercise in the previous 24 hours.

Compared with healthy-weight teenagers, those who were overweight consumed more calories at the food court. They also consumed 490 calories more on days they ate fast food than on days they didn't (that figure is based on the phone interviews, and what the overweight teens recalled their food intake to be in the previous 24-hour period). Healthy-weight teens ate the same number of calories each day, whether they ate fast food or not.[10] This suggests that compared to healthy-weight teenagers, overweight teens eat more calories from fast food when given carte blanche and are less likely to compensate for those extra calories. Other research has also linked eating more meals away from home with overweight among teens. Such eating habits contribute to higher calorie, fat, and sugar intakes.[11]

Encourage your teen to pack snacks and sandwiches to take to study groups, sports practices, and part-time jobs. If this isn't practical, speak to her about making healthy choices at the food court or fast food restaurants (you'll find plenty of tips in Chapter 7).

4. Cut Out Sugary Drinks

It's no surprise that studies have linked consumption of sugary beverages with obesity in kids.[12] In one study of children aged 6 to 13 years who attended a day camp, those who drank more than 12 ounces (355 ml) of sugary beverages per day consumed more calories, including those from the sugary beverages, and were more likely to gain weight by the end of camp than kids who drank less than 12 ounces (355 ml). What's more, these children also tended to drink less milk and consume less protein, calcium, magnesium, and vitamin A.[13]

Research suggests that we don't register—physically and mentally—liquid calories. They don't fill us up or put the brakes on our appetite as well as solid foods do. Scientists from the Department of Foods and Nutrition at Purdue University in Indiana gave people 450 calories' worth of either jelly beans or soda every day for four weeks. When people ate the jelly beans, they compensated by eating 450 fewer calories from other foods. When they consumed the sugary drink, the study participants didn't compensate—they ended up eating an extra 450 calories each day for one month. Not surprisingly, their weight climbed significantly over the study period.[14] It seems that liquid calories add on to, rather than displace, food calories. While it's easy to think twice about an extra 400 or 500 calories in food, people tend not to question the hidden calories in an extra-large bottle of fruit juice or cola.

And boy, have portion sizes of sweetened drinks gotten bigger. A kid's-sized soft drink at Wendy's provides 10 ounces (296 ml) of sugary beverage—that's 30% more than the fast food soft drink served in the 1950s. Wendy's Biggie soft drink weighs in at 16 ounces (473 ml) and almost 14 teaspoons (70 ml) of sugar. A large Fruitopia at McDonald's is 24 ounces (730 ml) and packs 23 teaspoons (115 ml) of sugar.

Teenagers don't have to eliminate pure unsweetened fruit juice from their diets, but they do need to limit their intake to no more than one small serving (3/4 cup or 175 ml) per day. Ounce for ounce, fruit juice has just as many calories as soft drinks. In this case, the calories are from naturally occurring sugars in fruit instead of refined sugars and syrups. But sugar supplies four calories per gram, regardless of the type of sugar. The bottom line: too much fruit juice can contribute to weight problems. Here are a few strategies to help teenagers reduce their intake of liquid calories:

- When ordering a sugary drink (if you must), ask for the kids' or small size. You'll get less sugar and fewer calories.

- Get an empty cup and split a sugary beverage with a friend. If free refills are part of the deal, ask for water instead of a pop refill.

- Don't have a high-calorie beverage as a snack to stave off hunger before a meal. It won't curb your appetite as well as solid food. Instead, try my power snack ideas listed earlier in the chapter, on page 168.

- Encourage your teen to drink water, tea, milk, soy milk, and vegetable juices instead of high-calorie sugar drinks.

- Opt for diet soft drinks over regular pop. But if teenagers guzzle caffeinated diet soda all day, they may experience anxiousness, irritability, and insomnia.

- Ask your teen to read the Nutrition Facts box the next time she chooses a bottle of juice or fruit drink at the corner store or school cafeteria. She might be surprised to see that many of the large bottles (16 ounce or 473 ml) of fruit drinks contain at least two servings. Most people assume that they're drinking one serving, regardless of the size of bottle.

5. Downsize Portions

It's important for teenagers to assess how much food they are eating. Paying attention to portion sizes can be a surefire way to shear off excess fat, sodium, and calories. Believe it or not, many people don't know what constitutes a serving size, partly because we've become so used to eating super-sized portions. When we eat a food, our portion often exceeds what's considered an official Food Guide serving. Research has shown that when people consume french fries, they eat almost two and a half servings at a time (10 french fries equals a Food Guide serving of potatoes). With baked potatoes, most people eat at least two or three servings at a meal. And with pasta, most people consume about three or four servings in one sitting.[15]

You'll see from the Canada Food Guide shown in Chapter 1 that the recommended number of servings from each food group is given as a range of servings. Overweight teens should choose the lower number of servings in each food group. You'll also find a list of foods and their serving sizes.

I strongly recommend that teenagers measure food portions to see what 3/4 cup (175 ml) of cereal, 1/2 cup (125 ml) of rice, 1 cup (250 ml) of pasta, and 3 ounces (90 grams) of meat looks like, or how 2 tablespoons (25 ml) of salad dressing covers a salad. They don't have to measure out food portions forever. But it's a wise idea to do so every once in a while since portion sizes can easily creep up. Here are a few tricks to help the whole family practice portion-size control:

- *Buy small packages of food.* Bonus-sized boxes of cookies, crackers, pretzels, and potato chips may be a deal at Costco, but they encourage overeating. If you resist the more-for-less way of thinking, you'll end up eating less.

- *Serve smaller portions at mealtime.* If you sit down to a plate overflowing with food, chances are good that you'll finish it. Most of us have a tendency to clear our plates, a habit rooted in childhood.

- *Use smaller plates.* A few of my clients find this trick really works. Instead of filling a large dinner plate with food, they serve less food on a luncheon-sized plate. Less food, but the plate still looks full.

- *Plate your snacks.* Never snack straight out of the bag, as you won't get a sense of how much food you're eating. It just doesn't register, and people usually end up eating more than they should. Whether your snack is crackers and low-fat cheese, popcorn, or baked tortilla chips and salsa, measure out your portion and put it on a plate.

- *Read the Nutrition Facts box.* Studies have shown that people who look at labels generally look at calories—they don't look at the serving sizes. But you should not assume that larger food packages yield one serving. Check the label to see how many servings one package contains.

- *Slow your pace.* Have a smaller portion of food, and savour it. Keep in mind that it takes 20 minutes to get the message to your brain that you've had enough. After each bite, put down your knife and fork and chew your food thoroughly. Avoid distractions such as watching television or reading while eating.

6. Don't Ban Favourite Foods—Plan a Weekly Treat

It's very important that teens trying to lose weight allow themselves to indulge in their favourite treat once a week. For some, this means a bowl of ice cream, a Starbucks Frappuccino, or a chocolate bar. For others it might be an order of french fries, cheesy nachos, or chicken wings. A weekly treat should be part of any weight loss plan, and teenagers should not feel guilty about eating it. A weekly splurge won't make a difference in one's weight loss progress. In fact, it can help teenagers stick to their healthy eating plan because they won't feel deprived of their favourite foods. Dietary changes need to be sustainable. Can you really see your teenager giving up sweets or french fries for good?

7. Get in Touch with Hunger and Satiety

Ideally, you should eat when you feel hungry. This is when your stomach is growling, telling you it needs food. But stomach hunger shouldn't be confused with mouth hunger, the desire to eat a food because it will taste good. Eating in response to how good your food looks or smells has to do with your appetite, not your hunger. If you're out of touch with how hunger feels to you, eat according to schedule for the next two weeks. Eat breakfast, lunch, and dinner at approximately the same time each day. You'll find that you will start to feel hungry before your meals.

Pay attention to your hunger signals and let them dictate how much you eat. When you sit down to a meal, rate your hunger on a scale of 1 to 10, 1 being so full you couldn't possibly eat another bite and 10 being ravenously hungry. Halfway through your meal, rate your hunger again. Let your score tell you whether it's time to stop eating.

Learning to stop eating when you feel full will help you eat less. Feeling full does not mean feeling stuffed. Satiety means that you no longer feel hungry and that, in fact, you feel good. Many of my clients are surprised to learn that it doesn't take much to feel satisfied.

8. Recognize What Triggers Overeating

We've all done it at some point—ordered the decadent dessert, despite feeling stuffed from dinner. Or devoured the entire bag of potato chips when we really wanted only a few. It is easy to overeat. Food is cheap, abundant, and often only an arm's-length away. And it doesn't take much overindulging to put on weight. If you munch an extra 100 calories each day, you'll gain 10 pounds (4.5 kilograms) per year. Those extra 100 calories can sneak up on you quickly. All it takes is grabbing an extra cookie after school or ordering the large versus medium fries.

There are many environmental triggers below our radar screens that make people unknowingly overeat. The size of a package, the shape of a glass, food proximity, variety, convenience, even the words on a menu can influence how much and what we eat. Take package size, for instance. Research shows that if you give people a large package, they'll pour more than they would from a smaller package, no matter whether it's pasta, vegetable oil, candy, pet food, or non-food items. Researchers believe we use products from large packages more freely because we perceive them as being less expensive than those from smaller ones. If you eat directly from a bigger package, research suggests you'll eat 25% more than you would from a smaller package. And if it's a snack food such as candy or chips, you'll eat 50% more. People have difficulty monitoring how much they eat when they eat from a large container.

The shape of an object can also influence how many calories people consume. Research has shown that kids pour—and consume—almost 75% more fruit juice when they use short, wide glasses rather than tall, narrow glasses. We tend to perceive tall, skinny glasses as holding more liquid than short, stubby ones. Our eyes focus on the height of an object, not allowing us to correctly account for its width.

Visibility and convenience can also prompt overeating. If food is in plain sight and it's nearby, we tend to nosh. (The best strategy here is to simply keep high-fat, high-sugar foods out of the house—out of sight, out of mind.) Some teenagers overeat because they feel sad, angry, or bored. Others overeat because people around them are eating. A food diary can help teenagers recognize the reasons they overeat and plan strategies to overcome these triggers.

9. Learn About Nutrition

Research shows that people who are successful at losing weight and keeping it off buy books and magazines related to nutrition and exercise. What's more, they continue to read about nutrition even after they've lost their unwanted weight. When you create an environment that fosters healthy eating, you're more likely to stay on track and make permanent changes. Reading this book is a great place for teenagers to start learning about nutrition. Other resources I recommend are the magazines *Vegetarian Times, Cooking Light, Shape,* and *Men's Fitness,* and the *Nutrition Action Healthletter* from the Center for Science in the Public Interest, at www.cspinet.org/nah.

10. Limit Screen Time, and Get Planned Exercise

By high school graduation, most teens have spent more time in front of the tube than in the classroom. In fact, some experts say that television viewing accounts for more of a teen's time than any other activity except sleeping. Excessive television watching encourages a sedentary lifestyle and unhealthy eating habits that promote weight gain. Teenagers should be encouraged to spend no more than one to two hours per day watching television and playing video and computer games.

Make it a practice to keep the television off during family meals. Parents need to set a good example for their kids by spending their free time doing activities other than watching TV. Encourage teenagers to engage in healthier pursuits—sports, hobbies, and reading. The majority of people who shed excess pounds permanently say they get one hour of scheduled exercise each day. Exercise makes you feel good about yourself and in turn makes you want to eat healthily. And there's a bonus: you can enjoy more food if you exercise regularly. In Chapter 10, I discuss how much exercise, and what types, teenagers should be getting.

Sedentary teenagers can start being active by adding little bits of activity to their daily routine. Small things—taking the stairs instead of the escalator, walking to school, or getting off the bus a few stops early—all burn calories. They will be amazed at how the calories burned in these small steps add up.

There's no need for teenagers to think that they need to be perfect when it comes to healthy eating. In fact, no one should. It's only natural to slip up from time to time. The key to successful weight loss is to consider lapses as momentary setbacks, not the ruin of all one's hard work. Forgive yourself—and keep trying. Teens are bound to stray from their healthy eating plan, whether they cave in and order a burger and fries instead of the grilled chicken sandwich or eat too much junk food with their friends on the weekend. It's all about dealing with small lapses when they occur, rather than waiting until they accumulate. We all need to tell ourselves that we're only human, and it's okay to slip a little. By doing so, you'll be amazed at how easy it is to return to your usual healthy routine. Don't dwell on the negative—think positively about all the healthy changes you have already made and keep on moving forward.

Fostering Healthy Habits in Your Teenager

It can be frustrating and upsetting to watch an overweight child engage in unhealthy behaviours, despite all the advice you offer them. Parents often find it difficult to convince teenagers of the benefits of healthy eating and exercise. But there are things parents can, and should, do to help foster healthy habits in their children.

Lead by example Teenagers are good at sensing the "do as I say, not do as I do" routine. Take a look at your own eating and exercise habits to see if you're setting a good example. Avoid fad diets and don't complain about your own weight, or anyone else's, in front of your kids. Try to avoid talking about dieting.

Encourage and support your teenager Don't criticize or blame your child for her weight. Talk to her about her concerns about weight and health. Encourage the whole family to eat well and be physically active. Focus and comment on qualities of your teenager other than the physical ones. Instill in her the belief that she is unique, valuable, and worthwhile regardless of her appearance. Teach her to feel good about herself whatever her body size.

Provide healthy food Don't simply lecture on the evils of french fries and chocolate bars. Stock the house with nutritious foods such as fruit, vegetables, low-fat dairy products, and whole grains. Keep healthy snacks in a place where your teenager can easily access them—front and centre in the fridge and cupboards. If your teen is trying to lose weight, don't bring home junk foods from the grocery store—nobody needs them.

Get professional help If your teen has shared her weight concerns with you and expressed an interest in losing weight, consider consulting a registered dietitian. Dietitians are trained professionals who can design a meal plan to suit your teenager's food preferences and busy schedule. Dietitians also offer ongoing support and nutrition education to help your child succeed at weight loss. To find a consulting dietitian in your community, visit www.dietitians.ca.

Leslie's Tips for Helping Teens Manage Their Weight

1. Keep a food diary for one week, and record the foods you eat, portion sizes, and the time of day you eat.

2. Measure food portions so you can compare how much you are eating with the recommended portion sizes outlined in Canada's Food Guide, shown in Chapter 1.

3. To lose weight safely, follow Canada's Food Guide, sticking to the lower number of servings in each food group. Or consult a registered dietitian to help plan a weight loss program that suits your schedule and meets your nutrient needs. Do not embark on a fad diet.

4. Avoid skipping meals, especially breakfast. To prevent hunger and overeating, eat three meals per day and two snacks, one mid-morning, and one mid-afternoon.

5. Choose snacks that contain carbohydrate and a little protein. Healthy and satisfying snacks include yogurt, fruit and nuts, smoothies, energy bars, raw vegetables and hummus, or a small bowl of high-fibre cereal and milk.

6. Avoid quickly digested snacks that don't satisfy your appetite. Such high glycemic index snacks include low-fat cookies, pretzels, bagels, low-fibre cereals, rice cakes, and cereal bars.

7. Pack lunch and snacks prepared at home to take with you to school. This decreases the chances that you will buy a high-calorie or processed snack on impulse.

8. Avoid sugary soft drinks, iced tea, and fruit drinks. Drink water when thirsty.

9. To help stick to a healthy eating plan designed for weight loss, indulge in your favourite higher-calorie treat once per week if you like.

10. Spend less time watching television or playing video and computer games. Limit yourself to two hours per day. Get involved in more active pursuits.

10

———— ⚏⚏⚏ ————

Nutrition Advice for Sports

It's hardly news that exercise is good for us, especially for teenagers. Regular physical activity helps kids grow and develop by boosting cardiovascular fitness, strength, flexibility, and bone density. In a decade-long study, researchers found that the more a teenage girl participated in sports, the stronger her bones were.[1] Girls form at least 40% of their bone density during adolescence.

Teenagers who are physically active also tend to have higher self-esteem and self-confidence compared with those who are not physically active.[2] Studies have found that teens aged 12 to 15 years who rarely or never participated in organized sports were more likely to report lower self-esteem and difficulty with friends. They were also more likely to smoke cigarettes.[3] Studies have also shown that regular exercise helps teenagers perform better at school. Daily activity is linked to better concentration and improved academic performance.

It's no surprise that physical activity can help teenagers manage their weight. Being active burns up calories and contributes to an efficient metabolism (the rate at which the body burns calories at rest). Plenty of research confirms the notion that physical inactivity increases the odds that teenagers will have weight problems. Among Canadian youth, both organized and unorganized sport and physical activity are negatively associated with being overweight (10% to 24% reduced risk) or obese (23% to 43% reduced risk). On the other hand, TV watching and playing video or computer games increased the risk of being overweight and obese by as much as 61%.[4]

We've all heard that regular workouts can help guard against heart disease and type 2 diabetes. Regular exercise might even help reverse the early stages of clogged arteries in obese kids. An eight-week study from Australia revealed that by participating in one-hour circuit training sessions (cardio plus weights, three times per week), obese teens were able to lose body fat and improve blood vessel function. At the start of the study, these teenagers had impaired blood vessel function, a sign of early heart disease.[5] The bad news is that the harmful effects of obesity on artery health is evident at an early age; the good news is that it can be reversed with regular exercise.

If exercise is so good for us, why aren't more teenagers getting off the couch? Today, more than one-half of Canadian teenagers are sedentary, accumulating less that one hour of walking per day. In fact, only 18% get enough daily exercise to meet international guidelines for optimal growth and development.[6] If your teenager isn't active outside school, don't expect physical education classes alone to give him the exercise he needs. According to a Canadian study, one out of every five teenagers opts out of physical education altogether, while only 23% of all students take classes daily.[7] Even if your child does take gym class, that doesn't mean he's participating in moderate or vigorous activity. And if he is getting his heart to beat faster, it might be only for a small portion of class time. If teenagers are going to meet physical activity recommendations, they need to get active outside of gym class.

How Much Exercise Do Teens Need?

International guidelines call for teenagers to engage in a variety of activities and expend 6 to 8 METs (metabolic equivalents) daily in physical activity. One MET is the amount of energy that's expended by your body as you sit quietly. The harder your body works during an activity, the higher the MET. Any activity that burns 3 to 6 METs is considered moderate-intensity physical activity. Any activity that burns more than 6 METs is considered vigorous-intensity physical activity.

To meet international guidelines of expending 6 to 8 METs daily, a teenager would need to play team sports for one hour or run for 30 minutes combined with an accumulated one hour of walking throughout the day. Here's a look at how different types of activity stack up in terms of intensity and energy expended. (Energy is measured in calories. The calorie measure used commonly to discuss the energy content of food, or the amount of energy the body burns during activity, is actually a kilocalorie or 1000 real calories. One kilocalorie, or kcal, is the amount of energy required to raise one kilogram of water—about 2.2 pounds—one degree Centigrade. The longer you exercise, or the more intense the activity, the more kilocalories the body burns.)

INTENSITY LEVELS OF VARIOUS ACTIVITIES

Light Intensity	Moderate Intensity	Vigorous Intensity
(Less than 3 METs or 3.5 kcal per minute):	*(3–6 METs or 3.5–7.0 kcal per minute):*	*(More than 6 METs or more than 7 kcal per minute):*
Bicycling, very light effort	Bicycling, 5–9 mph (8–14 k/h), level terrain, or with a few hills	Bicycling faster than 10 mph (16 k/h), or on steep uphill terrain
Dusting	Golfing, pulling or carrying clubs	Circuit training
Gardening	Mowing lawn with a power mower	Moving or pushing furniture
Golfing, powered cart	Tennis, doubles	Mowing lawn with a hand mower
Stretching lightly	Scrubbing floors	Speed walking, jogging, or running
Swimming, slow treading	Swimming, recreational	Swimming, laps
Vacuuming	Walking briskly	Tennis, singles
Walking slowly	Washing windows	
	Weight lifting, machines or free weights	

BE Ainsworth et al. Compendium of physical activities: Classification of energy costs of human physical activities. *Medicine and Science in Sports and Exercise* 1993, 25(1):71–80.

As a result of the increasing rates of obesity and inactivity among youth, Health Canada and the Canadian Society for Exercise Physiology have developed a Physical Activity Guide especially for kids aged 10 to 14 years.[8] The guide challenges Canadian youth to increase their daily physical activity and decrease their sedentary activities. It recommends that sedentary kids aged 10 to 14 years increase their physical activity to at least 30 minutes per day. This can be done in short 10-minute bouts, adding up to the 30-minute daily target. At the same time, sedentary kids are advised to reduce television and computer time by 30 minutes per day. Then, gradually over a period of five months, young teenagers should boost physical activity to at least 90 minutes per day.

What about older teenagers? Sedentary teens aged 15 to 19 years will also benefit from this advice. To date, there are no physical activity recommendations specific to this age group. But it makes sense that older teenagers should be following the same advice that's given to their parents. Experts recommend that we accumulate 60 minutes of physical activity every day to stay healthy or improve our health. The time that teens need to spend being active depends on the amount of effort the activity takes. In other words, the higher the exercise intensity, the shorter the duration of exercise needed to reap health benefits. But keep in mind that 45 minutes of moderate to vigorous activity may be needed to reduce the risk of breast and colon cancer.

Here's a list showing the level of exercise effort and duration of various activities. The activities that require moderate and vigorous effort are considered cardio, or aerobic, workouts (see below). Teens who do only light activities need to spend more time at them to reap health benefits.

EFFORT LEVELS OF VARIOUS ACTIVITIES

Light Effort	Moderate Effort	Vigorous Effort
60 minutes	30 to 60 minutes	30 minutes
Easy gardening	Biking	Aerobics
Light walking	Brisk walking	Basketball
Stretching	Dancing	Fast dancing
Volleyball	Raking leaves	Fast swimming
	Swimming	Hockey
	Water aerobics	Jogging
		Spinning

Source: *Handbook for Canada's Physical Activity Guide to Healthy Active Living,* Health Canada, 1998. Reproduced with the permission of the Minister of Public Works and Government Services, 2005.

Putting Together an Exercise Program for Teens

A well-rounded exercise program for teens includes activities that will strengthen their heart, lungs, and muscles, as well as improve the flexibility of their joints. Encourage your teen to participate in one or more activities in each of the following three categories: cardiovascular, strength, and flexibility. Keep in mind that some activities have more than one health benefit. For example, pilates and yoga are great for both muscle strengthening and flexibility.

Cardiovascular Activities

Aerobic or cardiovascular activities help a teenager maintain a healthy weight and get his heart, lungs, and circulatory system in shape. Aerobic exercise gets the heart pumping and the muscles using oxygen. Regular aerobic workouts strengthen the heart, making it more efficient in delivering oxygen to all parts of the body.

In addition to being active every day, experts recommend that teenagers get at least four 20-minute sessions a week of vigorous activity. Teenagers who play team sports are probably already getting more cardio than this. Team sports that give teenagers a great aerobic workout include competitive swimming, basketball, soccer, lacrosse, hockey, and rowing. If your teen does not play team sports, there are plenty of other ways to add cardio exercise to her weekly routine. Biking, running, swimming, dancing, in-line skating, cross-country skiing, hiking, and brisk walking are good options. Teenagers new to cardiovascular exercise should begin with activities that can be maintained continuously and don't require special skill. Group 1 activities in the table below provide constant intensity and are not dependent on skill; group 2 activities may provide constant or variable intensity, depending on skill; and group 3 activities provide variable intensity and are highly dependent on skill.

CARDIOVASCULAR ACTIVITIES (FOUR TO SEVEN DAYS PER WEEK)

Group 1 Activities	Group 2 Activities	Group 3 Activities
Cycling (indoor)	Aerobic dancing	Basketball
Jogging	Step aerobics	Handball
Walking	Hiking	Hockey
Rowing	In-line skating	Racquet sports
Stair climbing	Skipping rope	Soccer
Cross-country skiing	Swimming	Volleyball
Distance cycling	Water aerobics	Circuit training

Source: *Handbook for Canada's Physical Activity Guide to Healthy Active Living,* Health Canada, 1998. Reproduced with the permission of the Minister of Public Works and Government Services, 2005.

Strength Activities

Many teenagers discover strength (resistance) training when a coach or gym teacher suggests it to improve their performance in a particular sport. But there are plenty of reasons why teenagers should strength train. Regular weight workouts can improve endurance and strength in sports and fitness activities. Many teenage athletes I've counselled have spent time using weight machines to improve their game, be it tennis, swimming, or rugby. Strength training can also reduce the likelihood of sports injuries by protecting bones and joints. And there's more good news for teens who exercise with weights. Studies suggest that regular strength training can improve academic performance by helping kids concentrate better. For teenagers who exercise to maintain a healthy weight, resistance training can help the body burn more calories at rest. That's because increases in muscle mass increase a person's resting metabolism. That means they are burning a few extra calories when they're just sitting around doing nothing.

Many parents wonder if it is safe for teenagers to strength train. As soon as teenagers have started puberty, their bodies have begun making hormones necessary to help muscles grow and respond to resistance training. Because technique and proper form are important, if teenagers are mature enough to accept directions, they're old enough to start strength training. There are some risks involved, however. Teenagers' bodies are still growing and developing. That means their bones, joints, and tendons are more susceptible to strain and overuse injuries.

Teenagers need to start out slowly and give their bodies time to adjust to an increase in activity. And it's very important that teenagers get advice from a trainer or coach on how to safely use dumbbells and weight machines. Using weights safely, and properly stretching muscles, will reduce the risk of injury and muscle soreness. It's also a wise idea for teenagers who lift weights to have a spotter or coach supervising nearby.

STRENGTH ACTIVITIES (TWO TO FOUR DAYS PER WEEK)

Heavy yard work	Abdominal crunches	Cybex machines	Pilates
Raking and carrying leaves	Chin-ups	Free weights (dumbbells, barbells)	Yoga
Stair climbing	Lunges	Nautilus machines	
	Push-ups		
	Squats		

Source: *Handbook for Canada's Physical Activity Guide to Healthy Active Living,* Health Canada, 1998. Reproduced with the permission of the Minister of Public Works and Government Services, 2005.

Most experts recommend that teenagers who are new to strength training start out with two or three sessions per week, each 20 to 40 minutes in duration. Teenagers should never do the same workout on consecutive days; it's important to allow muscles to rest for 24 hours. Before teenagers hit the weight machines, they should start out lifting their own body weight by doing push-ups, chin-ups, pull-ups, and sit-ups. It's best to work out only two or three muscle groups per session. For example, teens can work out legs on one day; back, chest and shoulders another; and arms on the third exercise day.

Teens should follow these guidelines for safe strength training:

- Warm up with 5 to 10 minutes of light aerobic activity to get your circulation going and your joints moving.

- Stretch the muscles you plan to work out before each weight training session.

- Ask a personal trainer or coach to demonstrate proper technique in order to protect your shoulders, back, and joints.

- Perform three sets of 10 repetitions of each exercise. Start out with a light weight, then increase the weight slightly in the second and third sets.

- Breathe regularly when doing an exercise.

- Spend no more than 40 minutes in the weight room to avoid fatigue.

- Rest for at least one day between strength training sessions.

Flexibility Activities

Exercise helps the body stay flexible, which means muscles and joints can stretch and move fluidly. The more flexible teenagers are, the less likely they'll get injured during sports or other physical activities. Regular flexibility exercises can also help improve a teen's sports performance. Some sports, including martial arts, dance, and gymnastics, involve a great deal of flexibility. Pilates and yoga help people stay flexible, too. All sports, even baseball, football, and tennis, require some degree of flexibility. Gentle reaching, bending, and stretching your muscles all keep your joints flexible and your muscles relaxed.

FLEXIBILITY ACTIVITIES (FOUR TO SEVEN DAYS PER WEEK)

Gardening	Pilates	Bowling
Mopping	Stretching	Curling
Sweeping	Tai Chi	Dance
Vacuuming	Yoga	Golf
Yard work		

Source: *Handbook for Canada's Physical Activity Guide to Healthy Active Living,* Health Canada, 1998. Reproduced with the permission of the Minister of Public Works and Government Services, 2005.

Teens should follow these guidelines for safe stretching:

- Warm up with light activity for five minutes before stretching. This increases your body temperature and your range of motion. Or do your stretching after a cardio or weight workout.

- Stretch all your major muscle groups (back, chest, shoulders, arms, legs).

- Stretch slowly and smoothly, with no bouncing or jerking. Use gentle continuous movement or stretch and hold (for 10 to 30 seconds), whichever is right for the exercise.

- Focus on the target muscle that you're stretching. Relax the muscle and minimize the movement of other body parts.

- Stretch to the limit of the movement, but not to the point of pain. Aim for a stretched, relaxed feeling.

- Don't hold your breath. Keep breathing slowly and rhythmically while holding the stretch.

- If you're not sure what to do, get help from a coach, gym teacher, or personal trainer. Or pick up a book on stretching at your local bookstore.

Getting Inactive Teens Active

One of the biggest reasons people drop out of an exercise program is because they don't enjoy it. Exercise can become boring and monotonous if you don't choose activities that you have fun doing. When choosing an activity, inactive teenagers should consider their personalities. If they like to exercise by themselves on their own schedule, perhaps in-line skating, bike riding, or brisk walking is right for them. If teenagers prefer social interaction while they exercise, they are probably better suited for team sports or exercise classes at the community centre.

It's also important to consider barriers to exercise. Overweight teenagers may be reluctant to participate in sports that make them feel body-conscious. They may feel self-conscious about their bodies and feel embarrassed in exercise clothes. Encouraging activities in the privacy of your own home (treadmill, stationary bike, exercise videos) might be a way to get an overweight child to start exercising.

There are other ways parents can encourage teenagers to become active:

- Talk to your teen about physical activity being an important part of staying healthy.

- Find out what types of physical activity your teen would like to do.

- Consider activities that are non-competitive. This may increase the chance that your teen will enjoy an activity.

- Be patient as your teen learns new activities and praise his ability in order to build his confidence.

- Encourage weekend family outings that are active—hiking, cycling, and walking are good family activities.

- Commit to getting fit with your child. Plan to work out with your son or daughter a few times per week.

- Sneak exercise into your teen's daily routine. If appropriate, let your teen walk to and from school. Encourage her to ride her bike to a friend's house. Get her to help with household chores and yard work.

Foods That Fuel Exercise

Most teenagers who play sports attend practices, train in the gym, and get plenty of sleep the night before a big game. But many forget about one very important component of their training program: nutrition. There is no doubt that what you eat and drink, and the times you consume these foods, can help improve physical performance. The problem is that many teenage athletes don't realize that fine-tuning their diet can help them realize their fitness potential. Activity requires carbohydrate for fuel, protein to build and repair muscles, vitamins and minerals to support muscle building and energy metabolism, and fluids to cool the body. The following sections of this chapter give active teenagers plenty of tips for high-performance sports nutrition.

There are three potential sources of fuel from the foods we eat: protein, fat, and carbohydrate. Protein is used for fuel only during times of extreme deprivation, such as starvation. Fat is reserved for use when sufficient carbohydrate is not available (e.g., after a long run). Carbohydrate is the body's preferred fuel for daily activities and high-intensity exercise performance. In fact, many studies have shown that following a low-carbohydrate regime impairs athletic performance and causes athletes to fatigue prematurely.

When you eat a carbohydrate-rich food—bread, cereal, pasta, fruit, or yogurt, for example—the carbohydrate is digested and absorbed into the bloodstream as glucose. Whatever glucose is not used immediately for energy purposes is stored in the liver and muscles as glycogen. Glycogen in your liver helps replenish your blood glucose level, while muscle glycogen fuels exercise. Glycogen is vital to physical activity of all types—sports, running, walking, even weight lifting. During exertion, your liver releases its glucose into the bloodstream. Your muscles use both this glucose and their own private glycogen stores to fuel their work.

The body constantly uses and replenishes its glycogen stores. And the more glycogen your muscles store, the longer you'll be able to exercise before feeling tired. How do muscles build up their glycogen supply? By using the carbohydrates in your diet. How long your glycogen stores will last during exercise also depends on the intensity of the activity. Intense exercises (running, spinning) burn through glycogen quickly. Less intense workouts (brisk walking, dancing) use glycogen more slowly. Most people run out of muscle glycogen within two hours from the onset of intense exercise.

How your muscles use glycogen to fuel a workout depends not only on the intensity of the exercise but also on its duration. Within the first 20 minutes of moderate activity, your muscles use mainly glycogen, or carbohydrate, for fuel. As your muscles use up their glycogen stores, they burn glucose in the bloodstream that's released from the liver. (Consuming a carbohydrate-rich snack during exercise can also supply glucose.) After 20 minutes, your muscles start to use less and less glycogen and more and more fat (that's why marathon runners are so lean). Your muscles will continue to use glycogen, however, and if the exercise lasts long enough (about two hours of strenuous exercise), glycogen stores become depleted. When your glycogen stores run out, you've "hit the wall."

To keep your muscle glycogen stores topped up, make sure that all your meals and snacks contain carbohydrate-rich foods—whole-grain breads, cereals, pasta, rice, fruit, starchy vegetables, beans, lentils, dairy products, or soy milk. Sugary foods such as candy, sweets, and pop also contribute to muscle glycogen stores, but they're not recommended since they don't offer important vitamins and minerals needed for exercise. Read Chapter 2 to learn more about carbohydrates.

Pre-Exercise Meals and Snacks

The goal of a pre-game or pre-exercise meal is to ensure that you have energy in your body to exercise without getting tired too early in your activity. Eating too much food before a game or workout can have negative effects, including stomach upset and cramps. Eating too little food can leave athletes feeling lethargic and light-headed. A pre-workout snack, eaten one to two hours before exercise, may help reduce muscle tissue damage from weight training. And research suggests that as little as 6 grams of protein consumed before strength training can enhance post-exercise muscle repair. Remember, one pre-exercise meal won't make up for a poor training diet. You should eat plenty of healthy, high-carbohydrate foods every day to ensure your muscle's energy stores get replenished after exercise.

The ideal pre-exercise meal is high in carbohydrate, low in fat and fibre, and contains a little protein. Such a meal or snack is easier to digest and will empty from the stomach faster. Foods high in protein (e.g., meat, eggs, and tuna) and high in fat (e.g., peanut butter, fast food, and cookies) take longer to digest and can leave athletes feeling uncomfortable during exercise. To prevent stomach upset, pre-workout meals should be smaller the closer they are eaten to the time you begin exercise. In general, allow three to four hours for a large meal to digest, two to three hours for a smaller meal, and one to two hours for a small snack or liquid meal such as a smoothie or power shake.

These are only guidelines. Some athletes can handle a large meal with no problem within an hour of a big game, and others can eat nothing for a few hours prior. To find out what's right for you, you will have to experiment during training to determine which foods settle comfortably, when you should eat them, and how much you can eat. Always eat familiar foods before a big game or race—don't try anything new that might upset your stomach.

For morning workouts, games, and practices, teenagers need to eat a high-carbohydrate dinner and bedtime snack the night before. In the morning, they should eat a light carbohydrate-rich snack before heading out the door. For afternoon workouts, games, and practices, it's important to eat breakfast and lunch, and then a light snack one to two hours before exercising. You can see that to fuel your muscles properly for sports, meal skipping is not allowed. Here are a few suggestions for high-carb pre-exercise meals and snacks that will energize your body and delay fatigue during exercise:

Breakfasts:

- Cereal with 1% or skim milk and banana or raisins
- Whole-wheat toast with jam and unsweetened fruit juice

- Low-fat muffin with yogurt and unsweetened fruit juice
- Whole-grain bagel with jam and yogurt
- Blender smoothie made with milk, banana, and frozen berries, and toast with jam
- French toast or pancakes topped with fruit—but no butter

Lunches:

- Sandwich with turkey or ham with mustard and a glass of low-fat milk
- Chicken noodle, bean, or minestrone soup with low-fat crackers and glass of low-fat milk
- Thick-crust pizza (single cheese, vegetables, no fatty meat) and glass of milk

Snacks:

- Low-fat crackers
- Whole-grain bagel
- Toast with jam only
- Canned fruit or applesauce—no sugar added
- Yogurt and a piece of fruit
- Small turkey sandwich
- Blender smoothie made with milk, banana, and frozen berries
- 1 Sun-Rype FruitSource plus Veggie bar
- 1 energy bar (e.g., Clif Bar, Clif Luna Bar, ZonePerfect Bar, PowerBar Harvest, PowerBar Pria)

Dinners:

- Pasta with tomato sauce
- Chicken (only a little chicken) stir-fry with rice or noodles
- Sweet or baked potato and vegetables with small serving of chicken or fish

Fuelling Muscles During Exercise

If you are exercising for longer than one hour, feed your muscles carbohydrate. Consuming a source of carbohydrate during exercise helps maintain blood glucose levels at a time when your muscle glycogen stores are diminishing. Carbohydrate feedings have been shown to improve performance in endurance sports such as running, cycling, and swimming. But they also reduce fatigue in stop-and-go sports such as soccer, rugby, and basketball. These sports require repeated bouts of high-intensity, short-duration effort. In general, athletes are advised to consume 30 to 60 grams of carbohydrate every hour during exercise. One energy gel (a small portable package that provides pure glucose to fuel working muscles during exercise, available in sporting good stores) provides 25 grams of carbohydrate, 2 cups (500 ml) of sports drink (e.g., Gatorade, Powerade, All Sport) has 30 grams, and one medium banana has about 26 grams. If you drink Gatorade during exercise, all you need is one snack per hour.

Good choices for carbohydrate include sports drinks, energy gels, energy bars, bananas, fig bars, low-fat granola bars, and dried fruit snacks. Which snack you choose will depend on what kind of exercise you're doing. For instance, if your sport involves running, you'll want a food that's easy to consume—sports drinks, energy gels, and small pieces of an energy bar work well. If you're cycling or taking a break on the bench or sidelines, portable snacks such as fruit, yogurt, granola bars, and fruit bars are fine. But keep in mind that solid foods require water for digestion—so drink up.

Recovery Foods

After exercise, replenish your glycogen stores by eating a carbohydrate-rich snack. This is particularly important for teenagers who train day after day. Ideally, do so within 30 minutes after exercise. This is when your muscles are more likely to take up glucose. If you wait too long after exercise to eat your carbs, you can reduce muscle glycogen storage and impair recovery. To help muscles recover, teenage athletes should eat something immediately after exercise, and then again two hours later.

Research suggests that high glycemic foods may speed muscle recovery in the first 24 hours after exercise. High glycemic foods are those that are quickly digested and converted to blood glucose rapidly. That means your muscles receive the glucose from these foods sooner than from foods that are digested more slowly. Usually, nutritionists encourage people to consume low glycemic, or slow-acting, carbs for good health. But when it comes to recovering from exercise, high glycemic foods do have a place. Adding a little bit of protein to a post-workout snack may also enhance muscle recovery. The recovery snacks listed below provide carbohydrate and a little bit of protein. Not all are high glycemic index, but that's okay. The most important thing is to consume carbohydrates right after exercise.

- Blender smoothie made with low-fat milk or soy milk and fruit
- Yogurt and a banana
- Energy bar (e.g., PowerBar, Clif Bar)
- Low-fat granola bar and a glass of 1% or skim milk
- Commercial shakes (e.g., President's Choice Ultrashake, Ensure High Protein)

- Low-fat cheese string and a glass of unsweetened fruit juice

- Small sliced turkey or chicken sandwich

- Bowl of high glycemic cereal (e.g., Corn Flakes, Cheerios, Rice Krispies) with low-fat milk

The World of Energy Bars

Energy bars are a great option to energize your muscles before, during, and after exercise. They provide a portable and compact source of carbohydrate for working muscles. They're convenient, they don't need refrigeration, and they travel well. Most energy bars provide 200 to 250 calories and have added vitamins and minerals. Not all energy bars are created equal, however. Some are packed with sugar and some are higher in artery-clogging fat. Here's how energy bars differ.

High Carbohydrate Bars

(Clif Bar, Gatorade Energy Bar, GeniSoy Extreme, Geobar, Greens+ express, Kashi Golean Roll, PowerBar, PowerBar Harvest)

These are the original energy bars marketed to athletes to boost energy. They provide roughly 230 to 290 calories and are low in fat. Most have about 45 grams of carbohydrate and less than 10 grams of protein. They are made mainly of high-fructose corn syrup (sugar), fruit juice, and added vitamins and minerals. Depending on the brand, they can pack anywhere from 5 to 8 teaspoons (25 to 40 ml) of sugar per bar. This category of bars tends to have the most healthful flavours—honey, fruit, grains, and molasses.

Moderate-Carbohydrate/Moderate-Protein Bars (40/30/30 Bars)

(Balance Bar, Clif Luna Bar, Detour, Interactive SoyOne Bar, Life SuperBar, U-Turn, ZonePerfect)

These are moderate-carbohydrate and higher-protein bars; they usually contain between 190 and 250 calories and approximately 20 grams of carbohydrate and 10 to 15 grams protein. Many people prefer these bars as midday snacks because the protein in them helps to keep them feeling full longer. Protein and fat slow down the rate at which food is emptied from the stomach. The sugar content tends to be a little lower—anywhere from 3 to 5 teaspoons (15 to 25 ml) per bar. This category tends to have more candy-like flavours.

High-Protein Bars

(BigWhey, BioProtein, Lean Body, Meso-Tech, PowerBar Protein, Promax, Protein 2 Go)

These bars are often higher in calories (some have as many as 420 calories) than other energy bars. Most have 20 to 35 grams of protein (that's the same amount of protein found in 3 to 5 ounces/90 to 150 grams of chicken). These are popular with guys who lift weights at the gym. However, as you'll read below, there's little reason to think that teenagers who consume adequate calories need a protein supplement. Many high-protein bars have a chemical aftertaste.

Choose an energy bar that has at least 20 to 25 grams carbohydrate for muscle fuel—don't waste your money on low-carb bars. Look for a bar that has at least 3 grams of fibre. And read labels to make sure the energy bar contains a high-quality protein, such as whey, casein, egg, or soy. Here's what you don't want in an energy bar: palm kernel oil and partially hydrogenated vegetable oil. Choose a bar that has less than 2 grams of saturated fat. Read ingredient lists and nutrition labels to see what you're getting.

Do Teen Athletes Need Extra Protein?

Athletes often think of protein in association with growing stronger and bigger muscles. Protein-rich foods, protein bars, and protein shakes are often recommended by coaches and trainers to help people bulk up and recover from exercise. Protein is an important nutrient in an athlete's diet. Protein-rich foods—meat, poultry, eggs, dairy, nuts, beans, and tofu— supply amino acids, the building blocks used for muscle growth and repair.

During the 1800s, it was widely believed that protein was the main fuel burned during exercise. But gone are the days when body builders downed pre-competition meals of eggs and steak. Today, we know that almost all the energy used to fuel exercise, be it weight training, running, tennis, or basketball, comes from carbohydrate and fat. During short bouts of exercise, protein contributes virtually no fuel to working muscles. If you're a long-distance runner or endurance cyclist, proteins stored in muscle contribute roughly 2% to 5% of total calories burned.

Despite this, adult athletes do have higher protein requirements than sedentary people. Extra protein is needed to repair muscle damage that occurs during exercise and to support muscle building. Sedentary individuals require 0.36 grams per pound (0.8 grams of protein per kilogram) of body weight per day. For a 130-pound (59-kilogram) woman, this translates into roughly 50 grams of protein. Studies suggest that endurance athletes, including runners and cyclists, need to consume 0.54 grams per pound (1.2 grams of protein per kilogram) of body weight per day. Resistance exercise such as weight lifting is thought to increase protein needs even more. It's recommended that strength athletes consume 0.73 to 0.77 grams per pound (1.6 to 1.7 grams of protein per kilogram) of body weight per day.

However, data assessing how much protein teenage athletes need are lacking. It is within reason, however, to believe that growing teenage athletes do need more protein than their sedentary peers. But as long as teenagers are meeting their daily calorie needs, they will be getting all the protein their active bodies need. (See Chapter 1, page 15, to determine how many calories active teenagers need each day.)

What about those protein shakes sold at the gym? To date, there is no solid evidence that protein supplements or special blends of amino acids work any better at aiding muscle repair or growth than the protein found in foods. Protein supplements can give kids a false sense of security if they mistakenly think that improvements in performance are a result of protein powders they're taking. Improvements in strength, power, and speed are the results of training, hard work, and a balanced diet—not a protein bar that's eaten before a workout.

That's not to say there is no place for protein supplements. For vegetarian athletes who avoid animal foods, protein powders made from soy or whey (a by-product of cheese making) can certainly help boost their protein intake. Protein supplements are not safe for all teenagers, though. Teens with kidney problems or diabetes should not use protein powders or bars. Excess protein from any source can stress the kidneys, and people with diabetes are more prone to kidney disorders. Teenagers who do use protein supplements need to ensure they're drinking adequate fluids during the day. That's because the body needs water to break down the products of protein digestion. If you're dehydrated and take in too much protein, you'll become even more dehydrated.

While some protein is a good thing, more is not better. If you're trying to build muscle mass, increasing your protein intake beyond the recommended levels won't build bigger muscles, since there's a limit to the rate at which protein can be synthesized into muscle. Unlike carbohydrate and fat, the body can't store protein. The excess will be either burned for energy or, if you're already getting the calories you need, tucked away as fat.

Teenagers need to keep in mind that protein can't do its job without an adequate supply of carbohydrate-rich foods. If a teenager's diet supplies too few calories, the extra protein he consumes will be used for energy-burning purposes rather than muscle building. Often I counsel clients who are training hard and getting enough protein but aren't seeing results at the gym. The problem: too few calories from carbs, the primary fuel for muscle-building exercises. Eating more calories from whole grains and fruit enables these clients to get the gains they want.

When it comes to fuelling exercise, timing is key. Since the body can't store protein, it makes sense to feed your muscles when they need it. A pre-workout snack, eaten one to two hours before exercise, may help reduce muscle tissue damage from weight training. And research suggests that as little as 6 grams of protein, consumed before strength training, can enhance post-exercise muscle repair. After any workout, eat a combination of protein and carbohydrate within 30 minutes, and again two hours later, to help your muscles recover, grow, and re-energize for your next workout.

The Importance of Fluids for Sports Performance

It used to be that water was the beverage of choice for athletes. But ever since 1966, when scientists at the University of Florida tested a special formula on the school's football team, the Gators, sports drinks have become increasingly popular. This original concoction of sugar, salt, and water was appropriately named Gatorade. Over the past few decades, sports drinks have come a long way, with refinements in amounts of sugar and sodium, and the addition of minerals.

Today there are even products for low-carb followers who don't want to gulp sugar along with their fluids. Low-carb sports drinks (Powerade T.X.L., Ultima Replenisher) replace the sugar with non-caloric sweeteners. These low-carb versions are gaining popularity with marathoners, who get their carbohydrate from energy gels or bars during long runs and want only the fluid and electrolytes from a sports drink.

Depending on your sport, these high-tech beverages just might give you a competitive edge. Numerous studies have shown that the fluid, electrolytes, and carbohydrate in sports drinks delay fatigue, enhance physical performance, and speed recovery in athletes. Evidence also suggests that sports drinks can enhance the physical and mental performance of individuals who engage in team sports that are played for a short duration but intensely.

Sports drinks are intended to rapidly replace fluids and electrolytes, such as sodium and potassium, which are lost through sweating during exercise. Hydration is critical to athletic performance: one of the most common reasons for early fatigue during exercise is dehydration. All it takes is losing as little as 2% of your body weight for the detrimental effects of dehydration to kick in. Sweating is your body's way of releasing heat from working muscles. If you don't drink enough during exercise and you lose too much sweat, your body temperature will rise and performance can suffer. The combined effects of dehydration and exercise in the heat can lead to life-threatening heat stroke.

The addition of sodium to sports drinks stimulates fluid absorption, maintains the desire to drink, and helps prevent low blood sodium (hyponatremia) in prolonged exercise. Most beverages contain 6% to 9% carbohydrate in the form of liquid sugar and/or high-fructose corn syrup to provide energy for working muscles. (By comparison, pop and fruit juice contain 10% to 15% carbohydrate.)

But not everyone needs to switch from water to sports drinks. If you're working out for less than one hour, water will do just fine. Sports drinks benefit people who engage in longer bouts of exercise—running, cycling, sport tournaments, and the like. Whether you hydrate with water or a sports drink, the key is to drink enough fluids before, during, and after exercise. This may sound like an easy task, but research indicates that many athletes fall short. The following guide will help teenagers stay well hydrated before, during, and after exercise:

FLUID REQUIREMENTS FOR EXERCISE

24 hours before exercise

* Follow a nutritionally balanced diet and drink adequate fluids.

2 hours before exercise

* Drink 2 cups (500 ml) of cool fluid.

During exercise

* Start drinking cool fluids early at a rate of 1/2 to 1 cup (125 to 250 ml) every 15 to 20 minutes.
* For exercise lasting less than one hour, plain water is the best fluid for hydration.
* For exercise lasting longer than one hour, sports drinks that contain 4% to 8% carbohydrate and electrolytes (sodium, chloride, potassium) may improve hydration and performance (e.g., Gatorade, Powerade, All Sport).

After exercise

* Drink 2 cups (500 ml) of fluid for every pound you lose during exercise.
* A sports drink that contains sodium may improve recovery, but it's not necessary as long as sodium is in the foods you eat.

VA Convertino et al. American College of Sports Medicine position stand. Exercise and fluid replacement. Med Sci Sports Exerc 1996; 28(1):i–vii.

You'll notice in the above chart that it's recommended that you drink 1/2 to 1 cup (125 to 250 ml) of fluid every 15 to 20 minutes during exercise. Keep a water bottle handy, and drink even if you don't feel thirsty. Use the alarm on your wristwatch to remind you when it is time to take a drink. After exercise, replenish the fluid you lose through sweat. Learn how much sweat you lose during exercise by weighing yourself before and after a workout. For every pound of weight you lose during exercise, drink 2 cups (500 ml) of fluid to rehydrate. Teenagers who are physically active outdoors in hot, humid weather will have markedly higher fluid requirements, so it's important that they pay attention to how much fluid they're drinking during exercise. Teens who need to drink more fluids should avoid taking in too much sugar and sodium by drinking water or diluted sports drinks, or alternating water with a sports drink.

SPORTS DRINK LINEUP

Per 1 cup (250 ml) serving

	Calories	Carbs (grams)	Sodium (milligrams)	Potassium (milligrams)	Sweetener
All Sport	70	18	75	55	glucose-fructose
Gatorade	63	15.5	107	28	sugar, glucose-fructose
Powerade	88	22	31	34	sugar/glucose-fructose
Powerade T.X.L.	27.5	6	24	16	sugar/glucose-fructose, acesulfame-potassium
Ultima Replenisher	12.5	3	37.5	75	maltodextrin, stevia leaf extract
Water	0	0	0	0	none

What About Vitamins and Minerals?

Physically active teenagers don't have higher requirements for any specific vitamins and minerals than do sedentary teens. However, dietary surveys show that many teens are lacking adequate iron and calcium. These two minerals are important not only for good health but also for optimizing athletic performance. Adequate calcium is necessary for bone development and reducing the risk of osteoporosis later in life. A calcium-rich diet can also help reduce stress fractures, injuries that can put athletes on the sidelines instead of in play. All teenagers need 1300 milligrams of calcium per day, from diet and supplements combined. You'll find a list of calcium-rich foods in Chapter 1.

Iron deficiency, even without overt anemia, can dramatically impair physical performance. Iron is used by red blood cells to carry oxygen to all cells, tissues, and muscles. Low iron stores can interfere with the muscle's ability to use oxygen, causing teenagers to become fatigued and more breathless during exercise. Too little iron can also impair cognitive function and reduce the motivation to exercise. Vegetarian teens and girls who are menstruating are most at risk for iron deficiency and need to pay close attention to their iron intakes.

To meet their growth needs, adolescents require, along with calcium and iron, more folate, B12, B6, riboflavin, and zinc than do adults. To ensure they are meeting their needs, teenagers should eat a variety of whole grains, dairy products, and protein-rich foods. But I am realistic and recognize that busy, active teenagers don't always eat well. That's why I routinely recommend an all-purpose multivitamin and mineral supplement for all teenagers, active or not. You'll find tips on how to choose a multivitamin in

Chapter 1, page 19. But keep in mind that a supplement cannot make up for an unhealthy diet. First and foremost, teenagers need to eat right.

Performance-Enhancing Supplements and Drugs

Sports supplements are big business. Just visit any pharmacy or health food store and you'll see shelves and shelves of performance-enhancing supplements that claim they can boost athletic performance, delay fatigue, increase muscle mass, and reduce body fat. Even more are available over the internet. What's more, many high school kids are using them. Some products are safe, but others can be downright dangerous. Here's the lowdown on a few supplements that your teenaged son or daughter might be tempted to take.

Creatine

This over-the-counter supplement is best known for its ability to enhance performance in sports that involve short bursts of intense activity—weightlifting, wrestling, and sprinting, for example. Studies suggest that 17% to 74% of athletes of various ages in a variety of sports use creatine supplements.[9] Creatine is a protein produced by the liver. We also get some creatine from our diet, mostly from meat, fish, and other animal products. The body uses it to produce energy for muscle contraction. Approximately 95% of the body's creatine is stored in muscles, where it's used to generate energy compounds called ATP (adenosine triphosphate). Exercise that involves brief, intense efforts rely heavily on ATP for fuel since it is the only form of energy that muscles can generate at a fast enough rate. But muscles can provide ATP at maximal rates for only a few seconds before their creatine stores become depleted. It's been hypothesized that, for this reason, people who increase their muscle creatine levels by taking creatine supplements will have more energy to perform high-intensity activities.

Many studies have found that creatine supplementation does improve performance of brief high-intensity exercise—exercise lasting less than 30 seconds. However, there's limited evidence to support its use during exercise lasting longer than 90 seconds. Creatine supplements taken during weight training may allow athletes to complete more repetitions per set of a given exercise and may allow them to recover more quickly between sets. Because creatine supplementation can make muscles appear larger by increasing muscle uptake of water, it may enhance motivation to work out harder. Studies in healthy individuals have not found any adverse side effects with moderate doses of creatine supplements.

Creatine supplements don't work for everyone, however. It's unclear why certain people are less likely to increase muscle creatine levels after taking supplements, but genes might be involved. Some athletes may be more predisposed to store more creatine in their muscles.

Should teenagers take creatine supplements to improve their sport? No. Scientists do not know the effects of creatine supplements in teenagers who are still growing. For this reason, experts advise that people younger than 19 years stay clear of creatine supplements.

Androstenedione

As a supplement, androstenedione—or andro as it is commonly referred to—is used to increase testosterone production to enhance athletic performance, boost energy, and enhance recovery and muscle growth from exercise. Despite its claims, studies have found that taking andro supplements do not significantly increase muscle strength, muscle size, or lean body mass when it's used for two to three months in conjunction with weight training.

Andro gained popularity as the supplement used by home run hitter Mark McGwire. It is not prohibited in Major League Baseball, but it is banned by the International Olympic Committee, the National Collegiate Athletic Association, the National Basketball Association, the National Football League, and the World Natural Bodybuilding Federation. And in May 2004, the U.S. Food and Drug Administration asked companies to stop distributing dietary supplements that contain andro.

Side effects of andro differ for males and females. In males, the supplement can actually decrease the body's production of testosterone and increase production of estrogen. Side effects may include acne, reduced sperm production, shrinking of the testicles, and enlargement of breasts. There is also preliminary evidence that androstenedione might stimulate prostate cancer cell growth. And there's concern that the supplement might increase risk of heart disease in men because it decreases high-density lipoprotein (HDL or "good" cholesterol) levels. In women, andro can lead to acne, rough skin, deepening of the voice, and male-pattern baldness.

In children and teenagers, andro might cause premature bone growth and decrease adult height. And it could cause early development of secondary sex characteristics in boys and disrupted menstrual periods in girls. There's no way around it: andro is not safe and should not be used by anyone, athlete or not, regardless of his or her age.

Anabolic Steroids

Teenagers may refer to these drugs as 'roids, juice, hype, or pump. Studies show that the use of anabolic steroids by young athletes has increased, primarily among weightlifters and gymnasts. Surveys in the United States have revealed that as many as 11% of high school boys have tried steroids. Canadian students are not immune from experimenting with anabolic steroids. In a study conducted among 16,119 Canadian students in the sixth grade and above, almost 3% said they had used steroids in the previous year. Even more alarming was that 29% of those kids said they injected the drug, and among them, 29% reported sharing needles in the course of injecting steroids.[10]

High school students might take muscle-building steroids to enhance athletic performance, improve self-confidence, and become more attractive to others. Young athletes say they are influenced by their athletic role models who use illicit substances.

Anabolic steroids are powerful drugs that build body tissues. Their use is more common among athletes involved in sports such as football that rely on strength and size, endurance sports such as track and field, and weight training or bodybuilding. Steroids can be taken orally or by injection. Regardless of how they are taken, anabolic steroids can cause side effects and serious health problems, liver tumours, increased blood pressure, and high cholesterol among them. In teenagers, steroid use can cause stunted growth because they signal the bones to stop growing sooner than normal. And there's no way to tell how steroid use affects a teenager's future fertility.

It's easier to tell if your teenager is taking steroids than it is other supplements. Signs of steroid use in males include severe acne and male-pattern baldness. In girls, steroids can cause acne, a deepening of the voice, and dark facial hair.

By nature, teenagers are risk takers. But they also are less likely to understand the health risks or be concerned with potential side effects of supplements. Educate yourself about supplements so that you can tell your teenager about the long-term effects of performance-enhancing drugs. Encourage your child to get professional advice before trying any sports supplement. Educated coaches, physicians, and sport nutritionists are excellent resources and can be contacted through sport organizations or the Dietitians of Canada (see the Resources section at the back of this book). If you suspect your teen is taking a harmful supplement, talk with his or her coach or physical education teacher.

The bottom line: teenagers should not count on any supplement, safe or not, to give them a competitive edge. If they train hard, eat a healthy diet, and get ample rest, the results will follow.

Leslie's Tips for Teen Physical Activity

1. Encourage your sedentary teen to increase his physical activity to at least 30 minutes per day and to reduce television and computer time by 30 minutes per day.

2. To follow a well-rounded exercise program, teens should participate in cardiovascular exercises at least four days per week, strength exercises at least twice per week, and flexibility exercises at least four days each week.

3. To motivate sedentary teenagers to become active, commit to getting fit with your teen. Plan regular workouts together.

4. Physically active teens should eat carbohydrate-rich foods before workouts, practices, and games. You'll find a list of pre-exercise snacks and meals on page 186.

5. For exercise that lasts longer than one hour, encourage teens to consume a source of carbohydrate during exercise. Good choices include energy gels, energy bars, sports drinks, and bananas.

6. Teenagers who train hard day after day must allow their muscles to recover by eating a snack that includes carbohydrate and protein within 30 minutes after exercise. Best bets are yogurt, smoothies, energy bars, and commercial shakes.

7. When buying energy bars, choose one with at least 20 to 25 grams of carbohydrate, 3 grams of fibre, and less than 2 grams of saturated fat.

8. Ensure your active teen consumes adequate fluids before, during, and after workouts and games. For exercise lasting longer than one hour, sports drinks are a better choice than plain water, as they can improve hydration and thus performance.

9. Physically active teenagers should supplement their diet with a daily multivitamin and mineral to help meet nutrient needs.

10. Become informed about popular sports supplements and drugs so that you are able to talk to your teen about their long-term health consequences.

11

⟨⟨⟩⟩

Understanding Eating Disorders

Everywhere teenagers look, they're bombarded with the message that thin is beautiful. The waifish looks of ultra-thin models and celebrities have become our ideal—establishing standards of beauty that are not only unattainable but unhealthy. It's no wonder that so many Canadian teens struggle with their body image. By the time they reach adulthood, nearly half of all females have concerns about their weight, and many have already begun the vicious cycle of dieting and weight gain.

Some females, especially during the vulnerable teenage years, carry their struggle with body image to the extreme. Eating disorders usually begin with efforts to lose weight, often in an attempt at self-improvement. But somehow, a small percentage of these people go on to develop an eating disorder such as anorexia nervosa, bulimia nervosa, or binge eating disorder. While eating disorders affect females far more frequently than males, research does show that 10% of people with eating disorders are boys. Eating disorders are becoming increasingly common in young people. Today, they are the third most common chronic illness affecting teenage females. It's estimated that as many as 5% of young Canadian girls have an eating disorder, a rate that has risen dramatically over the past three decades.[1]

Perhaps your daughter has told you that she suspects a friend has an eating disorder. She's noticed that her friend has started avoiding the school cafeteria at lunch and spends all her free time exercising at the gym. Or maybe you're concerned that your own child is developing strange food rituals. At family meals you've watched her cut food into tiny pieces, move them around on her plate, but barely eat a thing. There are good reasons to be worried about your daughter, or her friend, and to address the problem as soon as possible. Eating disorders are categorized as mental illnesses, and they have serious and life-threatening physical effects on the body.

Anorexia Nervosa

Anorexia nervosa is characterized by an intense fear of gaining weight, even if one is underweight. People with anorexia nervosa are obsessed with being thin and have an unrealistic image of their body. When they look in the mirror, anorexics see themselves as fat, no matter how thin or emaciated they have become. To achieve weight loss, anorexics become obsessed with eating very little food. They may weigh their food before eating it or compulsively count the calories in everything they eat. Many people with anorexia also exercise excessively in an attempt to lose weight. Some people with anorexia will self-induce vomiting or misuse laxatives or diuretics as part of a binge-purge cycle, risking their health even further.

Even though anorexics deny themselves food, they become obsessive about it, frequently collecting recipes and making for other people elaborate meals that they will not eat themselves. They ritualize food preparation and will sometimes hide food in special places, but never eat it. They get pleasure from controlling their eating and, as they begin to starve, they may even achieve a sense of euphoria from being so disciplined and successful in achieving their goals.

Anorexia nervosa most commonly begins in adolescence or the early twenties, but its onset has been reported in children as young as eight years old. The eating disorder may be a sudden, limited episode. In other words, the person may lose a dramatic amount of weight in a period of a few months and then recover. Or the illness may work itself into the victim's life and go on for years. People with anorexia may fluctuate between spells of improvement and worsening, or they may become steadily more ill as the disease progresses in severity.

What Causes Anorexia Nervosa?

We don't know the exact cause of anorexia nervosa but there are a number of theories as to why people develop it. Scientists believe the disease is the result of a combination of psychological, social, and biological factors. Anorexia afflicts most people between the ages of 14 and 18, a time when many teenagers don't feel as though they have much control over anything. The physical and emotional changes that accompany adolescence can easily erode a teenager's self-confidence. By taking rigid control of their food intake, anorexics are able to maintain a sense of control over some aspect of their lives—their own bodies. Often individuals who develop anorexia nervosa have very low self-esteem. Some are depressed.

The eating disorder may be triggered by stress, anxiety, or anger toward family members or over other personal relationships.

It's also believed that people with eating disorders are responding to societal and cultural pressures to be thin. Girls typically develop more body fat during puberty than when they were younger, and this can make some teenagers very fearful of their new weight and changing figure.

In many cases, individuals who suffer from anorexia are perfectionists and over-achievers. By constantly striving to be perfect, they lay the foundation for failure. They are overly critical of themselves, set unreasonable standards of performance, and have a compulsive need to please others. Having low self-confidence and setting unrealistic goals often result in feelings of ineffectiveness that can lead to abnormal eating behaviours.

There may also be a biological explanation for eating disorders. Low levels of a brain chemical called serotonin are linked with depression and eating behaviours. Decreased serotonin activity has been associated with impulsive behaviour, and there is evidence to suggest that anorexics have lower levels of serotonin. Other theories suggest that the malfunctioning of the hypothalamus occurs in anorexia and may precede the illness. The hypothalamus is the part of the brain that controls hormone secretions, body temperature, fluid balance, and sugar and fat metabolism.

There is some evidence that eating disorders run in families. One reason may be that parents usually influence their children's attitudes toward food.

Warning Signs of Anorexia Nervosa

As I mentioned above, people with anorexia have a distorted vision of body image, feeling fat even when their weight is below normal. This may become apparent by things your teen says. Warning signs of anorexia nervosa include:

- A preoccupation with food and weight: excessive dieting, counting calories, checking body weight several times a day

- Significant weight loss, with no evidence of related illness

- Depression

- Denial of hunger, despite an extreme reduction in eating

- Strange eating habits: cutting food into small pieces, preferring food of specific texture or colour, refusing to eat in front of others

- Excessive exercise habits

- Withdrawal from social activities

- Complaints of feeling cold, because of dropping body temperatures

- Appearance of long, fine hair on the body as a way of conserving body heat

- Brittle hair and broken fingernails

- Dry, yellow skin

- Cessation of menstrual periods for three consecutive months

As the body starves, certain bodily processes slow down or stop. The illness does not spare any organ in the body. Blood pressure falls, breathing slows, menstruation ceases (or never begins), and the growth-regulating activities of the thyroid gland diminish. The skin becomes dry, and hair and nails become brittle. Light-headedness, cold intolerance, constipation, and joint swelling are other symptoms. Reduced body fat causes the body temperature to fall. Soft hair called lanugo forms on the skin for warmth. Dehydration sets in, and fainting spells are common. As the body loses potassium, sodium, and chloride, symptoms of fatigue, muscle weakness, irritability, muscle spasms, and depression can occur. In severe cases, these physical changes will cause irregular heartbeats, convulsions, and death due to kidney or heart failure. Approximately 1 in 10 women suffering from anorexia will die—a death rate that is among one of the highest for a psychiatric disease.

Depending on what stage of development teenagers are at when anorexia hits, some complications may be irreversible, such as growth retardation, delay of puberty, and impaired development of bone mass. If girls do not acquire adequate bone mass during their teen years, they will face a high risk of osteoporosis later in life.

Identifying Anorexia

Anorexia is usually diagnosed by the appearance of four specific symptoms:

- *Low body weight*—when an individual loses at least 15% of his or her body weight

- *Fear of gaining weight or becoming fat*—unhealthy weight control practices or obsessive thinking about food

- *Body image problems*—self-criticism about body shape and weight, even though he or she may be very thin

- *No menstrual periods*—failure to menstruate for at least three months

Because people with anorexia nervosa are very secretive about their eating habits, the illness can be hard to diagnose. Anorexics typically refuse to admit anything is wrong and may become angry or defensive when family or friends express concern. For this reason, the disorder may go undiagnosed for a long time. The most critical thing about any eating disorder is to recognize and address the problem as soon as possible. The longer the illness is left untreated, the more damage it does to the body and mind. And the more difficult it is to break unhealthy habits. The earlier the diagnosis, the more effective treatment will be.

Bulimia Nervosa

Bulimia nervosa is a quite different eating disorder from anorexia nervosa, as the person with bulimia does not avoid eating. Instead, she will eat large quantities of food in a short time and then get rid of it quickly by vomiting or by taking laxatives or diuretics. This behaviour is commonly referred to as bingeing and purging. Between binges, people with bulimia may fast or exercise excessively to combat weight gain caused by binge eating.

Bulimia usually begins in conjunction with a diet. But once the binge-purge cycle becomes established, it can get out of control. People suffering from bulimia may binge several times a day, sometimes consuming 10,000 calories or more in a matter of hours. Research has shown that the average binge lasts about one hour and results in the intake of about 3500 calories (a cheesecake, for example). Comfort foods that are sweet, soft, and high in calories (ice cream, cake, cookies, pastries) are common choices for bingeing. During the binge episode, people with bulimia nervosa feel a lack of control over their eating behaviour. Bulimics often spend $50 a day on food and may even steal money or food to support the obsession. Immediately after the binge comes the purge; some bulimics will use as many as 20 or more laxatives a day to rid their bodies of these huge quantities of food.

Like people with anorexia nervosa, bulimics are extremely fearful of becoming fat and are obsessed with body image. They fear food and yet they consume vast amounts of it. With anorexia nervosa, the extreme weight loss becomes an obvious outward sign of the illness. But people with bulimia usually look quite normal and often show few signs of their condition. Bulimics may appear average or even above-average weight. Although their body weight may fluctuate wildly, it usually stays within a normal range.

What Causes Bulimia?

Like other eating disorders, bulimia nervosa is thought to have psychological, social, and biological roots. It often affects high achievers who strive to conform to unrealistic ideals of thinness and beauty. It is thought that bulimics use food and weight as a means of controlling underlying emotional problems such as depression, anxiety, and low self-esteem. People with bulimia nervosa are very aware of their behaviour and feel guilty or remorseful. In this way, they are again quite unlike anorexics, who deny the existence of their illness.

Studies have shown that bulimics are particularly prone to impulsive behaviour. They have difficulty dealing with anxiety, have little self-control, and often indulge in drug or alcohol abuse or sexual promiscuity. They are also susceptible to depression, anxiety disorders, and social phobias. As with anorexia nervosa, people with bulimia have lower levels of brain neurotransmitters, such as serotonin, which may predispose them to developing these psychological disturbances.

Warning Signs of Bulimia Nervosa

In addition to the preoccupation with food and weight that is characteristic of most eating disorders, warning signs of bulimia include:

- Large amounts of food missing, stolen money or food
- Huge amounts of food being consumed but no weight gain
- Food cravings
- Complaints of stomach pain, which is caused by constant vomiting
- Excuses to go to the bathroom immediately after meals, to purge
- Development of "chipmunk cheeks," which occur when the salivary glands permanently expand from frequent vomiting
- Erosion of tooth enamel and other dental problems caused by frequent vomiting
- Feelings of shame, self-reproach, and guilt
- Emotional changes such as depression, irritability, or social withdrawal

The purging behaviour associated with bulimia can cause physical complications that are extremely dangerous to long-term health. Vomiting and purging can lead to imbalances in fluids and the electrolytes sodium, potassium, and chloride. When potassium levels fall too low, abnormal heart rhythms develop. Repeated vomiting can damage the esophagus and stomach, cause the gums to recede, and erode tooth enamel. In some cases, all teeth must be pulled prematurely because of constant contact with stomach acid. Other effects may be rashes, broken blood vessels in cheeks, and swelling around the eyes, ankles, and feet. Some bulimics use a medication called ipecac to induce vomiting. Overuse of this drug has been known to cause sudden death. The late singer Karen Carpenter, who suffered from anorexia nervosa, died after a build-up of ipecac irreversibly damaged her heart.

Identifying Bulimia Nervosa

Bulimia usually begins between the ages of 17 and 25. But because bulimics are deeply ashamed of their bingeing and purging and keep these behaviours a secret, the disorder can be hard to identify. Often a diagnosis is not made until a victim is well into her 30s or 40s and seeks help for the condition. Bulimia is usually suspected when the following symptoms are present:

- Binge eating: consuming a few to several thousand calories in a two-hour period accompanied by the feeling that one cannot stop or control eating.

- Purging: trying to undo the binge eating by vomiting, using laxatives or diuretics, or exercising excessively.

- Bingeing and purging more than twice a week for at least three months.

- Body image—self-evaluation and self-esteem are overly influenced by body weight and shape.

You can't necessarily tell that someone has bulimia nervosa by her body weight. In people with bulimia, weight can be normal, underweight, or overweight. However, weight can also dramatically shift, and large swings might be an indicator that someone has bulimia.

Binge Eating Disorder

Formerly called compulsive overeating, binge eating disorder (BED) has many similarities to bulimia nervosa. People with BED frequently eat huge quantities of food and feel out of control and powerless over their eating. After a binge, a person with BED feels ashamed or guilty. But unlike someone with bulimia, a person suffering from BED does not purge by vomiting or using laxatives. And although someone with BED eats compulsively, she does not exercise excessively as does someone with bulimia.

Most of us are guilty of overeating at one time or another, but binge eating disorder goes beyond normal overeating. People with BED regularly feel a powerful urge to overeat, and they don't stop eating when they feel full. Binge eating may be the means by which teenagers deal with difficult emotions: teenagers with a binge eating problem may be depressed, stressed, anxious, upset, hurt, or angry. Scientists are not sure whether depression is a symptom of BED or an underlying cause of the condition. Research is also investigating the link between brain chemicals and BED.

BED can lead to weight gain, unhealthy dieting, and emotional distress. Most people who binge eat are overweight and may become obese over time. Concerns about their body weight can lead people with BED to follow crash diets. Yo-yo dieting, the pattern of repeatedly losing then regaining weight, has its own set of health risks. Regular binge eating can lead to low energy, low self-esteem, and depression. Feelings of helplessness and hopelessness often surface when people are unable to stop binge eating.

What Causes Binge Eating Disorder?

There is no known single cause of binge eating. Experts believe that a combination of factors is responsible, including genetics, emotional issues, and learned behaviours. Some scientists believe that some people are more prone to overeating because the part of the brain that controls appetite fails to send proper messages about hunger and satiety. Serotonin, the brain chemical involved in mood, may be also involved in the development of BED. Patterns of overeating can begin in childhood, when food may be overused to comfort, reward, or punish. Some children may grow up thinking that negative emotions should be suppressed and may turn to food to deal with their feelings.

Warning Signs of Binge Eating Disorder

There are several warning signs of BED. Some of these signs may be apparent only to the person who has BED; nevertheless, as a parent, it is important to be aware of them to help you better understand the disorder.

- Frequently eating an abnormally large amount of food

- Feeling unable to control what or how much food is eaten

- Eating more rapidly than usual

- Eating until uncomfortably full

- Eating large amounts of food, even when not hungry

- Feelings of disgust, guilt, or depression after overeating

- Eating alone because of embarrassment at the quantity of food being eaten

Binge eating disorder occurs most often in people who are overweight and obese (BMI greater than 27) and it becomes more prevalent as body weight increases. It's estimated that between 30% and 90% of all people who are obese have binge eating problems. Obese people with BED become overweight at an earlier age than those without the disorder and may suffer more frequent bouts of losing and regaining weight. BED occurs slightly more often in women than in men and tends to appear in later years, affecting an older population than either anorexia or bulimia nervosa. While BED is typically diagnosed in adults, the age of onset is unknown. Triggers for the disorder, such as depression, strict dieting, and bingeing episodes, could begin in the teen years.

Identifying Binge Eating Disorder

BED can be very difficult to distinguish from other causes of obesity. Because people with the disorder are embarrassed about their behaviour, they work very hard to conceal their bingeing tendencies. Binge eating is defined as eating a large quantity of food in a discrete period of time, usually two hours or less, and feeling out of control while doing so. Someone is said to have BED if the binge eating occurs at least twice a week for six months. Doctors look for overeating habits that establish an out-of-control pattern and cause distress or problems in a teenager's life.

The Female Athlete Triad

Teenage girls who play sports are at risk of developing the female athlete triad, a combination of three interrelated conditions associated with training: disordered eating, amenorrhea (loss of one's menstrual period), and osteoporosis. A female athlete can have one, two, or all three parts of the triad. The true prevalence of disordered eating in sports is difficult to determine because of the tendency of those affected to hide their problem. However, some studies report that anorexia nervosa and bulimia nervosa occurs in 3% and 20% of athletes, respectively. When you include other types of disordered eating, the prevalence jumps to 15% to 60%, depending on the study.[2]

Teenage girls are faced with enormous pressure to be thin and have an attractive appearance. Some girls focus on thinness and an ideal body weight. For the teenage athlete, changes in body fat that occur naturally with puberty may be disconcerting. Sports-related pressures and expectations add to the physical and emotional challenges of adolescence. When all these factors are combined, it's easy to see why some female athletes develop an eating disorder.

Girls with the female athlete triad try to lose weight mainly to improve their sports performance. An offhand remark by a coach or parent about the need to lose a little bit of weight to get that competitive edge can trigger the development of an eating disorder. Sometimes the disordered eating that accompanies the condition isn't technically an eating disorder, but it can involve calorie counting, purging, and excessive exercise to lose weight.

Excessive exercise and weight loss can decrease the amount of estrogen in a girl's body. As a result, her period may become irregular or cease altogether. (If your daughter complains of a missed period and she is sexually active, she should be tested for pregnancy.) Girls who participate in sports from a young age may never get their first period. Other girls may have started menstruation, but as their training increases and their calorie intake declines, their periods may stop.

Low estrogen levels and a low-calorie diet that lacks calcium and vitamin D can lead to osteoporosis, the loss of bone density and inadequate formation of bone. The consequences of lost bone density can be devastating for a female athlete. Premature osteoporosis puts female athletes at increased risk of stress fractures as well as more devastating fractures of the hip or spine. Lost bone mineral density may never be regained. A poor diet may also lead to slow recovery and healing from sports injuries.

Who's at Risk of Female Athlete Triad?

Thankfully, not every girl who plays sports develops the female athlete triad. Those who do develop the triad tend to be highly competitive and participate in sports that put them at risk. Sports that classify athletes by weight, such as wrestling and rowing, increase the risk of disordered eating. So do sports that value a thin and lean body—gymnastics, dance, figure skating, swimming, and diving, for example. It's estimated that disordered eating may be as high as 62% in gymnastics and as high as 31% in males who compete in rowing and wrestling.[3]

Even sports that don't focus on body size for judging purposes may pressure girls to be thinner. Track and field, distance running, and cross-country skiing coaches might believe that a girl losing some body fat could improve her performance. Frequent weigh-ins, punitive consequences for weight gain, pressure to win at all costs, an overly controlling parent or coach, and social isolation caused by intensive involvement in sports may increase an athlete's risk of developing the triad.

Warning Signs of the Female Athlete Triad

The signs and symptoms of anorexia nervosa and bulimia nervosa listed above also apply to the female athlete triad. If a girl has risk factors for the triad, she may already be experiencing symptoms such as:

- Weight loss
- Irregular or missed periods
- Fatigue and difficulty concentrating
- Frequent comments about one's weight and body shape
- Refusing to eat with other people (e.g., teammates on road trips)
- Frequent trips to the bathroom after eating
- Criticism about the eating habits of other people
- Stress fractures and muscle injuries
- Abnormal anxiety about an injury
- Excessive exercise outside of the normal training regime
- Inability to relax

At first, the symptoms of the female athlete triad may be subtle. As soon as a coach, parent, or teammate suspects the condition in a female athlete, it is imperative to have her seek medical treatment. The doctor may recognize features of the triad during a routine exam, symptoms such as fatigue, anemia, electrolyte abnormalities, or depression caused by dieting. The doctor may also detect many of the common signs of an eating disorder. Because the risk of bone loss increases with the duration of amenorrhea, the doctor may order a special bone scan (dual energy X-ray absorptiometry or DEXA) in an athlete with amenorrhea lasting at least six months.

Preventing Female Athlete Triad

If your teenage daughter participates in sports, she needs to stay on top of her physical condition. She needs to educate herself about nutrition and eat regular meals and snacks. If she is serious about her sports performance, you might suggest she consult a registered dietitian who works with teen athletes. It's also important that she keep track of her menstrual periods. It's easy for girls to forget when they last got their period, so keeping track on a calendar is a good idea.

Teenage athletes also need to keep in mind that everyone is genetically unique. Some girls are predisposed to carrying more body fat than others and may not be able to lose weight without drastically reducing their food intake. Teenaged girls who understand this and accept their own body shape will be much less likely to engage in unhealthy dieting behaviours. Encourage your daughter to enjoy her sport for herself and no one else. If your daughter no longer enjoys her sport because of performance and weight pressures, encourage her to make a change. Make sure she knows she is not letting anyone down if she quits.

Preventing Eating Disorders

Parents can help prevent their child from developing an eating disorder by boosting their child's self-esteem. It is important for parents to reinforce exercising and healthy eating habits without emphasizing their child's weight and body image. Parents should also try to decrease competitiveness in young girls. Watch your child's reactions to models and other girls to see whether they are comparing themselves. Always discourage negative comments or statements about needing to lose weight.

Parents must also model the behaviour they wish to see in their children. Parents should exhibit healthy amounts of exercise and not openly criticize their own bodies. To do this, some parents may need to get in touch with their own eating habits and relationship with food. It's also important to try to eat together as a family so you are able to monitor your teenager's eating habits.

If You Suspect Your Teen Has an Eating Disorder

The severe health risks and the potential for eating disorders to become obsessive make it imperative that parents get professional help and treatment for their child if an eating disorder is suspected. But getting your child treatment may be a difficult task. She may deny the eating disorder, tell you that she has it under control, or be hostile to you.

Start by seeking help from your family physician or pediatrician. Ask for a referral to a treatment program for eating disorders. You will then need to explore the various options available to you and seek medical attention and some sort of therapy. Again, early treatment is crucial. As an eating disorder becomes more entrenched, the damage it causes becomes less reversible.

Keep an open line of communication with your child and never make her feel that her behaviour is bad or wrong. Doing so could cause her to hide her eating disorder and withdraw from the family. Critical comments and judgments are rarely helpful and only add to a teenager's feelings of self-criticism. Parents should also attempt to find out the underlying reason why their child has an eating disorder. This will be essential for offering support and helping your child heal.

For more information and literature on eating disorders, contact the National Eating Disorder Information Centre (see the Resources section at the back of this book for more details).

If Your Teen Suspects Her Friend Has an Eating Disorder

If your teen suspects that her friend has an eating disorder, she needs to confront this person in private and encourage her to seek medical help. She should tell her friend about the behaviours that she has noticed in a caring, non-judgmental way. She should listen carefully and be supportive of what her friend is going through. Your teen needs to know that it's normal for people with eating disorders to be defensive or angry when they are confronted for the first time. She should try not to be angry back. If her friend still seems in denial, your teen should discuss her concerns with a school counsellor or nurse, or her friend's parents. Although this isn't easy, it may be required to get her friend the help she needs.

Being a supportive friend also means learning about eating disorders and knowing how to behave around someone who is dealing with such an illness. Your teen should avoid talking about food and being overly watchful of her friend's eating habits or food choices.

Treatment Options for Teens with Eating Disorders

The goal of therapy for most eating disorders is to restore a normal weight, normalize eating patterns, overcome unhealthy attitudes about body image and self-worth, and provide support to family and friends who may be helping with the recovery process. Because eating disorders have such a widespread influence and affect so many aspects of daily life, effective treatment requires a collaborative effort from a team of health professionals. The team usually consists of a family physician to manage physical symptoms, a psychiatrist or psychologist to introduce behavioural modification, and a nutritionist to establish a healthy diet for recovery. The sooner an eating disorder is identified and treated, the better the eventual outcome. It is necessary to think of recovery in terms of months or years rather than weeks.

The National Eating Disorder Information Centre (see Resources) provides qualified referrals for the treatment of eating disorders.

Anorexia Nervosa

In the early stages, anorexia nervosa may be treated without hospitalization. But when weight loss is severe, hospitalization is necessary to restore weight and prevent further physical deterioration. A structured approach that involves careful observation of all eating and elimination (urinating, bowel movements, and vomiting) is the first stage of treatment. Once weight is restored and symptoms are stabilized, some type of psychotherapy is required to deal with the underlying emotional issues triggering the abnormal eating patterns. Family therapy is especially helpful for younger girls, and behavioural or cognitive therapy is also effective in helping replace destructive attitudes with positive ones. A nutritionist will add support by providing advice on proper diet and eating regimens. In some cases, antidepressant medication may be prescribed, but it should not be used as a substitute for appropriate psychological treatment.

Unfortunately, many people with anorexia nervosa have a tendency to relapse and return to dysfunctional eating habits. Long-term therapy and regular health monitoring are essential for a successful result. A strong network of love and support from family and friends is also crucial to the recovery process.

Bulimia Nervosa

In most cases, people with bulimia are treated without hospitalization. Because it is a psychological condition, cognitive and behaviour therapy are necessary to deal with the emotional issues underlying the symptoms of this disorder. As with anorexia nervosa, a multi-disciplinary approach to treatment works best. Physicians, nutritionists, and mental health professionals work together to address the many facets of this eating disorder. In particular, long-term psychotherapy is needed to help reduce destructive tendencies and develop better coping strategies. Antidepressant medication has proven to be an effective psychological intervention.

Binge Eating Disorder

Many of the medical problems related to obesity are also associated with binge eating disorder. Treatment may be necessary for related conditions such as high cholesterol, high blood pressure, diabetes, gallbladder disease, and heart disease. Other than the appropriate therapies for obesity-related disorders, there are no standard treatments for BED. As with most eating disorders, an approach that involves psychotherapy and anti-depressant medication seems to be most effective. It is essential to deal with the emotional issues of the illness. Because people with BED find it very difficult to stay on a treatment regimen and frequently return to unhealthy eating behaviours, long-term therapy is always recommended.

The Female Athlete Triad

Like other eating disorders, treatment of the female athlete triad involves the athlete working with a dietitian, psychologist or psychiatrist, and family doctor. But doctors also work with coaches, parents, and physical therapists to help their patients recover. Some girls may be prescribed the birth control pill, to supply their bodies with estrogen in order to resume their periods. Calcium and vitamin D supplementation is also recommended for girls who have suffered bone loss.

Leslie's Tips for Dealing with Eating Disorders

1. To help prevent an eating disorder in your teen, reinforce healthy eating and exercise without focusing on your teen's body weight.

2. As a parent, be a good role model. Make sure your teen sees you eating healthy meals and exercising. Don't be openly critical about other people's bodies, including your own.

3. Instill in your teen the belief that she is a unique, valuable, and worthwhile individual regardless of her body weight. Teach her to feel good about herself whatever her body size.

4. To help detect an eating disorder early, become familiar with the warning signs of anorexia, bulimia, binge eating disorder, and the female athlete triad.

5. Make sure your teen visits her doctor for an annual physical exam. Often physicians can recognize subtle features of an eating disorder during a routine exam.

6. If your teenager is serious about her sport, suggest she consult with a registered dietitian to learn about sports nutrition and get a meal plan that provides adequate calories, calcium, and iron.

7. If your teen no longer enjoys her sport because of body weight pressures, let her know that it is okay to quit. Encourage her to find a sport she enjoys.

8. If you suspect your teen has an eating disorder, confront her in a non-judgmental and caring way. Listen carefully and be supportive of what she is going through.

9. If your suspicions are correct, seek treatment immediately; ask your family physician for a referral to a treatment program for eating disorders.

10. Learn as much as you can about your teen's eating disorder and provide plenty of love and support during recovery. Be committed to being a part of the recovery process.

Part Four

———— ⁕⁕⁕ ————

The Recipes

BREAKFASTS ON THE GO

MUFFINS

Cranberry Flax Muffins

Flaxseeds add omega-3 fatty acids and soluble fibre to these tasty muffins. Their nutty taste, combined with the tartness of cranberries, makes for muffins that are sure to please everyone in the family.

1 cup	flaxseeds	250 ml
1 cup	each all-purpose flour, whole-wheat flour, and natural bran	250 ml
1 tbsp	baking powder	15 ml
1 tsp	each baking soda and cinnamon	5 ml
1/2 tsp	salt	2 ml
2	eggs	2
1 1/2 cups	buttermilk	375 ml
1 cup	packed brown sugar	250 ml
1/3 cup	vegetable oil	75 ml
1 1/2 cups	dried cranberries	375 ml

Set aside 2 tbsp (25 ml) of the flaxseeds.

In food processor, finely grind remaining flaxseeds; transfer to large bowl. Add all-purpose flour, whole-wheat flour, natural bran, baking powder, baking soda, cinnamon, and salt; whisk to combine.

In separate bowl, whisk together eggs, buttermilk, sugar, and oil; pour over dry ingredients. Sprinkle with cranberries; stir just until combined.

Spoon into 12 greased or paper-lined muffin cups; sprinkle with reserved flaxseeds. Bake in centre of 375°F (190°C) oven until tops are firm to the touch, about 20 minutes. Let cool in pan on rack for 5 minutes; transfer to rack and let cool completely.

Makes 12 servings.

Per muffin: about 338 cal, 8 g pro, 12 g total fat (1 g sat. fat), 54 g carb, 7 g fibre, 32 mg chol, 315 mg sodium. % RDI: 12% calcium, 25% iron, 2% vit A, 5% vit C, 29% folate.

Morning Sunshine Muffins

These muffins make a healthy breakfast-on-the-go. Just add a piece of fruit and a serving of yogurt and your teenager is good to go!

1 1/2 cups	each all-purpose and whole-wheat flours	375 ml
2 tsp	baking powder	10 ml
2 tsp	cinnamon	10 ml
1 tsp	baking soda	5 ml
1/2 tsp	ground ginger	2 ml
1/4 tsp	salt	1 ml
2	eggs	2
1 cup	packed brown sugar	250 ml
1 cup	mashed very ripe bananas	250 ml
2/3 cup	plain yogurt, full fat	150 ml
1/3 cup	vegetable oil	75 ml
2 cups	grated carrots (about 4)	500 ml
1 cup	chopped dates or raisins	250 ml
1/2 cup	chopped toasted pecans	125 ml
12	pecan halves	12

Grease 12 muffin cups or line with large paper liners; set aside.

In large bowl, whisk together all-purpose and whole-wheat flours, baking powder, cinnamon, baking soda, ginger, and salt.

In separate bowl, whisk together eggs, sugar, bananas, yogurt, and oil; pour over dry ingredients. Sprinkle with carrots, dates, and chopped pecans; mix just until dry ingredients are moistened.

Spoon into prepared cups until heaping but not spilling over; press pecan half into top of each. Bake in centre of 375°F (190°C) oven for about 30 minutes or until tester inserted in centre comes out clean. Let cool in pan on rack for 10 minutes. Transfer to rack and let cool completely. (Make-ahead: Store in airtight container for up to 1 day or wrap individually in plastic wrap and freeze in airtight container for up to 2 weeks.)

Makes 12 servings

Per muffin: about 361 cal, 7 g pro, 12 g total fat (1 g sat. fat), 60 g carb, 5 g fibre, 37 mg chol, 226 mg sodium. % RDI: 8% calcium, 17% iron, 44% vit A, 3% vit C, 15% folate.

CEREALS AND GRAINS

Deluxe Porridge

Here's a hearty, wholesome breakfast cereal with the delicious addition of nuts and raisins.

1 1/2 cups	large-flake rolled oats (not instant)	375 ml
1/3 cup	skim milk powder	75 ml
1/4 cup	packed brown sugar	50 ml
1/4 cup	natural bran	50 ml
1/2 tsp	cinnamon	2 ml
1/4 tsp	each salt and nutmeg	1 ml
2 tbsp	each raisins and chopped pecans	25 ml
2 tbsp	maple syrup	25 ml

In large saucepan, bring 3 1/2 cups (875 ml) water to boil. Using wooden spoon, gradually stir in oats. Reduce heat to medium; cover and simmer for 10 minutes.

Stir in skim milk powder, sugar, bran, cinnamon, salt, and nutmeg; cover and cook for about 10 minutes or until porridge is thick enough to mound on spoon.

Spoon into bowls. Top with raisins, pecans, and maple syrup.

Makes 6 servings.

Per serving: about 174 cal, 5 g pro, 3 g total fat (trace sat. fat), 34 g carb, 4 g fibre, 1 mg chol, 125 mg sodium. % RDI: 7% calcium, 11% iron (1.6 mg), 0% vit A, 0% vit C, 4% folate.

Microwave method: In large microwaveable casserole, microwave water at High for 3 minutes. Stir in all ingredients except raisins, pecans, and syrup. Microwave, uncovered, at High until thickened, 10 to 12 minutes. Spoon into bowls; add toppings.

OATMEAL TOPPERS

Jazz up your favourite bowl of hot cereal with a tempting topping.

• Dried fruits, such as raisins, cherries, cranberries, chopped apricots, dates, or figs

• Fresh or thawed frozen fruits, such as sliced strawberries, raspberries, blueberries, chopped apples, or pears (leave the skins on for extra fibre), bananas, sliced plums, or peaches

• Chopped toasted nuts or coconut

• Maple or fruit syrup

Hot Almond Honey Multigrain Cereal

Vary the flavour—and boost nutrition—by stirring in a handful of chopped dried fruit, such as dates or figs.

3 cups	low-fat milk	750 ml
1/2 tsp	salt	2 ml
1 cup	multigrain cereal (such as Red River or Sunny Boy)	250 ml
1/2 cup	slivered almonds	125 ml
1/4 cup	liquid honey	50 ml
Pinch	nutmeg or cinnamon	Pinch

In saucepan, bring milk and salt to boil.

Whisk in multigrain cereal, almonds, honey, and nutmeg. Reduce heat and simmer, whisking constantly, for 3 to 4 minutes or until desired thickness.

Makes 4 servings.

Per serving: about 349 cal, 14 g pro, 11 g total fat (2 g sat. fat), 53 g carb, 6 g fibre, 8 mg chol, 412 mg sodium. % RDI: 25% calcium, 16% iron, 10% vit A, 3% vit C, 12% folate.

Maple Walnut Multigrain Porridge

When buying shelled walnuts, look for ones that are plump, meaty, and crisp. Avoid those that appear shrivelled or dried out. And always store them tightly wrapped in a plastic bag.

3 cups	low-fat milk	750 ml
1/2 tsp	salt	2 ml
1 cup	multigrain cereal such as Red River or Sunny Boy	250 ml
1/2 cup	chopped walnuts	125 ml
2 tbsp	maple syrup	25 ml
1 tsp	vanilla extract	5 ml

Stove top: In saucepan, bring milk and salt to boil. Whisk in multigrain cereal, walnuts, maple syrup, and vanilla. Reduce heat and simmer, whisking constantly, for 6 to 7 minutes or until desired thickness.

Microwave: In 12-cup (3-L) microwaveable casserole dish, microwave milk with salt at High for 3 minutes or until boiling. Whisk in multigrain cereal, chopped walnuts, maple syrup, and vanilla. Microwave, covered, at High, stirring often, for 6 minutes or until desired thickness.

Makes 4 servings.

Per serving (based on 2% milk): about 349 cal, 14 g pro, 14 g total fat (3 g sat. fat), 45 g carb, 5 g fibre, 14 mg chol, 392 mg sodium. % RDI: 22% calcium, 9% iron, 9% vit A, 2% vit C, 17% folate.

Homemade Granola

Granola is almost as easy to make as it is to buy—and you control the ingredients. Customize by adding toasted pecans or almonds, chopped dried papaya or apricots, or flaked coconut with the cranberries.

3 cups	rolled oats	750 ml
2/3 cup	wheat germ	150 ml
1/2 cup	unsalted sunflower seeds, roasted	125 ml
1/2 cup	liquid honey	125 ml
1/4 cup	vegetable oil	50 ml
2/3 cup	dried cranberries or raisins	150 ml

In bowl, combine oats, wheat germ, and sunflower seeds.

In small saucepan set over medium heat, stir honey with oil just until steaming. Pour over oat mixture, stirring to coat.

Spread mixture on parchment paper–lined baking sheet and bake in 350°F (180°C) oven, stirring frequently, until golden brown, about 15 minutes. Remove from oven; stir in cranberries. Let cool, stirring occasionally to prevent clumping. (Make-ahead: Refrigerate in airtight container for up to 1 month.)

Makes about 4 1/2 cups (1.1 L) or 9 servings.

Per 1/2 cup (125 ml): about 309 cal, 8 g pro, 12 g total fat (1 g sat. fat), 46 g carb, 5 g fibre, 0 mg chol, 5 mg sodium. % RDI: 2% calcium, 15% iron, 0% vit A, 3% vit C, 20% folate.

Muesli Mix

Even though muesli is traditionally soaked and mixed with fruit for breakfast, this toasted mix is equally delicious not soaked and served with cold or warm milk.

4 cups	large-flake rolled oats	1 L
1 cup	wheat bran	250 ml
1 cup	chopped walnuts or almonds	250 ml
1 cup	chopped dried apricots	250 ml
1 cup	chopped dates, figs, or raisins	250 ml
1 cup	dried cranberries or cherries	250 ml

On large rimmed baking sheet, toast oats, bran, and walnuts in 350°F (180°C) oven, stirring 3 times, until golden and fragrant, about 12 minutes. Let cool.

In large airtight container, combine toasted oat mixture, apricots, dates, and cranberries. (Make-ahead: Store at room temperature for up to 3 weeks or freeze for up to 2 months.)
Makes 9 cups (2.25 L).

Serving suggestion: In bowl, combine 1/2 to 3/4 cup (125 to 175 ml) Muesli Mix with 1/3 cup (75 ml) milk or juice; refrigerate overnight. Top with dollop of plain or flavoured yogurt, a drizzle of honey, and sliced apple, banana, or fresh berries.

Per 1/2 cup (125 ml): about 195 cal, 5 g pro, 6 g total fat (1 g sat. fat), 34 g carb, 6 g fibre, 0 mg chol, 3 mg sodium. % RDI: 2% calcium, 14% iron, 5% vit A, 2% vit C, 9% folate.

Whole-Wheat Pancakes

By adding whole-wheat flour, wheat germ, and skim milk powder, you can increase fibre and calcium intakes without anyone even suspecting. The pancakes are as good with salsa or chili sauce as they are with syrup.

1 1/2 cups	all-purpose flour	375 ml
1/2 cup	whole-wheat flour	125 ml
3 tbsp	granulated sugar	50 ml
2 tbsp	each wheat germ and skim milk powder	25 ml
1 tbsp	baking powder	15 ml
1/4 tsp	each salt and ground nutmeg	1 ml
2	eggs	2
2 cups	2% milk	500 ml
3 tbsp	vegetable oil	50 ml

In bowl, whisk together all-purpose and whole-wheat flours, sugar, wheat germ, skim milk powder, baking powder, salt, and nutmeg.

In separate bowl, whisk together eggs, milk, and 2 tbsp (25 ml) of the oil; pour over flour mixture and stir just until combined.

Heat large non-stick skillet or griddle over medium heat; brush with some of the remaining oil. Using 1/4 cup (50 ml) batter for each pancake, pour batter into pan; cook until bubbles break on top but do not fill in, 2 to 3 minutes. Turn and cook until bottom is golden, about 1 minute.
Makes 18 pancakes or 4 to 6 servings.

Per each of 6 servings: about 314 cal, 10 g pro, 11 g total fat (2 g sat. fat), 44 g carb, 3 g fibre, 78 mg chol, 295 mg sodium. % RDI: 17% calcium, 16% iron, 8% vit A, 0% vit C, 23% folate.

Variation: Whole-Wheat Waffles: Heat waffle iron; brush lightly with some of the oil. Pour in 1/2 cup (125 ml) batter for each waffle, spreading to edges. Close lid and cook until crisp and golden and steam stops, 4 to 5 minutes.
Makes 8 waffles or 4 to 6 servings.

EGG DISHES

Eggs with Black Bean Salsa

Salsa and jalapeño pepper spice up these eggs, while black beans add a healthy dose of fibre, iron, protein, and magnesium.

1 tbsp	vegetable oil	15 ml
1	each small onion and clove garlic, chopped	1
2 tsp	minced jalapeño pepper	10 ml
1	can (19 oz/540 ml) black beans, drained and rinsed	1
2	plum tomatoes, chopped	2
1 cup	salsa	250 ml
2 tbsp	chopped fresh coriander	25 ml
1 tsp	cider vinegar	5 ml
8	eggs	8

In saucepan, heat oil over medium heat; cook onion, garlic, and jalapeño for 5 minutes or until softened. Stir in beans, tomatoes, and salsa; cook for 8 minutes or until thickened. Stir in coriander and vinegar.

Meanwhile, in large non-stick skillet over medium heat, cover and cook eggs, 4 at a time, for 3 minutes or until yolks are set.

Spoon salsa onto plates; nestle eggs in salsa.
Makes 4 servings.

Per serving: about 331 cal, 22 g pro, 14 g total fat (4 g sat. fat), 30 g carb, 8 g fibre, 429 mg chol, 554 mg sodium. % RDI: 10% calcium, 29% iron, 27% vit A, 30% vit C, 84% folate.

Skinny Omelette Roll-Up

Research shows that 75% of Canadians spend less than 15 minutes preparing breakfast. This single serving roll-up takes only a couple of minutes to prepare and a minute to cook, making it easy for everyone to stay on schedule.

1	egg	1
1 tbsp	2% milk	15 ml
Pinch	each salt and pepper	Pinch
1/4 tsp	vegetable oil	1 ml
1	7-inch (18 cm) flour tortilla	1
1 tbsp	shredded brick cheese	15 ml
1 tsp	chopped fresh parsley (optional)	5 ml

Whisk together egg, milk, salt, and pepper.

Heat 6-inch (15 cm) non-stick skillet over medium-high heat; brush with oil. Pour in egg mixture, tilting to spread evenly; cook, piercing any bubbles, for about 1 minute or until set.

Slide onto tortilla; sprinkle with cheese, and parsley (if using). Roll up.
Makes 1 serving.

Per serving: about 220 cal, 11 g pro, 10 g total fat (4 g sat. fat), 20 g carb, 1 g fibre, 194 mg chol, 263 mg sodium. % RDI: 9% calcium, 12% iron, 11% vit A, 0% vit C, 30% folate.

Tip: Try any combination of herbs and cheese, such as cheddar and chives, or mozzarella and basil.

Western Omelette Pockets

Fast enough to make and enjoy as breakfast on the run, this is a great meal for lunchtime, too. Use whole-wheat pita bread, and accompany with orange segments or unsweetened juice.

1 tsp	butter	5 ml
4	mushrooms, sliced	4
Half	sweet green pepper, chopped	Half
1/4 cup	chopped cooked ham	50 ml
1	green onion, chopped	1
Half	tomato, chopped	Half
4	eggs	4
1/4 tsp	dried basil	1 ml
Pinch	each salt and pepper	Pinch
2	6-inch (15 cm) whole-wheat pita breads	2
4	lettuce leaves (optional)	4

In non-stick skillet, melt butter over medium-high heat; cook mushrooms, green pepper, ham, and onion, stirring often, for about 3 minutes or until vegetables are slightly tender. Add tomato; cook just until heated through.

Whisk together eggs, basil, salt, and pepper; pour over vegetable mixture. Cook for 3 minutes or until almost set, gently lifting edges with spatula to allow uncooked eggs to flow underneath. Remove from heat; let stand for 3 minutes or until eggs are completely set.

Cut pitas in half to form pockets. Line each with lettuce leaf (if using). Cut omelette into 4 wedges; place in pockets.
Makes 4 servings.

Per serving: about 189 cal, 12 g pro, 7 g total fat (2 g sat. fat), 19 g carb, 3 g fibre, 193 mg chol, 358 mg sodium. % RDI: 5% calcium, 11% iron, 12% vit A, 23% vit C, 19% folate.

Variation: Quick Western Sandwich: Omit mushrooms. Cut omelette into quarters; place each between 2 slices of toast.

Tip: For an easy change, roll up the omelette and lettuce in a large tortilla instead of slipping them into pita pockets.

SMOOTHIES, DAIRY AND FRUIT

Frothy Fruit Smoothie

This creamy low-fat drink combines choices from two of the food groups. Serve with toast or a bagel for a balanced breakfast.

1 cup	milk	250 ml
1	can (14 oz/398 ml) peach halves, drained	1
1/2 cup	drained canned apricot halves	125 ml
1 tbsp	lemon juice	15 ml
1 tsp	liquid honey	5 ml
Pinch	cinnamon	Pinch

In blender, combine milk, peaches, apricots, lemon juice, honey, and cinnamon; purée until thick and frothy. **Makes 4 servings.**

Per serving: about 95 cal, 3 g pro, 1 g total fat (1 g sat. fat), 20 g carb, 1 g fibre, 5 mg chol, 35 mg sodium. % RDI: 7% calcium, 2% iron, 9% vit A, 8% vit C, 3% folate.

Fruity Tofu Smoothie

Tofu adds protein to this tasty morning drink. Custard-like silken tofu works best.

1 cup	fresh or frozen fruit (such as mixed tropical fruit, peaches, or strawberries)	250 ml
1 cup	orange juice	250 ml
1/2 cup	silken or soft tofu	125 ml
1/2 cup	plain low-fat yogurt	125 ml
2 tbsp	lemon juice	25 ml
2 tbsp	liquid honey	25 ml
1	banana	1

In blender, purée together fruit, orange juice, tofu, yogurt, lemon juice, honey, and banana until smooth. **Makes 2 servings.**

Per serving: about 276 cal, 8 g pro, 3 g total fat (1 g sat. fat), 59 g carb, 4 g fibre, 4 mg chol, 64 mg sodium. % RDI: 13% calcium, 7% iron, 7% vit A, 103% vit C, 35% folate.

Tip: Frozen bananas make smoothies thick and frosty. Wrap peeled ripe bananas tightly in plastic wrap, and freeze.

Fruity Yogurt Granola Trifle

This fun breakfast idea has endless variations. Try cubed cantaloupe, fresh raspberries, pineapple chunks, or even your favourite stewed fruit.

1 cup	low-fat plain or flavoured yogurt	250 ml
1 cup	granola	250 ml
3/4 cup	each sliced bananas, kiwifruit, and strawberries	75 ml
1 tbsp	liquid honey (optional)	15 ml

Spoon one-third of the yogurt into each of 2 glass dessert dishes. Top with one-third of the fruit, then half of the granola.

Repeat layers, ending with fruit on top. Drizzle with honey, if using.

Makes 2 servings.

Per serving: about 444 cal, 15 g pro, 14 g total fat (2.7 g sat. fat), 66 g carb, 7 g fibre, 7 mg chol, 93 mg sodium. % RDI: 23% calcium, 18% iron, 3% vit A, 70% vit C, 34% folate.

Sunrise Banana Split Parfait

Here, dairy and fruit are dressed up in a little morning indulgence—they're sure to make even the grumpiest of morning grumps smile. For a special treat, use frozen yogurt.

1/2 cup	sliced strawberries	125 ml
1 tsp	granulated sugar	5 ml
1	small banana, sliced	1
1 cup	vanilla-flavoured or plain yogurt, full fat	250 ml
2 tsp	chocolate syrup (optional)	10 ml
2 tsp	roasted sunflower seeds	10 ml

Mash strawberries with sugar. Divide half of the banana between 2 sundae cups or glass dessert bowls. Divide 2 tbsp (25 ml) of the strawberry sauce on top, then 1/2 cup (125 ml) of the yogurt. Divide remaining banana over top, then yogurt, then strawberry sauce.

Drizzle evenly with chocolate syrup (if using). Sprinkle with sunflower seeds.

Makes 2 servings.

Per serving: about 165 cal, 7 g pro, 5 g total fat (4 g sat. fat), 25 g carb, 2 g fibre, 17 mg chol, 60 mg sodium. % RDI: 15% calcium, 4% iron, 6% vit A, 47% vit C, 10% folate.

Fruity Breakfast Crisp

Although we think of crisp as a dessert, it also makes a healthy breakfast. Make it the night before for a quick spoon-it-up starter (warm it in the microwave, if you wish) or include it in a brunch buffet menu on a slowed-down Sunday.

4 cups	sliced, pitted and peeled peaches	1 L
4 cups	quartered pitted plums	1 L
2 tbsp	all-purpose flour	25 ml
2 tbsp	granulated sugar	25 ml
3/4 cup	whole-wheat flour	175 ml
3/4 cup	rolled oats	175 ml
1/2 cup	packed brown sugar	125 ml
1/4 cup	unsalted sunflower seeds, roasted	50 ml
1/4 cup	wheat germ	50 ml
1/3 cup	butter, melted	75 ml
1 tbsp	apple juice	15 ml

In large bowl, toss together peaches, plums, all-purpose flour, and granulated sugar; arrange in 8-inch (2 L) square glass baking dish.

In separate bowl, combine whole-wheat flour, oats, brown sugar, sunflower seeds, and wheat germ; stir in butter, and apple juice. Sprinkle over fruit mixture.

Bake in 375°F (190°C) oven for 45 to 55 minutes or until bubbly and golden brown. Let stand for 30 minutes. (Crisp can be covered, and refrigerated for up to 1 day.) Serve warm or at room temperature.

Makes 8 servings.

Per serving: about 325 cal, 6 g pro, 12 g total fat (5 g sat. fat), 54 g carb, 6 g fibre, 24 mg chol, 85 mg sodium. % RDI: 3% calcium, 13% iron, 13% vit A, 17% vit C, 13% folate.

Tip: Try unpeeled nectarines instead of peaches.

LUNCH BAG SAVIOURS

PITAS, WRAPS, AND SANDWICHES

Chicken Salad Apple Sandwich

A chicken sandwich doesn't sound so exciting—until you add a touch of fragrant curry, and the sweet crunch of apple to the mix. This chicken salad is also wonderful served on a bed of tender baby spinach or spooned into mini-pitas as an hors d'oeuvre.

2	cooked boneless skinless chicken breasts	2
1/3 cup	diced sweet red pepper	75 ml
1/3 cup	diced celery	75 ml
2	green onions, thinly sliced	2
Half	apple	Half
3	multigrain bagels	3
	Leaf lettuce	

Dressing:

1/3 cup	light sour cream	75 ml
2 tbsp	light mayonnaise	25 ml
1/2 tsp	minced gingerroot	2 ml
1/2 tsp	mild curry paste	2 ml
1/4 tsp	ground cumin	1 ml
1/4 tsp	salt	1 ml
Pinch	pepper	Pinch

In large bowl and using fingers, shred chicken finely to make about 2 cups (500 ml); add red pepper, celery, and green onions.

Dressing: In small bowl, stir together sour cream, mayonnaise, ginger, curry paste, cumin, salt, and pepper; add to chicken mixture, and stir to combine. (Make-ahead: Cover and refrigerate for up to 24 hours.)

Core apple half; cut into thin slices. Split bagels in half; line bottom halves with lettuce. Spread with chicken salad and top with apple slices.

Makes 3 sandwiches.

Per sandwich: about 422 cal, 31 g pro, 8 g total fat (2 g sat. fat), 60 g carb, 7 g fibre, 83 mg chol, 1062 mg sodium. % RDI: 14% calcium, 26% iron, 15% vit A, 62% vit C, 10% folate.

Bean Spread and Veggie Sandwich

For a vegetarian lunch, spread 2 tbsp (25 ml) bean spread over two slices of 12-grain bread. Top with tomato and cucumber slices, arugula leaves, and grilled zucchini or eggplant slices. For added convenience, and to ensure that your sandwich is as fresh and crunchy as can be, package each type of vegetable in a separate container and assemble at lunchtime.

Bean Spread:

1	can (19 oz/540 ml) white kidney beans, drained, and rinsed	1
2 tbsp	lemon juice	25 ml
2 tbsp	olive oil	25 ml
1/2 tsp	salt	2 ml
1/4 tsp	pepper	1 ml

In food processor, purée together all ingredients. Store in refrigerator for up to 3 days.

Makes 1 2/3 cups (400 ml).

Per serving: about 328 cal, 13 g pro, 8 g total fat (1 g sat. fat), 53 g carb, 7 g fibre, 0 mg chol, 668 mg sodium. % RDI: 2% calcium, 6% iron, 7% vit A, 33% vit C, 17% folate.

Hummus and Veggie Wrap

Hummus is easy to make, and smart cooks always keep a can or two of chickpeas in the cupboard. Tahini—somewhat less common—can be replaced by peanut butter or sesame oil.

4	large whole-wheat tortillas	4
1 cup	shredded romaine lettuce	250 ml
1/2 cup	each chopped tomato, cucumber, and green onion	125 ml

Hummus:

1	can (19 oz/540 ml) chickpeas, drained and rinsed	1
1/4 cup	lemon juice	50 ml
2 tbsp	tahini	25 ml
2 tbsp	chopped parsley	25 ml
2 tbsp	olive oil	25 ml
1	clove garlic, minced	1
1/2 tsp	ground cumin	2 ml
1/4 tsp	each salt and pepper	1 ml

Hummus: In food processor, purée chickpeas. Add lemon juice, tahini, parsley, olive oil, garlic, cumin, salt, and pepper; blend, adding a little water to thin, if desired. (Make-ahead: Refrigerate in airtight container for up to 2 days.)

Spread 1/2 cup (125 ml) hummus over each tortilla; sprinkle with lettuce, tomato, cucumber, and green onion.

Fold bottom of tortilla up about 1 1/2 inches (4 cm). Roll sides tightly toward centre. Wrap each bundle tightly in plastic wrap.

Makes 4 servings.

Per serving: about 367 cal, 12 g pro, 13 g total fat (2 g sat. fat), 62 g carb, 10 g fibre, 0 mg chol, 708 mg sodium. % RDI: 7% calcium, 27% iron, 7% vit A, 35% vit C, 54% folate.

Mango Chicken Salad Wrap

The sweetness of mango offsets the spiciness of jerk seasoning and wraps up everyday chicken salad with an appealing new look and taste.

1 tbsp	jerk seasoning	15 ml
1 tbsp	vegetable oil	15 ml
2	boneless skinless chicken breasts	2
1 cup	shredded lettuce	250 ml
1	mango, peeled, pitted, and diced	1
1/2	sweet red pepper, diced	1/2
1/4 cup	light mayonnaise	50 ml
1/4 tsp	grated lime rind	1 ml
1 tbsp	lime juice	15 ml
4	large flour tortillas	4

In bowl, whisk jerk seasoning with oil; add chicken and turn to coat. Place on foil-lined rimmed baking sheet; broil, turning once, for about 12 minutes or until no longer pink inside. Let cool slightly; cut into thin strips.

In large bowl, toss together chicken, lettuce, mango, red pepper, mayonnaise, lime rind, and lime juice. Divide among tortillas, placing in centre of each. Fold 2 sides over filling; roll up from end.

Makes 4 servings.

Per serving: about 380 cal, 22 g pro, 13 g total fat (1 g sat. fat), 44 g carb, 3 g fibre, 42 mg chol, 711 mg sodium. % RDI: 4% calcium, 18% iron, 30% vit A, 78% vit C, 10% folate.

Salmon Pitas with Celery Heart Salad

Teenagers will love this salmon sandwich flavoured with a vinaigrette. Mash any soft bones into the salmon for an extra hit of calcium.

2 tbsp	chopped fresh dill	25 ml
2 tbsp	lemon juice	25 ml
1 tbsp	extra-virgin olive oil	15 ml
1/4 tsp	each salt, and pepper	1 ml
1	small head celery	1
1/2 cup	thinly sliced radishes	125 ml
1/2 cup	thinly sliced red onion	125 ml
1/4 cup	light sour cream	50 ml
2	cans (each 7 1/2 oz/213 g) salmon, drained	2
4	lettuce leaves	4
4	whole-wheat pita pockets or tortillas	4

In large bowl, whisk 1 tbsp (15 ml) each of the dill, lemon juice, and oil, and half each of the salt and pepper; set aside.

Remove tough outer stalks from celery to leave 2-inch (5 cm) heart; reserve outer stalks for another use. Trim tops from heart to leave 5-inch (12 cm) long base; reserve tops for another use. Peel outside of celery heart to remove tough strings; trim bottom. Slice celery heart lengthwise into paper-thin slices; cut slices crosswise into thirds. Add to oil mixture along with radishes and onion; toss to coat.

In separate bowl, combine sour cream and remaining dill, lemon juice, salt, and pepper. Add salmon, flaking with fork.

Layer lettuce, celery mixture, and salmon mixture onto pitas and roll up. (Make-ahead: Wrap in plastic wrap and refrigerate for up to 24 hours.)
Makes 4 servings.

Per serving: about 363 cal, 25.5 g pro, 12 g total fat (3 g sat. fat), 42 g carb, 7.5 g fibre, 27 mg chol, 948 mg sodium. % RDI: 30% calcium, 25% iron, 5% vit A, 28% vit C, 48% folate.

Salsa Wrap

These wraps are loaded with flavour and can be made a day in advance. If your teenager is a vegetarian, substitute the ground beef for veggie ground round, a soy food sold in most grocery stores.

8 oz	lean ground beef	227 g
1/2 cup	chunky salsa	125 ml
10	6-inch (15 cm) whole-wheat tortillas	10
3/4 cup	light spreadable cream cheese	175 ml
5	leaves romaine lettuce, torn in half	5

In non-stick skillet, cook beef over medium-high heat, breaking up with spoon, until no longer pink, about 5 minutes. Drain off fat. Add salsa; cook over medium heat for 5 minutes. Let cool.

Spread each tortilla with rounded 1 tbsp (15 ml) cream cheese, leaving 1-inch (2.5 cm) border. Spoon about 2 tbsp (25 ml) of the beef mixture along centre of each; top with half of lettuce leaf. Fold up bottom edge of tortilla, then sides; roll up. (Make-ahead: Wrap individually in plastic wrap and refrigerate for up to 24 hours.)
Makes 10 servings.

Per wrap: about 154 cal, 9 g pro, 6 g total fat (3 g sat. fat), 20 g carb, 2 g fibre, 24 mg chol, 291 mg sodium. % RDI: 3% calcium, 9% iron, 4% vit A, 5% vit C, 8% folate.

Tofu Burritos

Tofu is a versatile, inexpensive, and high-protein ingredient. Because most tofu is coagulated using a calcium compound, it is often rich in calcium. Its bland nature means tofu works well with many different flavourings, like the Tex-Mex seasonings in these burritos.

1	pkg (12 oz/350 g) extra-firm tofu	1
1 tbsp	vegetable oil	15 ml
1	large onion, chopped	1
1	clove garlic, minced	1
1/2 tsp	each ground cumin and chili powder	2 ml
1/4 tsp	each salt and pepper	1 ml
1	sweet green pepper, chopped	1
1	jalapeño pepper, chopped	1
1 cup	drained chopped canned tomatoes	250 ml
4	large whole-wheat flour tortillas	4
3/4 cup	shredded light cheddar cheese	175 ml

Pat tofu dry; cut into 1/2-inch (1 cm) cubes. Set aside.

In skillet, heat oil over medium heat; cook onion, garlic, cumin, chili powder, salt, and pepper, stirring occasionally, until onion is softened, about 3 minutes.

Add tofu cubes, green and jalapeño peppers, and tomatoes; cook until peppers are softened, about 4 minutes.

Spoon about 1 cup (250 ml) of the tofu mixture along centre of each tortilla; sprinkle with one-quarter of the cheese. Fold up bottom edge, then sides; roll up.

Bake on greased rimmed baking sheet in 400°F (200°C) oven until golden and cheese is melted, about 15 minutes. Cut diagonally into halves.

Makes 4 servings.

Per serving: about 334 cal, 22 g pro, 14 g total fat (4 g sat. fat), 43 g carb, 5 g fibre, 13 mg chol, 750 mg sodium. % RDI: 31% calcium, 26% iron, 9% vit A, 62% vit C, 50% folate.

Tuna Melt Quesadillas

This twist on a tuna sandwich is low in fat and a good source of iron. For a boost of fibre, use whole-wheat tortilla shells.

2	cans (each 6 oz/170 g) water-packed tuna, drained	2
2	cloves garlic, minced	2
2 tsp	lime juice	10 ml
1/2 tsp	each salt, pepper, ground cumin, and ground coriander	2 ml
4	large flour tortillas	4
3/4 cup	shredded Monterey Jack cheese	175 ml
1/4 cup	each chopped fresh coriander and green onion	50 ml

In bowl, mix together tuna, garlic, lime juice, salt, pepper, cumin, and ground coriander. Spoon 1/2 cup (125 ml) onto half of each tortilla; sprinkle evenly with cheese, fresh coriander, and green onion. Fold uncovered half over filling.

In non-stick skillet or on greased grill, cook quesadillas over medium-high heat, in batches if necessary and pressing with spatula, until golden, 2 to 3 minutes per side. Cut each into 3 wedges.

Makes 4 servings.

Per serving: about 340 cal, 26 g pro, 11 g total fat (5 g sat. fat), 33 g carb, 2 g fibre, 37 mg chol, 877 mg sodium. % RDI: 18% calcium, 24% iron, 7% vit A, 3% vit C, 36% folate.

Tuna Pan Bagnat

A classic recipe from southern France, this sandwich is perfect to pack for picnics and summer events.

1	baguette (French stick)	1
3 tbsp	extra-virgin olive oil	50 ml
1 tbsp	red wine vinegar	15 ml
2 tsp	anchovy paste (optional)	10 ml
1/4 tsp	each salt and pepper	1 ml
1/2 cup	sliced sweet green pepper	125 ml
1/4 cup	sliced black olives	50 ml
1/4 cup	chopped red onion	50 ml
1	small tomato, sliced	1
2 tbsp	drained capers	25 ml
1	can (6 oz/170 g) solid white tuna, drained, and broken into chunks	1

Cut bread in half horizontally without cutting all the way through.

In small bowl, whisk together oil, vinegar, anchovy paste (if using), salt, and pepper; brush half over cut surfaces of loaf.

Arrange green pepper, olives, onion, tomato, capers, and tuna on bottom half of loaf; drizzle with remaining dressing. Close top of loaf over filling. (Make-ahead: Wrap in plastic wrap, and refrigerate up to 1 day.)

Makes 4 servings.

Per serving: about 363 cal, 16 g pro, 14 g total fat (2 g sat. fat), 43 g carb, 3 g fibre, 14 mg chol, 872 mg sodium. % RDI: 6% calcium, 19% iron, 4% vit A, 27% vit C, 37% folate.

Tip: Canned tuna comes in many varieties. Albacore, the most expensive, is the only one that can be called white. It is also a source of omega-3 fatty acids, a natural component of some fish oils.

Tip: It is traditional in pan bagnat to use an oil-packed tuna; however, water-packed is lower in fat and thus a lighter choice.

SOUPS AND SALADS

Black Bean Soup

Hearty and delicious, this soup also looks great, with its spoonful of sour cream swirled into each serving. If you like, purée the soup before adding the coriander; just reserve about 1/4 cup (50 ml) of the whole beans to garnish each bowlful.

1 tbsp	vegetable oil	15 ml
1	onion, chopped	1
3	cloves garlic, minced	3
1	sweet red pepper, chopped	1
1 tsp	ground cumin	5 ml
Pinch	cayenne pepper	Pinch
1	can (19 oz/540 ml) black beans, drained and rinsed	1
2 cups	vegetable or chicken stock	500 ml
2 tbsp	chopped fresh coriander (optional)	25 ml
2 tbsp	lime juice	25 ml
1/4 cup	sour cream	50 ml

In large saucepan, heat oil over medium heat; cook onion, garlic, red pepper, cumin, and cayenne, stirring occasionally, for 5 minutes or until onion is softened.

Add black beans and stock; bring to boil. Reduce heat and simmer for 10 minutes. Stir in coriander (if using) and lime juice. Dollop sour cream on each serving.

Makes 4 servings.

Per serving: about 178 cal, 9 g pro, 5 g total fat (1 g sat. fat), 26 g carb, 8 g fibre, 2 mg chol, 687 mg sodium. % RDI: 7% calcium, 17% iron, 12% vit A, 90% vit C, 30% folate.

Broccoli, Cauliflower, and Tofu Soup

This last-minute soup is a snap using frozen vegetables. To increase your calcium intake, look for tofu with calcium sulfate in the ingredient list.

1 tbsp	vegetable oil	15 ml
1	onion, chopped	1
2	cloves garlic, minced	2
1 tsp	dried basil	5 ml
1/4 tsp	pepper	1 ml
6 cups	vegetable stock	1.5 L
2 cups	each fresh or frozen broccoli and cauliflower florets	500 ml
1/2	pkg (17 1/2 oz/500 g pkg) soft tofu, cubed	1/2
1	carrot, grated	1
1 tbsp	chopped fresh parsley	15 ml

In saucepan, heat oil over medium heat; cook onion, garlic, basil, and pepper until onion is softened, about 5 minutes.

Add stock; bring to boil. Add broccoli and cauliflower; reduce heat, cover, and simmer until vegetables are tender, about 5 minutes. Add tofu and heat through. In batches, transfer to blender and blend until smooth. (Make-ahead: Let cool for 30 minutes; refrigerate until chilled. Cover and refrigerate for up to 2 days.)

Topping: In small bowl, mix carrot with parsley; sprinkle over each serving.

Makes 4 servings.

Per serving: about 127 cal, 6 g pro, 7 g total fat (1 g sat. fat), 13 g carb, 3 g fibre, 0 mg chol, 964 mg sodium. % RDI: 6% calcium, 10% iron, 61% vit A, 82% vit C, 20% folate.

Ginger Noodle Soup

Make this soup ahead of time and divide into individual containers for a lunch that can be quickly reheated. Complete the meal with sliced fresh fruit for dessert.

1 lb	lean ground pork	500 g
1	onion, chopped	1
3	cloves garlic, minced	3
1/3 cup	hoisin sauce	75 ml
2 tbsp	chopped gingerroot	25 ml
2 tbsp	soy sauce	25 ml
4 cups	chicken stock	1 L
1	carrot, shredded	1
1/2 cup	sliced mushrooms	125 ml
5 oz	rice vermicelli noodles	142 g
1	green onion, thinly sliced	1
1/2 cup	bean sprouts	125 ml
4	sprigs coriander	4

In saucepan, brown pork over medium-high heat, stirring to break up meat, 5 to 7 minutes. Drain off fat. Add onion, garlic, hoisin sauce, ginger, and soy sauce; cook for 2 minutes.

Add chicken stock and bring to boil. Add carrot and mushrooms; reduce heat and simmer for 10 minutes.

Stir in vermicelli noodles; simmer for about 5 minutes or until noodles are tender. Ladle into large soup bowls. Garnish with sliced green onion, bean sprouts, and coriander sprigs.
Makes 4 servings.

Per serving: about 463 cal, 29 g pro, 16 g total fat (6 g sat. fat), 48 g carb, 3 g fibre, 75 mg chol, 1735 mg sodium. % RDI: 6% calcium, 19% iron, 46% vit A, 10% vit C, 17% folate.

Variation: Vegetarian Ginger Tofu Soup: Omit pork. Use 1 tbsp (15 ml) vegetable oil to sauté onion mixture. Replace chicken stock with vegetable stock and add 1 cup (250 ml) diced firm tofu along with the stock.

Tortellini Bean Soup

Vegetables and pasta are a winning combination in this substantial soup. Look for fresh tortellini in the deli section of your grocery store. You can use the leftover canned beans for lunch the next day either tossed in a salad or added to rice pilaf.

2 tsp	vegetable oil	10 ml
4	carrots, chopped	4
1	onion, chopped	1
2	cloves garlic, minced	2
1 tsp	dried basil	5 ml
1	bay leaf	1
3 cups	chicken stock	750 ml
1	can (19 oz/540 ml) tomatoes	1
8 oz	fresh meat-filled tortellini	227 g
1 cup	canned black beans, drained and rinsed	250 ml
1/4 tsp	pepper	1 ml
1/4 cup	freshly grated Parmesan cheese	50 ml

In large saucepan, heat oil over medium heat; cook carrots, onion, garlic, dried basil, and bay leaf, stirring occasionally, for about 5 minutes or until onion is softened.

Add chicken stock and tomatoes, breaking up with back of spoon; bring to boil. Add tortellini; return to boil. Reduce heat to medium-high; cook, stirring occasionally, for about 10 minutes or until pasta is tender but firm. Stir in beans and season with pepper; heat until simmering. Discard bay leaf. Serve sprinkled with Parmesan cheese.
Makes 4 servings.

Per serving: about 375 cal, 20 g pro, 10 g total fat (4 g sat. fat), 51 g carb, 8 g fibre, 38 mg chol, 1400 mg sodium. % RDI: 23% calcium, 31% iron, 19% vit A, 38% vit C, 25% folate.

Tip: For a vegetarian version, use vegetable stock and cheese-filled tortellini.

Curried Corn and Chicken Salad

Subtle overtones of curry in a creamy dressing turn leftovers into a special meal.

3 cups	corn kernels, cooked	750 ml
2 cups	cubed cooked chicken	500 ml
1 cup	shredded red cabbage (or coarsely chopped tomato)	250 ml
1	sweet green pepper, chopped	1
1	carrot, diced	1
1/3 cup	chopped red onion	75 ml

Dressing:

1/2 cup	plain yogurt	125 ml
1/4 cup	light mayonnaise	50 ml
1 tsp	each curry powder, brown sugar, and cider vinegar	5 ml
1/2 tsp	each ground cumin, salt, and pepper	2 ml

In large bowl, combine corn, chicken, cabbage, green pepper, carrot, and onion.

Dressing: Whisk together yogurt, mayonnaise, curry powder, sugar, vinegar, cumin, salt, and pepper; toss with salad.

Salad can be covered and refrigerated for up to 4 hours.

Makes 4 servings.

Per serving: about 415 cal, 37 g pro, 15 g total fat (3 g sat. fat), 37 g carb, 4 g fibre, 70 mg chol, 492 mg sodium. % RDI: 8% calcium, 15% iron, 63% vit A, 72% vit C, 28% folate.

Mexican-Style Bean Salad

With two different kinds of beans plus corn, this is a colourful salad. All it needs is crusty rolls and a plate of sliced tomatoes and cucumbers to round out the menu.

1	can (19 oz/540 ml) black or kidney beans	1
1	can (19 oz/540 ml) romano beans	1
1 cup	cooked corn kernels	250 ml
1/2 cup	thinly sliced onion	125 ml
1/2	sweet red pepper, chopped	1/2
4	black olives, sliced	4
2 tbsp	chopped fresh coriander or parsley	25 ml

Dressing:

1/3 cup	lemon juice	75 ml
2 tbsp	vegetable oil	25 ml
2 tsp	granulated sugar	10 ml
1/4 tsp	salt	1 ml
Pinch	pepper	Pinch

Drain and rinse black and romano beans; place in bowl. Add corn, onion, red pepper, and olives.

Dressing: In small bowl, whisk together lemon juice, oil, sugar, salt, and pepper; pour over bean mixture. Sprinkle with coriander; toss to coat.

Makes 6 servings.

Per serving: about 250 cal, 12 g pro, 6 g total fat (1 g sat. fat), 39 g carb, 9 g fibre, 0 mg chol, 586 mg sodium. % RDI: 5% calcium, 18% iron, 7% vit A, 43% vit C, 47% folate.

Salmon Pasta Salad

Look for whole-wheat pastas in your grocery store or at health food stores. Elbow macaroni, farfalle, or fusilli would also work well for this salad.

4 cups	small shell pasta	1 L
1 cup	frozen peas	250 ml
1	can (7 1/2 oz/213 g) sockeye salmon, drained	1
1/2 cup	plain low-fat yogurt	125 ml
1/3 cup	finely diced red onion	75 ml
1/4 cup	light mayonnaise	50 ml
6	radishes, thinly sliced	6
2 tbsp	chopped fresh dill (or 2 tsp/10 ml dried dillweed)	25 ml
1/2 tsp	each salt, pepper, and hot pepper sauce	2 ml
12	leaves romaine lettuce	12

In large saucepan of boiling salted water, cook pasta for 7 minutes. Add peas; cook until pasta is tender but firm, about 1 minute. Drain and rinse under cold water; shake out excess water.

Meanwhile, in small bowl, flake salmon with fork, mashing in any bones; remove skin if desired. Set aside.

In large bowl, stir together yogurt, onion, mayonnaise, radishes, dill, salt, pepper, and hot pepper sauce.

Tear 4 of the lettuce leaves into bite-size pieces; add to yogurt mixture along with pasta mixture and salmon, and toss to combine. To serve, spoon onto remaining lettuce leaves.

Makes 4 servings.

Per serving: about 484 cal, 24 g pro, 10 g total fat (2 g sat. fat), 74 g carb, 6 g fibre, 26 mg chol, 985 mg sodium. % RDI: 18% calcium (202 mg), 24% iron (3.4 mg), 13% vit A, 25% vit C (15 mg), 87% folate (192 mcg).

Variations: Shrimp Pasta Salad: Replace salmon and peas with cooked salad shrimp and chopped red or yellow pepper.

Crab Pasta Salad: Replace salmon and peas with crabmeat and frozen broccoli florets.

Sesame Chicken Salad

Anchovy paste is the secret ingredient that enriches the flavour of this dish, but you'll never taste it separately. Look for it chilled in the dairy section of the grocery store.

1 tbsp	sesame oil	15 ml
4	boneless skinless chicken breasts	4
1/2 tsp	each salt, and pepper	2 ml
1/4 cup	light mayonnaise	50 ml
2	cloves garlic, minced	2
1 tbsp	lemon juice	15 ml
1 tsp	Dijon mustard	5 ml
1/2 tsp	anchovy paste	2 ml
1/2	English cucumber (6 inches/15 cm)	1/2
4 cups	torn romaine lettuce	1 L
4	radishes, thinly sliced	4
2	green onions, thinly sliced	2
1/2 cup	sesame bread sticks (2 inches/5 cm) or croutons	125 ml

Brush 2 tsp (10 ml) of the oil over chicken; season with half each of the salt and pepper. Place on greased grill over medium-high heat or 6 inches (15 cm) from broiler; close lid and grill or broil until no longer pink inside, turning once, about 12 minutes. (Make-ahead: Let cool; wrap and refrigerate for up to 24 hours.) Cut into thin strips.

Meanwhile, in large bowl, whisk together mayonnaise, garlic, lemon juice, mustard, anchovy paste, and remaining oil, salt, and pepper. Peel, and halve cucumber lengthwise; with spoon, scoop out fleshy core. Thinly slice crosswise; add to bowl along with lettuce, radishes, onions, bread sticks, and chicken; toss to coat.

Makes 4 servings.

Per serving: about 276 cal, 33 g pro, 11 g total fat (2 g sat. fat), 10 g carb, 2 g fibre, 84 mg chol, 549 mg sodium. % RDI: 5% calcium, 14% iron, 16% vit A, 35% vit C, 46% folate.

Vegetable Tofu Salad

Let the tofu marinate in the dressing until lunchtime. Keep your vegetables in a separate container, and then toss everything together once the lunch bell chimes.

1	pkg (12 oz/350 g) extra-firm tofu	1
2 cups	cherry tomatoes	500 ml
1	sweet green pepper	1
2	carrots	2
2 cups	small mushrooms	500 ml

Dressing:

1/3 cup	red wine vinegar	75 ml
1/4 cup	chopped fresh basil (or 2 tsp/10 ml dried)	50 ml
1/4 cup	olive oil	50 ml
1	clove garlic, minced	1
1/4 tsp	dry mustard	1 ml
1/4 tsp	each salt and pepper	1 ml

Drain and pat tofu dry; cut into 1/2-inch (1 cm) cubes. Add to dressing; let stand for 10 minutes.

Meanwhile, cut tomatoes in half. Cut green pepper in half lengthwise; seed and core. Cut in half crosswise; cut lengthwise into strips. Slice carrots. Add vegetables to bowl along with mushrooms; toss with dressing to coat.

Dressing: whisk together vinegar, basil, oil, garlic, mustard, salt, and pepper until combined in a large bowl.

Makes 4 servings.

Per serving: about 250 cal, 11 g pro, 19 g total fat (3 g sat. fat), 14 g carb, 3 g fibre, 0 mg chol, 174 mg sodium. % RDI: 14% calcium, 20% iron, 119% vit A, 73% vit C, 24% folate.

Tip: This salad is also tasty with cooked sliced chicken or turkey breast, sliced hard-cooked eggs, or cubed low-fat cheese.

QUICK DINNERS ON THE FLY

FISH, MEAT, AND POULTRY

Curried Salmon Fillets

There is just a wisp of curry on these fillets. Serve with new potatoes, sugar snap peas, and sprouts.

4	salmon fillets (with skin), 1 1/2 lb (680 g) total	4
1/4 cup	plain yogurt	50 ml
1 tbsp	lemon juice	15 ml
1 tsp	mild curry paste	5 ml
Pinch	each salt and pepper	Pinch
2 tbsp	chopped fresh coriander	25 ml

Place salmon in shallow dish. Whisk together yogurt, lemon juice, curry paste, salt, and pepper; pour over fish, turning to coat.

Reserving yogurt mixture, place fillets, skin side down, on greased grill over medium-high heat. Close lid and cook, turning and brushing both sides with yogurt mixture halfway through, for 10 minutes per inch (2.5 cm) of thickness or until fish is opaque and flakes easily when tested with fork. Serve sprinkled with coriander.

Makes 4 servings.

Per serving: about 232 cal, 31 g pro, 10 g total fat (2 g sat. fat), 1 g carb, 0 g fibre, 87 mg chol, 78 mg sodium. % RDI: 4% calcium, 10% iron, 2% vit A, 1% vit C, 17% folate.

Garlicky Tuna Toss

With a few cans of tuna on your pantry shelves, dinner is only an arm's-length—and a few minutes—away.

1 tbsp	olive oil	15 ml
2	cloves garlic, minced	2
1	small sweet red pepper or roasted pepper, chopped	1
4	green onions, chopped	4
1 cup	chicken stock	250 ml
2	cans (each 6 oz/170 g) tuna, drained and broken in chunks	2
1/4 tsp	each salt and pepper	1 ml
4 cups	fusilli pasta	1 L

In skillet, heat oil over medium heat; cook garlic, red pepper, and half of the onions for 2 minutes.

Stir in chicken stock; bring to boil. Reduce heat; simmer for 5 minutes. Add drained tuna, salt, and pepper; heat through.

Meanwhile, in large pot of boiling salted water, cook fusilli for about 8 minutes or until tender but firm. Drain and return to pot. Add tuna sauce; toss to coat. Serve sprinkled with remaining green onions.

Makes 4 servings.

Per serving: about 437 cal, 29 g pro, 6 g total fat (1 g sat. fat), 65 g carb, 4 g fibre, 20 mg chol, 786 mg sodium. % RDI: 4% calcium, 19% iron, 8% vit A, 55% vit C, 14% folate.

Tip: Choose water-packed tuna instead of oil-packed to keep the dish as low in fat as it is high in flavour. Chunk or whole tuna won't fall apart when tossed with the pasta.

Steamed Fish with Couscous

Bell pepper adds a splash of colour and plenty of vitamin C to this scrumptious fish dish. To get more fibre, use whole-wheat couscous, which is available at many health food stores.

1	zucchini, thinly sliced	1
1	onion, thinly sliced	1
3	cloves garlic, minced	3
1 cup	uncooked couscous	250 ml
3/4 cup	tomato juice	175 ml
3/4 tsp	salt	3 ml
1/4 tsp	pepper	1 ml
1/2 cup	chopped fresh basil (or 1/4 tsp/1 ml dried)	125 ml
4	sole or haddock fillets (about 1 lb/454 g)	4
1	sweet red, yellow, or green pepper, chopped	1
4 tsp	butter	20 ml

Cut 4 pieces of heavy-duty or double-thickness foil 15 inches (38 cm) long. Onto centre of each, slightly overlap zucchini slices; top with onion and garlic. Top each with 1/4 cup (50 ml) couscous. Gather foil sides up into bowl shape.

In measuring cup, combine tomato juice, 1/2 cup (125 ml) water, half of the salt and the pepper; drizzle evenly over couscous. Sprinkle with basil. Top each with fish fillet; sprinkle with red pepper and remaining salt. Dot each with 1 tsp (5 ml) butter. Seal foil, leaving room in package for steam.

Place packets, seam side up, on grill over medium heat; close lid and cook until fish flakes easily when tested, about 15 minutes. Let stand for 5 minutes or until couscous has absorbed all the liquid.

Makes 4 servings.

Per serving: about 347 cal, 29 g pro, 6 g total fat (3 g sat. fat), 45 g carb, 4 g fibre, 65 mg chol, 733 mg sodium. % RDI: 6% calcium, 12% iron, 19% vit A, 93% vit C, 25% folate.

Tuna Burgers

Serve these tuna burgers in whole-wheat pitas with slices of avocado and tomato, and lettuce. For an alternative that's just as tasty and nutritious, substitute two cans of salmon for the tuna.

2	eggs	2
1/3 cup	dry bread crumbs	75 ml
1 tbsp	chopped fresh dill (or 1 tsp/5 ml dried dillweed)	15 ml
1 tbsp	horseradish	15 ml
2 tsp	Dijon mustard	10 ml
1/4 tsp	pepper	1 ml
Pinch	salt	Pinch
2	cans (each 6 1/2 oz/170 g) water-packed tuna	2
2	green onions, minced	2
1	stalk celery, chopped	1
1 tbsp	vegetable oil	15 ml
4	whole-wheat hamburger buns	4
	Alfalfa sprouts	

In bowl, lightly beat eggs; mix in bread crumbs, dill, horseradish, mustard, pepper, and salt. Drain tuna; mix into bowl along with onions and celery. Shape into four 1/2-inch (1 cm) thick patties.

In non-stick skillet, heat oil over medium heat; cook patties, turning once, for 10 minutes or until golden brown, and set. Sandwich in buns. Garnish with sprouts.

Makes 4 burgers.

Per serving: about 360 cal, 32 g pro, 9 g total fat (2 g sat. fat), 40 g carb, 5 g fibre, 113 mg chol, 667 mg sodium. % RDI: 11% calcium, 26% iron, 6% vit A, 3% vit C, 20% folate.

Balsamic Honey Pork Tenderloin

Succulent pork tenderloin is perfect for the grill. It needs little time for cooking and is a great medium for marinades and spices. This sweet yet sour marinade glazes the meat and turns into a tangy crust.

2 tbsp	liquid honey	25 ml
2 tbsp	grainy mustard	25 ml
2 tbsp	balsamic vinegar	25 ml
1 tbsp	olive oil	15 ml
1	clove garlic, minced	1
1/4 tsp	each salt and pepper	1 ml
2	pork tenderloins	2

In large bowl, combine honey, mustard, vinegar, oil, garlic, salt, and pepper; add pork, turning to coat. (Make-ahead: Cover and refrigerate for up to 24 hours.)

Reserving marinade, place pork on greased grill over medium-high heat; brush with marinade. Close lid and cook, turning occasionally, for about 18 minutes or until just a hint of pink remains inside.

Transfer to cutting board; tent with foil and let stand for 5 minutes. Cut into 1/2-inch (1 cm) thick slices.

Makes 6 servings.

Per serving: about 182 cal, 27 g pro, 5 g total fat (1 g sat. fat), 5 g carb, 0 g fibre, 61 mg chol, 167 mg sodium. % RDI: 1% calcium, 10% iron, 0% vit A, 0% vit C, 2% folate.

Beef and Bulgur Pitas

Increase the amount of grains in your diet by adding them to a pita stuffing. Not only do grains add valuable nutrients, but they also let you reduce the amount of meat in a meal.

1/2 cup	bulgur (medium or coarse)	125 ml
8 oz	extra-lean ground beef	227 g
1	each carrot and zucchini, grated	1
1	onion, chopped	1
2	cloves garlic, minced	2
1 tbsp	chili powder	15 ml
1 tsp	ground cumin	5 ml
1/4 tsp	pepper	1 ml
1 cup	no-salt-added tomato juice	250 ml
1/2 cup	chopped fresh coriander or parsley	125 ml
2 tsp	lime juice	10 ml
4	whole-wheat pitas	4
4	leaves leaf lettuce	4
16	slices English cucumber	16
16	cherry tomatoes, halved	16
1/4 cup	plain low-fat yogurt	50 ml

In saucepan, bring 3/4 cup (175 ml) water to boil; stir in bulgur. Reduce heat to low; cover and simmer until no liquid remains, about 10 minutes.

Meanwhile, in non-stick skillet, sauté beef over medium-high heat, breaking up with spoon, until no longer pink, about 5 minutes. Drain off any fat from pan.

Add carrot, zucchini, onion, garlic, chili powder, cumin, and pepper; cook over medium heat, stirring occasionally, until onion is tender, about 5 minutes. Add tomato juice and bring to boil; reduce heat and simmer until liquid is almost evaporated, about 5 minutes. Stir in bulgur, 1/4 cup (50 ml) of the coriander, and lime juice.

Cut top third off each pita; place inside each bottom. Line each with lettuce leaf and some of the cucumber. Spoon in beef mixture; top with remaining cucumber, tomatoes, yogurt, and remaining coriander.

Makes 4 servings.

Per serving: about 372 cal, 23 g pro, 7 g total fat (2 g sat. fat), 59 g carb, 9 g fibre, 32 mg chol, 413 mg sodium, % RDI: 8% calcium, 35% iron, 60% vit A, 35% vit C, 36% folate.

Stroganoff Toss for Two

Economical ground beef with flavourful notes of caraway and paprika will be a hit that can easily be doubled to serve four. Serve with steamed peas and carrots, and crusty rolls.

8 oz	lean ground beef	227 g
1 tsp	vegetable oil	5 ml
3 cups	quartered mushrooms	750 ml
1	onion, chopped	1
2	cloves garlic, minced	2
2 tsp	paprika	10 ml
1/2 tsp	each salt and pepper	2 ml
1/2 tsp	caraway seeds, crushed	2 ml
1/2 cup	beef stock	125 ml
1 tbsp	wine vinegar	15 ml
1/2 cup	light sour cream	125 ml
1 tbsp	horseradish	15 ml
4 cups	curly broad egg noodles	1 l
1/4 cup	chopped fresh parsley	50 ml

In non-stick skillet, brown beef, breaking up with spoon. Drain off any fat. Remove and set aside.

Add oil to skillet; cook mushrooms, onion, garlic, paprika, salt, pepper, and caraway seeds over medium heat, stirring often, for 8 minutes or until mushrooms are softened.

Stir in beef stock and vinegar. Return beef to pan. Remove from heat. Stir in sour cream and horseradish.

Meanwhile, in pot of boiling salted water, cook noodles for 8 minutes or until almost tender; drain and return to pot. Add meat mixture and parsley; toss to coat.

Makes 2 servings.

Per serving: about 759 cal, 44 g pro, 21 g total fat (7 g sat. fat), 99 g carb, 10 g fibre, 170 mg chol, 1422 mg sodium. % RDI: 19% calcium, 72% iron, 21% vit A, 22% vit C, 113% folate.

20-Minute Chicken Chili

Here's a quick, warming answer to dinnertime during those chilly months. Double the recipe if you like and serve half for dinner, then freeze the remainder in individual take-along containers for up to 2 weeks. Serve as is or spoon into whole-wheat tortillas and sprinkle with cheese to make burritos.

1 lb	boneless skinless chicken breasts	454 g
1 tbsp	vegetable oil	15 ml
1	onion, chopped	1
1	sweet green pepper, chopped	1
1 tbsp	chili powder	15 ml
2 tsp	dried oregano	10 ml
1/2 tsp	salt	2 ml
1/4 tsp	pepper	1 ml
1	can (28 oz/796 ml) diced tomatoes	1
1	can (19 oz/540 ml) black or kidney beans, drained, and rinsed	1
1/2 cup	corn kernels	125 ml

Trim any fat from chicken breasts; cut into 1-inch (2.5 cm) cubes. In large heavy saucepan, heat oil over medium-high heat; cook chicken until no longer pink inside, about 5 minutes. Transfer to plate.

Add onion, green pepper, chili powder, oregano, salt, and pepper to pan; cook over medium heat, stirring often, until vegetables are softened, about 5 minutes. Add tomatoes and beans; increase heat, and boil, stirring often, for 10 minutes. Add corn. Return chicken to pan; heat through.

Makes 4 servings.

Per serving: about 359 cal, 38 g pro, 6 g total fat (1 g sat. fat), 40 g carb, 9 g fibre, 66 mg chol, 929 mg sodium. % RDI: 10% calcium, 33% iron, 21% vit A, 72% vit C, 75% folate.

Micro-Grilled Lemon Thyme Chicken

This chicken dish is low in fat, and big on taste. Marinating the chicken overnight in the lemon sauce increases the flavour.

1/4 cup	lemon juice	50 ml
1 tbsp	chopped fresh thyme (or 1/2 tsp/2 ml dried)	15 ml
1 tbsp	Dijon mustard	15 ml
1 tbsp	liquid honey	15 ml
1/2 tsp	each salt and pepper	2 ml
4	skinless chicken breasts or legs	4

In microwaveable dish, whisk together lemon juice, thyme, mustard, honey, salt, and pepper. Add chicken; turn to coat. Cover and microwave on high for 7 minutes. Transfer chicken to plate. Microwave lemon mixture, uncovered, on high for 3 minutes or until reduced to 1/3 cup (75 ml).

Meanwhile, place chicken on greased grill over medium-high heat; close lid and cook, turning once, for 8 minutes. Brush with half of the lemon sauce; cook for 2 minutes longer or until no longer pink inside. Serve with remaining sauce.

Makes 4 servings.

Per serving: about 179 cal, 33 g pro, 2 g total fat (1 g sat. fat), 6 g carb, trace fibre, 84 mg chol, 411 mg sodium. % RDI: 1% calcium, 6% iron, 1% vit A, 5% vit C, 2% folate.

Micro-Grilled Salsa Chicken

Warm things up with this hot and spicy grilled chicken. In addition to the great taste, this recipe is low in fat and high in vitamin C.

8	boneless skinless chicken thighs	8
3/4 cup	salsa	175 ml
2 tbsp	tomato paste	25 ml
1 tbsp	lemon juice	15 ml
1 tbsp	liquid honey	15 ml
1	green onion, chopped	1
1	clove garlic, minced	1
1/4 tsp	each salt and pepper	1 ml

Place chicken in single layer in microwaveable dish. Combine salsa, tomato paste, lemon juice, honey, onion, garlic, salt, and pepper; set aside 1/2 cup (125 ml) for basting. Pour remainder over chicken and turn to coat. Cover and microwave on high for 5 minutes.

Discarding salsa mixture in dish, place chicken on greased grill over medium-high heat; close lid and cook, turning once, for 10 minutes. Baste with reserved salsa mixture; cook until juices run clear when chicken is pierced, about 4 minutes.

Makes 4 servings.

Per serving: about 200 cal, 25 g pro, 7 g total fat (2 g sat. fat), 9 g carb, 1 g fibre, 95 mg chol, 367 mg sodium. % RDI: 4% calcium, 14% iron, 7% vit A, 25% vit C, 7% folate.

Quick Chicken for Two

This chicken favourite is packed with flavour and it's high in iron—perfect for growing teenagers.

2	boneless skinless chicken breasts	2
3 cups	sliced mushrooms (about 8 oz/227 g)	750 ml
1	zucchini, sliced	1
1 tsp	Italian seasoning	5 ml
1/2 cup	light sour cream	125 ml

Sprinkle chicken breasts with pinch each salt and pepper. In non-stick skillet, heat 2 tsp (10 ml) oil over medium-high heat; cook chicken, turning once, for about 12 minutes or until no longer pink inside. Transfer to plate and keep warm.

Return skillet to medium heat and add mushrooms, zucchini, and Italian seasoning; cook, stirring often, for 8 minutes or until about 1 tbsp (15 ml) liquid remains in pan. Remove from heat; stir in sour cream. Spoon sauce over chicken to serve.

Makes 2 servings.

Per serving: about 273 cal, 33 g pro, 9 g total fat (3 g sat. fat), 14 g carb, 3 g fibre, 77 mg chol, 134 mg sodium. % RDI: 14% calcium, 21% iron, 5% vit A, 12% vit C, 14% folate.

LEGUMES AND SOY

Chickpea Patties in Pitas with Coriander Yogurt

Legumes such as chickpeas are an essential part of vegetarian diets. Not only are they versatile, they're also high in fibre and protein. Even meat lovers will want more of these low-fat, no-cholesterol patties.

2	cans (19 oz/540 ml each) chickpeas, drained and rinsed	2
2	eggs	2
2 tbsp	Cajun seasoning	25 ml
1/2 tsp	each salt and pepper	2 ml
1/4 cup	fresh bread crumbs	50 ml
3	green onions, thinly sliced	3
2	cloves garlic, minced	2
3 tbsp	vegetable oil	50 ml
3	large whole-wheat pita breads	3
1 1/2 cups	shredded carrots	375 ml
1 1/2 cups	thinly sliced cucumber	375 ml

Coriander Yogurt:

1/2 cup	plain yogurt	125 ml
2 tbsp	chopped fresh coriander	25 ml

In food processor, pulse together chickpeas, eggs, Cajun seasoning, salt, and pepper until smooth; transfer to bowl. Add bread crumbs, green onions, garlic, and 2 tbsp (25 ml) of the Coriander Yogurt; stir to combine. Using wet hands, shape into six 1/2-inch (1 cm) thick patties. (Make-ahead: Cover and refrigerate patties and yogurt for up to 24 hours.)

In large non-stick skillet, heat oil over medium heat; fry patties, turning once, until golden and crisp, about 10 minutes.

Cut each pita in half; stuff each pocket with patty. Spread Coriander Yogurt on patties; top with carrots and cucumber.

Coriander Yogurt: In small bowl, mix yogurt with coriander; set aside.

Makes 6 servings.

Per serving: about 391 cal, 15 g pro, 12 g total fat (2 g sat. fat), 59 g carb, 10 g fibre, 64 mg chol, 904 mg sodium. % RDI: 11% calcium, 27% iron, 89% vit A, 17% vit C, 57% folate.

Tip: Replace fresh coriander with mint for a twist on the yogurt sauce.

Cumin Carrot Tofu Patties

We all know about salmon and tuna patties, but why not try something new and use tofu? Tofu, with its bland taste, has an extraordinary ability to absorb other flavours, as seen in this recipe inspired by Middle Eastern cuisine. Be sure to use extra-firm tofu, since the other types will have too soft a consistency for the patties to hold together.

1 tbsp	olive oil	15 ml
1	onion, chopped	1
1/2 cup	grated carrot	125 ml
2	cloves garlic, minced	2
1/4 tsp	ground cumin	1 ml
Pinch	cayenne pepper	Pinch
1	pkg (12 oz/350 g) extra-firm tofu	1
1/4 cup	tahini (sesame paste)	50 ml
1/2 cup	chopped fresh parsley	125 ml
1/4 cup	dry bread crumbs	50 ml
2 tbsp	lemon juice	25 ml
1/4 tsp	each salt and pepper	1 ml
1 cup	pasta sauce	250 ml
1 tsp	grated lemon rind	5 ml
Pinch	cinnamon	Pinch

In non-stick skillet, heat 1 tsp (5 ml) of the oil over medium heat; cook onion, carrot, garlic, pinch of the cumin, and cayenne pepper, stirring occasionally, for 5 minutes or until onion is softened. Set aside.

In food processor, blend tofu with tahini. Add onion mixture, half of the parsley, the bread crumbs, lemon juice, salt, and pepper; pulse to combine. Form into 8 1/2-inch (1 cm) thick patties.

Heat remaining oil in clean non-stick skillet over medium heat; cook patties, in batches, for 4 minutes per side or until golden.

Meanwhile, in saucepan, combine pasta sauce, lemon rind, cinnamon, and remaining cumin and parsley; bring to simmer over medium-high heat, stirring often, about 3 minutes. Serve over patties.

Makes 4 servings.

Per serving: about 284 cal, 14 g pro, 18 g total fat (3 g sat. fat), 20 g carb, 4 g fibre, 0 mg chol, 480 mg sodium. % RDI: 18% calcium, 29% iron, 37% vit A, 23% vit C, 26% folate.

Teriyaki Tofu with Mushrooms and Cabbage

In addition to being a great source of vegetarian protein, tofu adds a nutritional boost with omega-3 fatty acids, B vitamins, and iron.

1 cup	shredded cabbage	250 ml
1 cup	bean sprouts	250 ml
1 cup	sliced mushrooms	250 ml
1	pkg (16 oz/454 g) medium-firm tofu	1
2	cloves garlic, minced	2
2 tbsp	teriyaki sauce	25 ml
1 tbsp	grated gingerroot	15 ml
1 tbsp	light soy sauce	15 ml
1/4 tsp	pepper	1 ml
1 1/2 tsp	cornstarch	7 ml
1	green onion, chopped	1

Place greased rack in shallow pan or bamboo steamer in wok; pour in enough water to come about 1 inch (2.5 cm) below rack. Cover and bring to boil; reduce heat to medium high.

Meanwhile, spread cabbage in 9-inch (23 cm) pie plate; add bean sprouts and mushrooms. Cut tofu vertically into 4 slices; place on mushrooms. In small bowl, whisk together garlic, teriyaki sauce, ginger, soy sauce, and pepper; drizzle over tofu.

Place pie plate on rack in pan; cover and steam until cabbage is tender, about 15 minutes.

In small saucepan, whisk cornstarch with 1 tbsp (15 ml) water. Drain liquid from pie plate into saucepan; bring to boil over medium heat, whisking, until thickened, about 1 minute. Spoon over tofu. Sprinkle with green onion.

Makes 4 servings.

Per serving: about 122 cal, 11 g pro, 5 g total fat (1 g sat. fat), 10 g carb, 2 g fibre, 0 mg chol, 509 mg sodium. % RDI: 18% calcium, 18% iron, 1% vit A, 13% vit C, 27% folate.

Tofu Vegetable Curry

Freshness is essential to tofu. Fresh tofu smells sweet, mild, and slightly nutty. Tofu past its prime has a sour odour and should be discarded. Check the best-before date. Serve with a dollop of yogurt.

1	eggplant (about 1 lb/454 g)	1
2	large potatoes (1 lb/454 g)	2
1	pkg (12 oz/350 g) extra-firm tofu	1
1 tbsp	vegetable oil	15 ml
1	onion, chopped	1
1/2 cup	chopped fresh coriander	125 ml
1 tbsp	mild curry paste	15 ml
1/2 tsp	salt	2 ml
1 cup	vegetable stock	250 ml
1	can (28 oz/796 ml) tomatoes	1
2 cups	small cauliflower florets	500 ml
1 cup	frozen peas	250 ml

Cut eggplant into 1/2-inch (1 cm) cubes. Scrub potatoes; cut into same-size cubes. Set vegetables aside. Pat tofu dry; cut into 3/4-inch (2 cm) cubes. Set aside.

In shallow Dutch oven, heat oil over medium-high heat; cook onion, half of the coriander, the curry paste, and salt, stirring occasionally, for 3 minutes. Add eggplant, potatoes, and vegetable stock; cook, stirring often, for about 8 minutes or until vegetables are softened.

Add tomatoes; bring to boil, scraping up brown bits from bottom of pan and breaking up tomatoes with back of spoon. Cover and cook, stirring occasionally, for 15 minutes.

Add cauliflower and tofu; cook, covered, for about 7 minutes or until potatoes and cauliflower are tender. Add peas and remaining coriander; cook for 1 minute or until hot.

Makes 4 servings.

Per serving: about 320 cal, 16 g pro, 11 g total fat (1 g sat. fat), 46 g carb, 10 g fibre, 0 mg chol, 794 mg sodium. % RDI: 25% calcium, 30% iron, 16% vit A, 102% vit C, 51% folate.

Vegetarian Hummus Burgers

Chickpeas add plant protein, fibre, and B vitamins to these veggie burgers. Serve them on a crusty whole-grain bun with tahini sauce, lettuce, and slices of tomato.

1/2 cup	bulgur	125 ml
1	can (19 oz/540 ml) chickpeas, drained and rinsed	1
2 tbsp	lemon juice	25 ml
1	clove garlic, minced	1
1/2 tsp	each salt and ground cumin	2 ml
1/4 tsp	each ground coriander and pepper	1 ml
1	egg	1
1/2 cup	chopped roasted or fresh sweet red pepper	125 ml
1/4 cup	dry bread crumbs	50 ml
2 tbsp	chopped fresh parsley	25 ml
1 tbsp	vegetable oil	15 ml

Tahini Sauce:

1/4 cup	each water and tahini (sesame paste)	50 ml
2 tbsp	lemon juice	25 ml
1 tsp	chopped fresh parsley	5 ml
1 tsp	grated lemon rind	5 ml
1	clove garlic, minced	1
Pinch	sugar (optional)	Pinch

Pour 1 cup (250 ml) boiling water over bulgur; cover and let stand for 10 minutes. Drain well.

In food processor, finely chop chickpeas. Add bulgur, lemon juice, garlic, salt, cumin, coriander, pepper, and egg; pulse to combine. Stir in red pepper, bread crumbs, and parsley. Shape into 8 patties.

In non-stick skillet, heat half of the oil over medium-high heat; cook patties, in batches and adding remaining oil, for 4 to 6 minutes per side or until golden.

Makes 4 servings.

Tahini Sauce: Mix together water, tahini paste, lemon juice, parsley, lemon rind, garlic, and sugar. Stir in up to 2 tbsp (25 ml) more water for desired consistency. Drizzle over burgers.

Makes 1/2 cup (125 ml).

Per serving: about 266 cal, 12 g pro, 7 g total fat (1 g sat. fat), 42 g carb, 5 g fibre, 54 mg chol, 563 mg sodium. % RDI: 5% calcium, 18% iron, 10% vit A, 57% vit C, 32% folate.

SNACK ATTACK

HEALTHY COOKIES AND ENERGY BARS

Bodybuilder Cookies

The surprise ingredient (cheddar cheese) in these energy-extending morsels may intrigue you, but the delicious taste and crunch will win you over.

3/4 cup	butter or margarine	175 ml
1 cup	packed brown sugar	250 ml
1	egg	1
1 tsp	vanilla extract	5 ml
1 3/4 cups	all-purpose flour	425 ml
1/2 tsp	each baking powder, baking soda, and salt	2 ml
3 cups	flaked bran cereal, slightly crushed	750 ml
1/2 cup	shredded light cheddar cheese	125 ml
1/2 cup	raisins	125 ml
1/2 cup	chopped toasted pecans or walnuts	125 ml

In large bowl, beat butter with sugar until light and fluffy. Beat in egg and vanilla.

In separate bowl, stir together flour, baking powder, baking soda, and salt; stir into butter mixture just until combined. Stir in crushed cereal, cheddar cheese, raisins, and pecans to make slightly crumbly mixture.

Using 1 rounded tablespoonful (15 ml) per cookie, squeeze batter into balls; place about 2 inches (5 cm) apart on ungreased baking sheets. Bake in top and bottom thirds of 350°F (180°C) oven for about 15 minutes or until lightly browned, switching and rotating pans halfway through.

Let cool on pans on racks for 5 minutes. Transfer to racks and let cool completely. (Make-ahead: Store in airtight container at room temperature for up to 1 week or freeze for up to 1 month.)

Makes about 42 cookies.

Per cookie: about 101 cal, 2 g pro, 5 g total fat (2 g sat. fat), 14 g carb, 1 g fibre, 16 mg chol, 122 mg sodium. % RDI: 2% calcium, 6% iron, 3% vit A, 0% vit C, 5% folate.

Carrot Apricot Bran Muffin Bars

Adding grated carrot to muffin bars is another way to consume vegetables—every little bit counts. Vary the dried fruits by choosing your family's favourite.

1 1/3 cups	buttermilk	325 ml
3/4 cup	natural wheat bran	175 ml
3/4 cup	All-Bran or 100% bran cereal	175 ml
2 cups	all-purpose flour	500 ml
3/4 cup	whole-wheat flour	175 ml
1/2 cup	packed brown sugar	125 ml
4 tsp	baking powder	20 ml
2 tsp	baking soda	10 ml
1/2 tsp	cinnamon	2 ml
1/4 tsp	salt	1 ml
3/4 cup	fancy molasses	175 ml
1/3 cup	vegetable oil	75 ml
1	egg	1
2 tsp	vanilla	10 ml
1 1/2 cups	grated carrot	375 ml
1/2 cup	chopped dried fruits, such as dried apricots	125 ml

In bowl, stir together buttermilk, natural bran, and cereal; let stand for 10 minutes. Meanwhile, in large bowl, whisk together all-purpose and whole-wheat flours, sugar, baking powder, baking soda, cinnamon, and salt.

Whisk molasses, oil, egg, and vanilla into bran mixture; pour over flour mixture. Sprinkle with carrot and dried fruit; stir just until combined.

Scrape into parchment paper–lined or greased 13- x 9-inch (3.5 l) metal cake pan. Bake in centre of 350°F (180°C) oven until cake tester inserted in centre comes out clean, about 25 minutes. Let cool in pan on rack. Cut into 12 large or 24 small bars. (Make-ahead: Wrap whole cake or individual bars in plastic wrap and store at room temperature for up to 2 days or freeze in airtight container for up to 1 month.)

Makes 12 large or 24 small cookies.

Per large bar: about 300 cal, 6 g pro, 7 g total fat (1 g sat. fat), 57 g carb, 5 g fibre, 16 mg chol, 419 mg sodium.

% RDI: 13% calcium, 27% iron, 36% vit A, 2% vit C, 17% folate.

Variation: Carrot Apricot Bran Muffins: Spoon batter into greased muffin cups. Bake in centre of 375°F (190°C) oven until tops are firm to the touch, about 25 minutes. Let cool in pan on rack for 2 minutes. Transfer to rack and let cool completely.
Makes 12 large or 18 medium-sized muffins.

Coco-Coconut Energy Bars

These no-bake energy bars are easy to tuck into a backpack for an energy-boosting after-school snack. Substitute your favourite dried fruit and nuts to suit your tastebuds.

1 1/3 cups	granulated sugar	325 ml
1/2 cup	unsweetened cocoa powder	125 ml
1/2 cup	milk	125 ml
1 tbsp	butter	15 ml
2 cups	quick-cooking rolled oats	500 ml
1/2 tsp	salt	2 ml
1 cup	unsweetened desiccated coconut	250 ml
3/4 cup	dried cherries or raisins	175 ml
1/2 cup	chopped toasted pecans	125 ml
1 tsp	vanilla extract	5 ml

Line 8-inch (2 L) square cake pan with foil; grease foil and set aside.

In saucepan, whisk together sugar, cocoa, milk, and butter over medium-low heat until sugar is dissolved and butter is melted; bring to boil. Stir in rolled oats and salt until combined; remove from heat. Stir in coconut, dried cherries, pecans, and vanilla.

Scrape into prepared pan, using back of wet spoon to smooth and pat down. Cover and refrigerate for about 1 hour or until chilled. Cut into bars.

Bars can be individually wrapped in plastic wrap and stored at room temperature for up to 2 days or frozen for up to 2 weeks.
Makes 18 bars.

Per bar: about 184 cal, 3 g pro, 7 g total fat (4 g sat. fat), 30 g carb, 3 g fibre, 2 mg chol, 95 mg sodium. % RDI: 2% calcium, 7% iron, 1% vit A, 0% vit C, 2% folate.

Tip: To toast pecans, spread on baking sheet and toast in 350°F (180°C) oven or toaster oven for about 8 minutes or until fragrant.

Farmland Flax Cookies

The flaxseed in these wholesome, crunchy cookies is a source of soluble fibre and alpha-linolenic acid, an essential fatty acid. Like all nuts and seeds, flaxseed should be stored in the refrigerator.

1/2 cup	butter, softened	125 ml
1/2 cup	packed brown sugar	125 ml
1/3 cup	granulated sugar	75 ml
1	egg	1
1/2 tsp	vanilla extract	2 ml
1 cup	all-purpose flour	250 ml
3/4 cup	quick-cooking rolled oats	175 ml
2/3 cup	flaxseeds	150 ml
1 tsp	baking soda	5 ml

In bowl, beat together butter, and brown and granulated sugars until light; beat in egg and vanilla. In separate bowl, whisk together flour, oats, flaxseeds, and baking soda; stir into butter mixture until soft dough forms.

Drop by level tablespoonfuls (15 ml), 2 inches (5 cm) apart, on ungreased rimless baking sheets. Bake in top and bottom thirds of 350°F (180°C) oven, rotating and switching pans halfway through, until golden, about 12 minutes. Let cool on pan on racks for 2 minutes.

Transfer cookies to racks; let cool. (Make-ahead: Layer between waxed paper and freeze in airtight container for up to 1 month.)

Makes about 40 cookies.

Per cookie: about 69 cal, 1 g pro, 3 g total fat (2 g sat. fat), 9 g carb, 1 g fibre, 11 mg chol, 57 mg sodium. % RDI: 1% calcium, 4% iron, 2% vit A, 0% vit C, 5% folate.

Hermit Cookies

Mix the dry ingredients together ahead of time and store in an airtight container. When ready to bake, just add the wet ingredients and pop in the oven for a warm snack.

Hermit Cookie Mix:

1 cup	chopped blanched almonds	250 ml
1/2 cup	chopped prunes	125 ml
1/2 cup	chopped dried apricots	125 ml
1 cup	dried cranberries	250 ml
2 1/2 cups	all-purpose flour	625 ml
1 1/2 tsp	baking powder	7 ml
1/2 tsp	each baking soda and salt	2 ml
1 1/2 tsp	cinnamon	7 ml
1 tsp	ground nutmeg	5 ml
1/2 tsp	each ground allspice and cloves	2 ml
2/3 cup	packed brown sugar	150 ml
2/3 cup	granulated sugar	150 ml

In tall, wide-mouthed jar with tight-fitting lid large enough to hold 6 cups (1.5 L), neatly layer almonds, prunes, apricots, and cranberries, packing each layer well.

In bowl, whisk together flour, baking powder, baking soda, and salt; spoon half over cranberries. In small bowl, mix together cinnamon, nutmeg, allspice, and cloves; sprinkle around edge of flour mixture in jar. Spoon remaining flour mixture over top.

Cut 8-inch (20 cm) round of waxed paper. Spoon brown and granulated sugars on centre; bundle up and place on flour mixture in jar. Seal jar. (Make-ahead: Store for up to 1 month.)

Makes 6 cups (1.5 L) of mixture.

Hermit Cookies:

1/2 cup	butter, softened	125 ml
1/2 cup	shortening	125 ml
	Hermit Cookie Mix	
2	eggs	2
1 tsp	vanilla extract	5 ml

Grease or line rimless baking sheets with parchment paper; set aside.

In large bowl, beat together butter, shortening, and brown and granulated sugars from Hermit Cookie Mix until light and fluffy. Beat in eggs, 1 at a time; beat in vanilla. Stir in flour and spice mixtures, then cranberries, apricots, prunes, and almonds from Hermit Cookie Mix.

Drop dough by tablespoonfuls (15 ml), about 2 inches (5 cm) apart, onto prepared pans. Bake in top and bottom thirds of 350°F (180°C) oven until golden, about 15 minutes, rotating and switching pans halfway through. (Make-ahead: Store in airtight container for up to 5 days or freeze for up to 1 month.)

Makes about 80 cookies.

Per cookie: about 69 cal, 1 g pro, 3 g total fat (1 g sat. fat), 9 g carb, 1 g fibre, 8 mg chol, 41 mg sodium. % RDI: 1% calcium, 3% iron, 2% vit A, 0% vit C, 2% folate.

Oatmeal Snack Squares

These moist, flat cake-like squares are reduced in fat but high in flavour—a welcome addition to kids' lunches or a school bake sale.

1 cup	packed brown sugar	250 ml
2/3 cup	plain low-fat yogurt	150 ml
1/3 cup	vegetable oil	75 ml
2	eggs	2
1 tsp	vanilla extract	5 ml
1 1/2 cups	rolled oats (not instant)	375 ml
1 cup	whole-wheat flour	250 ml
1 tsp	baking powder	5 ml
1/2 tsp	salt	2 ml
1/2 cup	each raisins and chocolate chips	125 ml

In large bowl, whisk together sugar, yogurt, and oil. Whisk in eggs and vanilla until smooth. Combine oats, flour, baking powder, and salt; stir into yogurt mixture just until blended. Stir in raisins and chocolate chips. Spread in greased 13- x 9-inch (3.5 L) baking pan.

Bake in centre of 350°F (180°C) oven for 20 to 25 minutes or until lightly browned and firm to the touch. Let cool in pan on rack. Cut into squares.

Squares can be individually wrapped in plastic wrap and refrigerated for up to 1 day or wrapped and stored in an airtight container and frozen for up to 1 week.

Makes 36 squares.

Per square: about 91 cal, 2 g pro, 4 g total fat (1 g sat. fat), 14 g carb, 1 g fibre, 12 mg chol, 48 mg sodium. % RDI: 2% calcium, 4% iron, 1% vit A, 0% vit C, 1% folate.

Power Bars

Firm and tasty, these high-energy bars make satisfying snacks.

2 cups	whole-wheat flour	500 ml
1/2 cup	packed brown sugar	125 ml
1/4 cup	skim milk powder	50 ml
1/4 cup	wheat germ	50 ml
1 tsp	baking powder	5 ml
1 1/2 cups	raisins or chopped dried apricots	375 ml
1/2 cup	unsalted sunflower seeds	125 ml
2	eggs	2
1/2 cup	vegetable oil	125 ml
1/2 cup	molasses	125 ml
1/3 cup	peanut butter	75 ml

In bowl, combine flour, sugar, skim milk powder, wheat germ, and baking powder; stir in raisins and sunflower seeds. Combine eggs, oil, molasses, and peanut butter; add to dry ingredients, blending well.

Spread in greased 9-inch (2.5 L) square cake pan. Bake in 350°F (180°C) oven for 35 minutes or until browned and firm to the touch. Let cool completely. Cut into 24 bars. Bars can be stored in airtight container for up to 5 days.

Makes 24 bars.

Per bar: about 190 cal, 4 g pro, 9 g total fat (1 g sat. fat), 26 g carb, 2 g fibre, 16 mg chol, 44 mg sodium. % RDI: 4% calcium, 10% iron, 1% vit A, 0% vit C, 8% folate.

Power-Packed Wheat Squares

Puffed wheat cereal makes a lightweight, nutritious square perfect for breakfast or a snack.

5 cups	puffed wheat cereal	1.25 L
2 cups	toasted oat cereal Os with nuts and honey	500 ml
3/4 cup	roasted unsalted peanuts, coarsely chopped	175 ml
1/2 cup	roasted salted sunflower seeds	125 ml
1 1/2 cups	granulated sugar	375 ml
3/4 cup	corn syrup	175 ml
1/3 cup	butter	75 ml
1 tbsp	vanilla extract	15 ml

Line 13- x 9-inch (3.5 L) cake pan with foil; grease foil. Set aside.

In large bowl, stir together puffed wheat and toasted oat cereals, chopped peanuts, and sunflower seeds; set aside.

In saucepan, cook sugar, corn syrup, and butter over medium-low heat, stirring with wooden spoon, for about 6 minutes or until sugar is dissolved. Increase heat to medium and bring to rolling boil, stirring constantly. Boil, without stirring, for 6 minutes. Remove from heat and stir until bubbling stops; stir in vanilla. Pour over cereal mixture; stir to coat well.

Using spatula, press cereal mixture into prepared pan. Let cool completely; peel off foil and cut into squares.

Squares can be wrapped individually in foil and set aside for up to 3 days.

Makes 18 squares.

Per square: about 225 cal, 3 g pro, 8 g total fat (3 g sat. fat), 35 g carb, 1 g fibre, 11 g chol, 103 mg sodium. % RDI: 1% calcium, 7% iron, 3% vit A, 0% vit C, 9% folate.

MUFFINS AND LOAVES

Anything Goes Muffins

You can substitute raisins, dried cranberries, or chocolate chips for the blueberries. Or make two kinds of muffins at once by dividing the batter between two bowls and adding 1/2 cup (125 ml) of different add-ins to each bowl.

2 cups	all-purpose flour	500 ml
3/4 cup	packed brown sugar	175 ml
2 tsp	baking powder	10 ml
1/2 tsp	baking soda	2 ml
1/2 tsp	cinnamon	2 ml
1/4 tsp	salt	1 ml
2	eggs	2
1 cup	2% milk	250 ml
1/4 cup	vegetable oil	50 ml
1 tsp	grated orange rind	5 ml
1 tsp	vanilla extract	5 ml
1 cup	blueberries	250 ml

Place oven rack in middle of oven. Preheat oven to 375°F (190°C). Lightly grease muffin cups or place paper liner in each; set aside.

In large bowl and using wooden spoon, stir together flour, brown sugar, baking powder, baking soda, cinnamon, and salt until mixed and there are no lumps of sugar.

In separate bowl and using wire whisk, beat together eggs, milk, oil, orange rind, and vanilla until all one colour; pour liquid ingredients over dry ingredients. Using wooden spoon, stir until only a few streaks of flour remain.

Gently stir blueberries into batter. With large spoon or ice-cream scoop, drop batter into muffin cups, scraping off spoon with spatula. Bake for 20 to 25 minutes or until golden. Insert toothpick in centre of one muffin; if it comes out clean, muffins are done. Let cool in pan on cooling rack for 10 minutes, then run knife around muffins to loosen and lift out. Transfer to rack and let cool completely.

Makes 12 muffins.

Per muffin: about 200 cal, 4 g pro, 6 g total fat (1 g sat. fat), 32 g carb, 1 g fibre, 33 mg chol, 166 mg sodium. % RDI: 6% calcium, 10% iron, 2% vit A, 2% vit C, 14% folate.

Tip: To make grated orange rind, rub an orange against the smallest holes on a cheese grater.

Apple Oat Muffins

Start your day with a hearty muffin that combines whole wheat and oats with apples and warm spices.

1 3/4 cups	quick-cooking rolled oats	425 ml
1 3/4 cups	plain 1% or 2% yogurt	425 ml
2	eggs	2
1 cup	shredded peeled apple	250 ml
1/4 cup	vegetable oil	50 ml
1 tsp	vanilla extract	5 ml
2 cups	whole-wheat flour	500 ml
3/4 cup	packed brown sugar	175 ml
4 tsp	baking powder	20 ml
2 tsp	cinnamon	10 ml
1 tsp	baking soda	5 ml
1/2 tsp	each nutmeg and salt	2 ml
3/4 cup	raisins or dried cranberries	175 ml

In bowl, combine oats and yogurt; let stand for 10 minutes. Whisk in eggs, apple, oil, and vanilla. In large bowl, combine flour, sugar, baking powder, cinnamon, baking soda, nutmeg, and salt. Pour yogurt mixture over dry ingredients. Sprinkle with raisins; stir just until moistened. Spoon into greased or paper-lined muffin cups.

Bake in centre of 375°F (190°C) oven for 35 minutes or until golden brown and tops are firm to touch. Let cool in pan on rack for 5 minutes; transfer to rack and let cool completely.

Mix can be stored in airtight container for up to 1 day or frozen for up to 2 weeks.

Makes 12 large muffins.

Per muffin: about 278 cal, 8 g pro, 7 g total fat (1 g sat. fat), 49 g carb, 5 g fibre, 37 mg chol, 322 mg sodium. % RDI: 13% calcium, 16% iron, 2% vit A, 2% vit C, 7% folate.

Date and Banana Loaf

This perfect pick-me-up snack contains magnesium-packed whole-wheat flour and wheat germ, and vitamin B6–packed banana. As a bonus, it will truly satisfy your sweet tooth.

1/2 cup	granulated sugar	125 ml
1/2 cup	plain yogurt, full fat	125 ml
1/4 cup	vegetable oil	50 ml
2	eggs	2
1 cup	mashed banana	250 ml
1 tsp	vanilla extract	5 ml
1 cup	all-purpose flour	250 ml
3/4 cup	whole-wheat flour	175 ml
1/4 cup	wheat germ	50 ml
2 tsp	baking powder	10 ml
1/2 tsp	baking soda	2 ml
1/2 cup	chopped dates	125 ml

In bowl, whisk together sugar, yogurt, oil, and eggs; stir in banana and vanilla.

In large bowl, whisk together all-purpose and whole-wheat flours, wheat germ, baking powder, and baking soda; stir in dates. Stir in banana mixture until combined.

Pour into greased 8- x 4-inch (1.5 L) loaf pan. Bake in centre of 350°F (180°C) oven for about 1 hour or until tester inserted in centre comes out clean. Let cool in pan on rack for 15 minutes. Remove from pan; let cool on rack. (Make-ahead: Wrap in plastic wrap and store for up to 2 days, or wrap in foil and freeze for up to 2 weeks.)

Makes 1 loaf or 12 slices.

Per serving: about 203 cal, 5 g pro, 6 g total fat (1 g sat. fat), 34 g carb, 3 g fibre, 37 mg chol, 110 mg sodium. % RDI: 4% calcium, 9% iron, 2% vit A, 3% vit C, 12% folate.

TRAIL MIXES

Grab-a-Snack Mix

In a rush with no time to eat in the morning? This snack mix is the perfect breakfast for you and your kids to munch on while on your way to work or school. (Bring along a small carton of milk or unsweetened fruit juice.) It's even great to snack on during the day or while watching a movie in the evening.

1 cup	whole-wheat cereal squares	250 ml
1/2 cup	raisins	125 ml
1/3 cup	banana chips, broken	75 ml
1/4 cup	dried apricots, quartered	50 ml
2 tbsp	chopped toasted almonds	25 ml

In glass bowl, mix together cereal squares, raisins, banana chips, dried apricots, and almonds.

Mix can be covered with plastic wrap or transferred to resealable plastic bag for up to 2 weeks; do not store in airtight container.

Makes 2 cups (500 ml).

Per 2/3 cup (150 ml) serving: about 255 cal, 4 g pro, 6 g total fat (3 g sat. fat), 50 g carb, 5 g fibre, 0 mg chol, 149 mg sodium. % RDI: 4% calcium, 26% iron, 8% vit A, 3% vit C, 7% folate.

SUPER CEREAL

Add fibre and vitamins A and C to your bowl by topping cereal with a couple of spoonfuls of one, or a juicy combination, of the following: blueberries, raspberries; sliced bananas, peaches, strawberries, or nectarines; dried cranberries.

For an extra 4 grams of fibre, sprinkle your favourite cereal with 2 tbsp (25 ml) Kellogg's All-Bran Buds with Psyllium.

Hiker's Happy Trail Mix

Trail mix is wonderfully easy and portable. Keep a small airtight container in your bag for a convenient snack or try sprinkling it over yogurt for a quick breakfast.

4 cups	toasted-oat cereal rounds	1 L
4 cups	waffle-weave wheat cereal squares	1 L
2 cups	raisins	500 ml
1 1/2 cups	banana chips	375 ml
1 1/2 cups	multibran cereal flakes	375 ml
1 cup	shredded sweetened coconut	250 ml
1 cup	pecan halves	250 ml
1/2 cup	mini chocolate chips	125 ml

In large bowl, gently toss together cereal rounds, wheat cereal squares, raisins, banana chips, multibran flakes, coconut, pecans, and chocolate chips.

Store in airtight container at room temperature for up to 1 month.

Makes about 15 cups (3.75 L).

Per 1/2 cup (125 ml): about 290 cal, 4 g pro, 11 g total fat (5 g sat. fat), 47 g carb, 6 g fibre, 0 mg chol, 199 mg sodium. % RDI: 3% calcium, 31% iron, 0% vit A, 3% vit C, 9% folate.

Hit-the-Road Mix

This grab-and-go snack can be mixed ahead of time and divided into individual portions. It provides both carbs and protein to generate fuel for those after-school activities.

1 cup	corn-and-bran cereal squares	250 ml
1 cup	multigrain cereal circles	250 ml
1 cup	raisins	250 ml
3/4 cup	chopped dried pineapple rings or chunks	175 ml
1/3 cup	unsalted sunflower seeds, roasted	75 ml
1/4 cup	flaked or shredded coconut	50 ml
1/4 cup	each roasted unsalted cashews and peanuts	50 ml

In large bowl, mix together cereal squares and circles, raisins, dried pineapple, sunflower seeds, coconut, cashews, and peanuts.

Mix can be stored in glass bowl covered with plastic wrap or in sealable plastic bag for up to 1 month; do not store in airtight container.

Makes 4 cups (1 L).

Per 1/2 cup (125 ml): about 230 cal, 5 g pro, 9 g total fat (2 g sat. fat), 38 g carb, 5 g fibre, 0 mg chol, 77 mg sodiium. % RDI: 3% calcium, 19% iron, 0% vit A, 2% vit C, 12% folate.

MORE SMOOTHIES AND FRUIT

Banana Orange Shake

Cool down with a frosty vitamin and mineral shake-up. Wrap peeled ripe bananas in plastic wrap and keep them in the freezer, ready to blend with juice for after-school thirst quenchers.

1	frozen peeled ripe banana	1
1 cup	orange juice	250 ml

Cut banana into chunks; transfer to blender or food processor. Pour in juice; blend or purée until smooth. Pour into glasses.
Makes 2 servings.

Per serving: about 105 cal, 1 g pro, trace total fat (trace sat. fat), 26 g carb, 1 g fibre, 0 mg chol, 2 mg sodium. % RDI: 1% calcium, 2% iron, 1% vit A, 83% vit C, 28% folate.

MORE BLENDER BLASTS

Fruity Milk Sipper: Blend 1 1/2 cups (375 ml) milk or soy beverage with 1/4 cup (50 ml) raspberry, cranberry, or pineapple juice concentrate.

Mango Lassi: Blend together 1 cup (250 ml) plain yogurt, 1 ripe mango, peeled, and chopped, and 1 tbsp (15 ml) liquid honey. (If mangoes are unavailable, use 1 1/2 cups/375 ml mango juice or nectar and 1/2 cup/125 ml plain yogurt.)

Choco-Berry Smoothie: Blend 1 cup (250 ml) chocolate milk with 1 cup (250 ml) frozen or fresh strawberries.

Fruity Blender Buzz

Not always up to eating first thing in the morning? Shake things up with a frothy fruit beverage to get your engine running. Instead of berries, you can use sliced, peeled, and pitted peaches or mangos.

1 cup	milk or soy beverage	250 ml
2 tbsp	skim milk powder	25 ml
1	ripe banana	1
1 cup	frozen or fresh strawberries, blueberries, or raspberries	250 ml

In blender, purée together milk, skim milk powder, banana, and berries until smooth. Pour into 2 glasses.
Makes 2 servings.

Per serving: about 155 cal, 6 g pro, 3 g total fat (2 g sat. fat), 28 g carb, 2 g fibre, 10 mg chol, 87 mg sodium. % RDI: 20% calcium, 6% iron, 8% vit A, 62% vit C, 14% folate.

Tropical Smoothie

Look for canned pineapple tidbits packed in juice instead of those packed in syrup, which contains a lot of added sugar. Tuck a few peeled bananas into the freezer to have on hand for smoothie cravings.

1	can (14 oz/398 ml) pineapple tidbits	1
1	mango, chopped (or 1 cup/250 ml frozen peaches)	1
Half	banana, frozen	Half

In blender or food processor, whirl together pineapple with juice from can, mango, and banana until smooth.
Makes 2 servings.

Per serving: about 219 cal, 2 g pro, 1 g total fat (trace sat. fat), 57 g carb, 5 g fibre, 0 mg chol, 4 mg sodium. % RDI: 4% calcium, 6% iron, 41% vit A, 85% vit C, 14% folate.

Variation: Creamy Tropical Smoothie: Add 1/2 cup (125 ml) plain or vanilla-flavoured low-fat yogurt to blender.

Peach Leather

This chewy, textured peach leather has an intense flavour.

4 cups	chopped unpeeled peaches or nectarines (about 5)	1 L
2 tbsp	granulated sugar	25 ml

In blender or food processor, purée peaches with sugar until smooth.

Microwave method: Pour purée into large microwaveable bowl; microwave at High, stirring occasionally, for 15 minutes or until thickened and reduced by half. Line 10-inch (25 cm) microwaveable pie plate with plastic wrap. Spread 1/4 cup (50 ml) of the purée in 6-inch (15 cm) circle in centre. Microwave on medium for about 6 minutes or until no longer sticky in centre. Repeat with remaining purée.

Oven method: Pour purée into deep saucepan and bring to boil; reduce heat and simmer, stirring often, for 30 minutes or until reduced by half. Let cool to room temperature. Line two baking sheets with foil; grease foil. Spread 1/4 cup (50 ml) of the purée into each of the six 6-inch (15 cm) circles of foil. Bake in 175°F (80°C) oven for 2 to 3 hours or until no longer sticky in centre, rotating pan halfway through.

Both methods: Transfer fruit leather on plastic wrap or foil to rack; let stand, uncovered, at room temperature overnight or until completely dry.
Roll up in plastic wrap and store in refrigerator for up to 2 weeks.
Makes 6 servings.

Per serving: About 50 cal; 1 g pro; trace total fat (trace sat. fat); 12 g carb, 2 g fibre, 0 mg chol, 0 mg sodium. % RDI: 1% calcium, 1% iron, 5% vit A, 8% vit C, 1% folate.

Resources

Diet, Nutrition, and Weight Control

Canadian Partnership for Consumer Food Safety Education
1755 Courtwood Crescent, Suite 500
Ottawa, Ontario, Canada K2C 3J2
www.canfightbac.org
This national association is committed to educating Canadians about the ease and importance of food safety in the home. You'll find plenty of practical information and tips on
safe food-handling practices in the consumer section of the site.

Center for Science in the Public Interest
www.cspinet.org/nah
The Center publishes the 10-issues-a-year Nutrition Action Healthletter. Archived issues
are posted on the website, and you can subscribe online or order from:
Nutrition Action Healthletter
PO Box 70373
Toronto Station A
Toronto, ON M5W 2X5

Dietitians of Canada
480 University Avenue, Suite 604
Toronto, Ontario M5G 1V2
Tel: 416-596-0857
Fax: 416-596-0603
www.dietitians.ca
The Dietitians of Canada is an association of food and nutrition professionals committed
to the health and well-being of Canadians. Visit the website to learn about nutrition
resources or to find a registered dietitian in your community.

Health Canada Online
www.hc-sc.gc.ca
Visit Health Canada's main site to find information about nutrition, physical activity, health care, and diseases and conditions. You'll also find the latest headlines and advisories.

You can also visit more specific nutrition sites, such as www.hc-sc.gc.ca/hppb/nutrition, where you'll find Canada's Food Guide to Healthy Eating and plenty of information on nutrition labelling and healthy weights.

International Food Information Council
1100 Connecticut Avenue, NW
Suite 430
Washington, DC, USA 20036
Tel: 202-296-6540
E-mail: foodinfo@ific.org
www.ific.org
The mission of this site is to communicate science-based information on food safety and nutrition. You'll find brochures and fact sheets that discuss child and adolescent nutrition, weight management, food additives, and a lot more. The Q&A centre provides answers to questions about today's food safety issues, from fish and trans fat to pesticides and artificial sweeteners.

Eating Disorders

National Eating Disorder Information Centre
www.nedic.ca
ES 7-421
200 Elizabeth Street
Toronto, Ontario M5G 2C4
Tel: 416-340-4156 or 1-866-633-4220 (toll-free)
Fax: 416-340-4736
This organization provides information, literature, and qualified referrals for the treatment of eating disorders.

General

Familydoctor.org
http://familydoctor.org/x5575.xml
Produced by the American Academy of Family Physicians, this website gives a brief overview of a number of conditions and issues that affect teens. Its value is its brevity: teens will get a quick look at a topic and find links to related information without being overwhelmed by information. For some, it will be a good place to start their search for health information.

4 Girls Health

www.4girls.gov

Sponsored by the U.S. Office on Women's Health in the Department of Health and Human Services, this website is aimed specifically at girls between the ages of 10 and 16 and promotes healthy, positive behaviours. The nutrition page contains information on portions, vitamins, and minerals; reading food labels; body image; vegetarianism; and bone health. The fitness page includes a self-test for fitness levels and a heart-rate calculator, and offers fitness-planning advice for girls.

Go Ask Alice!

www.goaskalice.columbia.edu/Cat3.html

This website provides teens with a health question-and-answer service produced by Alice!, Columbia University's Health Education program, a division of Health Services at Columbia. Answers to teen-related questions on health, nutrition, and body issues are provided by qualified health care professionals. The website offers plenty of specific information on vegetarianism, nutrition, fitness, and eating disorders. Although the website is aimed at older teens and university-age students, much of the information is relevant for younger teens, too.

TeenGrowth.com

www.teengrowth.com

Reviewed by experts in the U.S. pediatric community, this website provides plenty of facts about puberty, sexual health, healthy eating, and fitness. It also has interactive sections where teens can submit questions to doctors and offer their advice to other teens around the world on a variety of topics.

Teen Health Website

www.chebucto.ns.ca/Health/TeenHealth

This general website delves into issues of interest to teens, including healthy eating, sports, and exercise. It's associated with Dalhousie University School of Medicine, in Nova Scotia. Each section provides useful links to other sites.

TeensHealth

www.teenshealth.org

Created by the Nemours Foundation's Center for Children's Health Media, this website is for teens looking for accurate, up-to-date, and jargon-free information about their bodies, health conditions, nutrition, food, and fitness. The website includes a lengthy question-and-answer section that covers topics such as dieting, puberty, hygiene, illnesses, and emotional health.

Vegetarianism

Physician's Committee for Responsible Medicine

www.pcrm.org

Founded in 1985, this non-profit organization is composed of doctors and laypersons working together for compassionate and effective medical practice, research, and health promotion. There is an entire section on the website devoted to vegetarianism. You can also download a Vegetarian Starter Kit, which includes recipes, tips for dining out, and a list of vegetarian food products available in the marketplace.

Vegan Society

www.vegansociety.com

This educational charitable organization based in the United Kingdom is committed to providing education about vegan lifestyles.

Vegetarian Resource Group

www.vrg.org

This non-profit organization based in Baltimore, Maryland, is dedicated to providing information on all types of vegetarianism and the interrelated issues of health, nutrition, ecology, ethics, and world hunger. The group also produces and sells cookbooks, other books, and pamphlets.

Vegetarian Society

www.vegsoc.org

An educational charity based in the United Kingdom, the Vegetarian Society promotes understanding and respect for all types of vegetarian lifestyles. Since its foundation in 1847, the Society has been a basic source of reference for local and national vegetarian societies and individuals worldwide.

Vegetarianteen.com

www.vegetarianteen.com

This website is dedicated to vegetarian teenagers and teenage life. Topics covered include food and nutrition, school life, activism, fashion, and dating. There's even a section for parents and list of links to other teen vegetarian sites.

VegSource

www.vegsource.com

This website provides plenty of support for vegetarians via recipes, newsletters, articles about health, book reviews, discussion boards, live chats, and email.

Endnotes

Introduction

1. Growing up healthy? Supplement to Health Reports, volume 14, 2003. Statistics Canada, Catalogue 82–003.

2. Canadian Population Health Initiative. Overweight and obesity in Canada: A population health perspective. Canadian Institute for Health Information (August 2004).

3. Canadian Community Health Survey 2000/2001. Statistics Canada. Available at www.statcan.ca/english/freepub/82–221–XIE/00502/tables/html/2165.htm.

4. 2002 physical activity monitor. Canadian Fitness and Lifestyle Research Institute. Available at www.cflri.ca/cflri/pa/index.html.

5. How healthy are Canadians? 2003 Annual Report. Catalogue no. 82–003 SIE. Supplement to volume 14, 2003. Statistics Canada, Ottawa.

2   All About Carbohydrates

1. Steffen, LM, et al. Whole grain intake is associated with lower body mass and greater insulin sensitivity among adolescents. *Am J Epidemiol* 2003, 158(3):243–50.

2. Ludwig, DS, et al. High glycemic index foods, overeating and obesity. *Pediatrics* 1999, 103(3):E26.

3. Ebbeling, CB, et al. A reduced-glycemic load diet in the treatment of adolescent obesity. *Arch Pediatr Adolesc Med* 2003, 157(8):773–79.

4. Spieth, LE, et al. A low-glycemic index diet in the treatment of pediatric obesity. *Arch Pediatr Adolesc Med* 2000, 154(9):947–51.

5. Schultz, MB, et al. Sugar-sweetened beverages, weight gain, and incidence of type 2 diabetes in young and middle aged women. *JAMA* 2004, 292(8): 927–34.

3   A Primer on Protein

1. Cooper, C., et al. Dietary protein intake and bone mass in women. *Calcif Tissue Int* 1996, 58(5):320–25.

2. Xiao, Ou Shu, et al. Soyfood intake during adolescence and subsequent risk of breast cancer among Chinese women. *Cancer Epidemiology Biomarkers & Prevention* 2001, 10(5):483–88.

3. Bazzano, LA, et al. Legume consumption and risk of coronary heart disease in US men and women: NHANES I Epidemiologic Follow-up Study. *Arch Intern Med* 2001, 161(21):2573–78.

4. Hu, FB, et al. Frequent nut consumption and risk of coronary heart disease in women: prospective cohort study. *BMJ* 1998; 317(7169):1341–45.

5. Jiang, R, et al. Nut and peanut butter consumption and risk of type 2 diabetes in women. *JAMA* 2002, 288(20):2554–60.

4   The Facts on Fat

1. Gary-Donald, K, et al. Food habits of Canadians: reduction of fat over a generation. *Can J Public Health* 2000, 91(5):381–85.

2. Dorgan, J, et al. Diet and sex hormones in girls: Findings from a randomized controlled clinical trial. *J Natl Cancer Inst* 2003, 15(2):132–41.

3. Siscovick, DS, et al. Dietary intake of long-chain n-3 polyunsaturated fatty acids and the risk of primary cardiac arrest. *Am J Clin Nutr* 2000, 71(1 Suppl):208S–12S.

4. He, K, et al. Accumulated evidence on fish consumption and coronary heart disease mortality: A meta-analysis of cohort studies. *Circulation* 2004, 109(22):2705–11.

5. Djousse, L, et al. Relation between dietary linolenic acid and coronary artery disease in the National Heart, Lung, and Blood Institute Family Heart Study. *Am J Clin Nutr* 2001, 74(5):612–19; Hu, FB, et al. Dietary intake of alpha linolenic acid and the risk of fatal ischemic heart disease among women. *Am J Clin Nutr* 1999, 69(5):890–97.

5 Water and Other Fluids

1. Wyshak, G. Teenaged girls, carbonated beverage consumption, and bone fractures. *Arch Pediatr Adolesc Med* 2000, 154(6):610–13.

2. Lloyd, T, et al. Dietary caffeine intake and bone status of postmenopausal women. *Am J Clin Nutr* 1997, 65(6):1826–30.

3. Harris, SS, and B Dawson-Hughes. Caffeine and bone loss in healthy menopausal women. *Am J Clin Nutr* 1994, 60(4): 573–78.

4. Vlachopoulos, C, et al. Caffeine increases aortic stiffness in hypertensive patients. *Am J Hypertens* 2003, 16(1):63–66.

5. Savoca, MR, et al. The association of caffeinated beverages with blood pressure in adolescents. *Arch Ped Adolesc Med* 2004, 158(5):473–77.

6. Office of Inspector General. Youth and alcohol: Dangerous and deadly consequences. Washington, DC: U.S. Department of Health and Human Services, 1992.

7. Presley, C, and P Meilman. Alcohol and drugs on American college campuses. Carbondale: Student Health Program Wellness Center, Southern Illinois University, 1992.

8. American Academy of Pediatrics. Alcohol advertising: Fiction vs. fact. 1998.

9. American Academy of Pediatrics. Underage drinking. 1998.

8 Nutrition Advice for Vegetarian Teens

1. Beef Information Centre. Canadian Eating Trends Study. Ottawa: Agriculture and Agri-Foods Canada, 1998.

2. Greene-Finestone, LS, et al. Dietary intake among young adolescents in Ontario: Associations with vegetarian status and attitude toward health. *Prev Med* 2005, 40 (1):105–11.

3. Fraser, GE. Associations between diet and cancer, ischemic heart disease, and all-cause mortality in non-Hispanic white California Seventh-day Adventists. *Am J Clin Nutr* 1999, 70(3 Suppl): 532S–38S.

4. Appleby, PN, et al. The Oxford Vegetarian Study: An overview. *Am J Clin Nutr* 1999, 70(3 Suppl):525S–31S.

5. Deegan, H. Assessment of iron status in adolescents. Master of science thesis, University of Alberta, 2000; Gibson, RS, et al. Are young women with low iron stores at risk of zinc as well as iron deficiency? Trace elements in man and animals 10, edited by Roussel et al., New York: Klower Academic/Plenum Publishers, 2000.

9 Weight Control Strategies for Teens

1. Tremblay, MS, et al. Temporal trends in overweight and obesity in Canada, 1981–1996. *Int J Obes* 2002, 26 (4):538–43.

2. Janssen, I, et al. Associations between overweight and obesity with bullying behaviors in school-aged children. *Pediatrics* 2004, 113(5):1195–1203.

3. Field, AE, et al. Relation between dieting and weight change among preadolescents and adolescents. *Pediatrics* 2003, 112(4):900–6.

4. Stice, E, et al. Naturalistic weight-reduction efforts prospectively predict growth in relative weight and onset of obesity among female adolescents. *Consult Clin Psychol* 1999, 67(6):967–74.

5. Patton, GC, et al. Onset of adolescent eating disorders: Population based cohort study over 3 years. *BMJ* 1999, 318(7186):765–68; Grigg, M, et al. Disordered eating and unhealthy weight reduction practices among adolescent females. *Prev Med* 1996, 25 (6):748–56.

6. Krowchuk, DP, et al. Problem dieting behaviours among young adolescents. *Arch Pediatr Adolesc Med* 1998, 152(9):884–888; Calderon, LL, et al. Dieting practices in high school students. *JADA* 2004, 104(9):1369–74.

7. Fabry, P, et al. The frequency of meals: Its relation to overweight, hypercholesterolaemia, and decreased glucose tolerance. *Lancet* 1964, 18:614–15; Fabry, P, et al. Effect of meal frequency in schoolchildren: Changes in weight-height proportion and skinfold thickness. *Am J Clin Nutr* 1966, 18 (5):358–61.

8. Iwao, S, K. Mori, and Y. Sato. Effects of meal frequency on body composition during weight control in boxers. *Scand J Med Sci Sports* 1996, 6(5):265–72.

9. Pollitt, E, et al. Fasting and cognition in well- and undernourished schoolchildren: A review of three experimental studies. *Am J Clin Nutr* 1998, 67(4):779S–84S; Vaisman, N, et al. Effect of breakfast timing on the cognitive functions of elementary school students. *Arch Pediatr Adolesc Med* 1996, 150(10):1089–92; Michaud, C, et al. Effects of breakfast-size on short-term memory, concentration, mood and blood glucose. *J Adolesc Health* 1991, 12(1):53–57.

10. Ebbeling, CB, et al. Compensation for energy intake from fast food among overweight and lean adolescents. *JAMA* 2004, 291(23):2828–33.

11. Gillis, LJ, and O Bar-Or. Food away from home, sugar-sweetened drink consumption and juvenile obesity. *J Am Coll Nutr* 2003, 22(6):539–45.

12. Ludwig, DS, et al. Relation between consumption of sugar-sweetened drinks and childhood obesity: A prospective, observational analysis. *Lancet* 2001, 357(9255):505–8.

13. Mrdjenovic, G, and DA Levitsky. Nutritional and energetic consequences of sweetened drink consumption in 6- to 13-year-old children. *J Pediatr* 2003, 142(6):604–10.

14. DiMeglio, DP, and RD Mattes. Liquid versus solid carbohydrate: Effects on food intake and body weight. *Int J Obes Relat Metab Disord* 2000, 24(6):794–800.

15. Young, LR, and M Nestle. Variation in perceptions of a 'medium' food portion: implications for dietary guidance. *J Am Diet Assoc* 1998, 98(4):458–59.

10   Nutrition Advice for Sports

1. Lloyd, T, et al. Lifestyle factors and the development of bone mass and bone strength in young women. *J Pediatr* 2004, 144(6):776–82.

2. Ekeland, E, et al. Exercise to improve self-esteem in children and young people (Cochrane Review). In *The Cochrane Library*, no. 3. Chichester, UK: John Wiley and Sons, 2004.

3. Statistics Canada Health Reports. How healthy are Canadians? Supplement to Volume 14, 2003. Available at www.statcan.ca/english/freepub/82-003-SIE/2003000/pdf/82-003-SIE2003001.pdf.

4. Tremblay, MS, and JD Willms. Is the Canadian childhood obesity epidemic related to physical inactivity? *Int J Obes Relat Metab Disord* 2003, 27(9):1100–5.

5. Watts, K, et al. Exercise training normalizes vascular dysfunction and improves central adiposity in obese adolescents. *J Am Coll Cardiol* 2004, 43(10):1823–27.

6. 2002 physical activity monitor. Ottawa: Canadian Fitness and Lifestyle Research Institute. Available at www.cflri.ca/cflri/pa/index.html.

7. Ibid.

8. Canada's physical activity guide to healthy living. Family guide to physical activity for youth 10–14 years of age. Health Canada and the Canadian Society for Exercise Physiology. Available www.phac-aspc.gc.ca/pau-uap/paguide/child_youth/index.html.

9. Rawson, Eric S., and Priscilla M. Clarkson. Gatorade Sports Science Institute. Scientifically debatable: Is creatine worth its weight? *Sports Science Exchange* 91; 2003, 16(4).

10. Melia, P, et al. The use of anabolic-androgenic steroids by Canadian students. *Clin J Sport Med* 1996, 6(1):9–14.

11   Understanding Eating Disorders

1. Health Canada. A report on mental illnesses in Canada, chap 6. Ottawa: 2002. Available at www.phac-aspc.gc.ca/publicat/miic-mmac/index.html.

2. Gatorade Sports Science Institute. Eating disorders in athletes: The dietician's perspective. Roundtable 18, 1994, 5(4).

3. Ibid.

Subject Index

academic performance, 93, 151, 162, 177
acidic foods, 34
adenosine, 88
adolescence, xiii, 3
adult onset diabetes. *See* diabetes (type 2)
aerobics, 180–81
Agaston, Arthur, 162
alcohol, 87, 91–95
alcohol poisoning, 92
alcoholism, 93–94
alfalfa, 113
all-dressed burger, 125
allergies, 104
almonds: fat content, 74; fibre content, 38; nutrients derived from, 16, 17, 18; protein content, 51; and weight loss, 169
alpha-lineolic acid (ALA), 62, 73, 74
amenorrhea. *See* menstruation
American Dietetic Association, 146
amino acid supplements, 191
amino acids, 48, 49–50, 148–49
anabolic steroids, 196–97
anchovies, 79
androstenedione (andro), 196
anemia, xiv, 161, 194
anorexia nervosa, 200–3, 207, 211
antibodies, 48

antioxidants, 19, 30
anxiety: and caffeine, 89; and eating disorders, 201, 203, 204, 205, 208
appearance: and diet, 3–4; and eating disorders, 202, 204; effect of andro on, 196; nutrients for, 17, 47
appetite control, 166
apples, 33, 36, 37, 38
apricots, 17, 36, 38, 151
Arby's, 126, 127, 128, 132
arthritis, 60
artichokes, 17
Asian food, 133, 135–36; fast food, 129
asparagus, 17
atherosclerosis, 109
Atkins, Robert C., 161
Atkins diet, 161–62
ATP (adenosine triphosphate), 195
attention, 151
avocados, 17, 18, 67, 74

B vitamins: functions of, 17; in multivitamins, 19, 20; sources of, 10, 11, 17
back problems, xv
bacteria, 84–85, 111, 113, 142
baked beans, 18, 35, 51, 155
baked goods: fat content, 65
baldness, 196
bananas: for exercise, 188; fibre content, 38; GI

value of, 33, 34, 36; nutrients derived from, 17, 18; shopping for, 108
barley, 35, 37
basketball, 180, 181
batch cooking, 114
bean soup, 168
beans (legumes): fibre content, 37, 38; GI values of, 35–36; iron content, 151; protein content, 51; serving size, 11
beef: cholesterol content, 76; fat content, 65, 71; iron content, 151; nutrients derived from, 17, 18; shopping for, 109
beef liver, 17, 18
beer, 92, 141
bell peppers, 18
beta-carotene, 17, 18, 19
bicycling, 179, 180, 181
binge drinking, 92
binge eating, 160
binge eating disorder (BED), 205–7, 212
bingeing and purging, 203, 205
black beans, 38, 57
blackstrap molasses, 18, 151
bloating, 38
blood clotting, 18, 30, 48
blood fats, 29
blood formation, 18
blood pressure, 18, 34, 202; high, xiv, xv, 22, 54, 89, 146
blood sugar, 27, 37, 48

cantaloupe, 18
carbohydrates, 26–45; calories in, 42; defined, 26–27; in energy bars, 189; and exercise, 188–89; functions of, 26, 27; and glycemic index, 31–36; needs, 27–28; for physical activity, 185, 187–88; and protein, 48; in snacks, 114; sources of, 10, 11, 28–32, 192; tips for, 45–47 (*See also* low-carb diets; sugar)
cardiovascular activities, 180–81
Carpenter, Karen, 204
carrots, 17, 33, 34, 38, 169
Casey's Bar and Grill, 121, 132
cashews, 18, 39, 74
cataracts, 18
cauliflower, 18
cavities, 44–45
cells, 18
cellulose, 27
Centers for Disease Control and Prevention, 21
cereal, breakfast: fibre content, 38, 39; GI values of, 33, 34, 35; high-fibre, 39–41; iron content, 151; nutrients derived from, 17, 18; serving size, 11; shopping for, 110–11; as starch, 27; sugar content, 45; in vegetarian diet, 149; for weight loss, 169; whole-grain, 30, 31–32
cereal bars, 33
Chartwells Dining Services, xvi, 138
cheese: and cavities, 44; cholesterol content, 76; fat content, 66, 70, 78; nutrients derived from, 17; protein content, 51; serving size, 11; shopping for, 109; substitutes, 156

cheese strings, 169
chicken. *See* poultry
chicken burgers and strips, 125–26
chickpeas, 11, 36, 38, 57
children (younger), xiv, xv
chili, 128
Chinese food, 133; fast food, 129
chipmunk cheeks, 204
chloride, 82, 202, 204
chocolate, 34, 36, 66, 70, 90
cholesterol (blood), 69–70; and BMI-for-age, 22; in boys, 62; and carbohydrates, 29, 30; and dietary cholesterol, 75; and fast foods, 117; and fats, 63, 70, 72; and fibre, 37; and heart disease, xiv; and obesity, xv; and particular foods, 56, 58
cholesterol (dietary), 62, 75–76, 103
"cholesterol free," 105
chopsticks, 133
chromium, 20
circuit training, 179, 181
citrus fruits, 18, 33, 37
cleaning, 112
clover, 113
cocaine, 94
coffee, 83, 90 (*See also* caffeine)
cola. *See* soft drinks
colon cancer, 29, 147, 179
comfort foods, 203
complementary proteins, 148–49
compulsive overeating, 205–7
computer games, xv, 174, 177, 179
concentration, 18, 53, 151, 177, 208
constipation, 31, 36, 37, 202

convenience, 174
cookies, 35
cooking, tips for, 111–14
cooking spray, 111
copper, 20, 30
corn, 27, 35, 39, 149
cottage cheese, 156
couscous, 35
cracked wheat, 32
crackers, 35, 110
crash diets, 161
cravings, 204
creatine, 195–96
cross-contamination, 112–13
cross-country skiing, 181, 208
curling, 183
curries, 136
cutting boards, 113

dairy products: cholesterol content, 76; fat content, 66, 70–71, 78; nutrients derived from, 17, 18; protein content, 51; shopping for, 108–9 (*See also* milk products)
Dairy Queen, 132
dance, 180, 181, 183, 208
dates, 18, 33, 34, 36
De Dutch Pannekoek House, 132
defrosting, 114
dehydration, 82, 83, 192, 202
deli meats, 110
deli-style sandwiches, 126–27
depression, 201; and eating disorders, 200, 201, 202, 203, 204, 205; and fats, 60; and obesity, xv
desserts, 66, 71, 90, 109, 119
development: and dieting, 161, 162; nutrients for, 17, 18
dextrose, 27
DHA (docosahexanaeonic acid), 73

Pop-Tarts, 33
pork, 17, 18, 71, 76
portion size: of breads, 110; and glycemic index, 34; at restaurants, 119–20; of soft drinks, 42, 170; vs. serving size, 119; and weight loss, 171–72
potassium, 18, 82, 202, 204
potato chips, 66
potatoes: fat content, 65; fibre content, 39; GI values of, 33, 35; instant, 111; nutrients derived from, 17; protein content, 52; serving size, 11, 171; as starch, 27; for vegetarians, 155
poultry: cholesterol content, 76; at fast food restaurants, 125–26; fat content, 65, 71, 77–78; food safety, 112, 142; nutrients derived from, 17, 18; protein content, 51; serving size, 11; shopping for, 109
poutine, 128
premenstrual syndrome (PMS), 150
President's Choice, 106, 107
pretzels, 66
processed foods, 28–29
produce. *See* fruit; vegetables
progesterone, 64
prostate cancer, 147
protein, 47–59; in the body, 48; complementary, 148–49; deficiency, 53–54; development, 18; digestion of, 17; in energy bars, 189–90; in excess, 54; and fats, 61; functions of, 47–49; needs, 50–51, 190–91; for physical activity, 185, 186, 190–91; sources of, 11, 47, 49–53, 54–59; supplements, 191;

tips for, 59; for vegetarians, 49–50, 146, 148–49
protein powder, 52, 57
prune juice, 151
prunes, 18, 38
psyllium husks, 37
puberty, 21
pumpkin seeds, 18

quinoa, 32

racquet sports, 181
radish sprouts, 113
raisins, 18, 33, 36, 38, 44, 66
rashes, 204
reading while eating, 172
recipes: choosing and using, 111–12; modification for vegetarians, 156
recovery foods, 188–89
red blood cells, 17, 18
Red Bull, 87, 90
Red Lobster, 123
"reduced," on packaging, 105
refined foods, 28–29
refried beans, 134
refrigerator temperature, 114
resistance training, 181–82
respiratory illness, xv
responsible drinking, 94–95
restaurants: family-style, 121–23; fats and oils in, 77; frequent of use of, 117; healthy eating in, 118–23 (*See also* fast food restaurants)
retinol, 20
rheumatoid arthritis, 60
riboflavin (vitamin B2): functions of, 17; in multivitamins, 20; sources of, 10, 11, 17, 85; and urine colour, 83
rice, 11, 27, 35, 38, 52, 111; brown, 33, 38, 111
rice beverages, 11, 17, 18, 85, 149

rice cakes, 35
rickets, xiv
rowing, 180, 181, 208
running, 179, 181, 208
rye, 27

salad bar, 139
salad dressing, 11, 34, 67, 77, 111
salads: adding fibre to, 39; at fast food restaurants, 127–28; fat content, 66, 67; Italian, 134; at restaurants, 119; serving size, 11; for vegetarians, 155
salmon, 18, 51, 76, 79, 110
salmonella, 113
salsa, 119
sandwiches, 119, 125, 126–27, 155–56
sardines, 18, 79
sashimi, 136
satiety. *See* fullness
saturated fats, 69, 70–71; limiting, 77–78; on packaging, 103, 105; risks of, 63
Schlosser, Eric, 124
school. *See* academic performance; cafeterias; university
seafood, 112, 142 (*See also* fish)
Sears, Barry, 163
secondary sex characteristics, 196
sedentary lifestyles, 174–75, 177, 178, 184
seeds: nutrients derived from, 17, 18; protein content, 51–52, 149; serving size, 11, 67
selenium, 19, 20, 30
self-confidence, 177, 200
self-consciousness, 184
self-esteem: and alcohol, 95; and body weight, xv, 159;

Recipe Index